I0828378

The Gallatin Way *to* Yellowstone

DUNCAN T. PATTEN

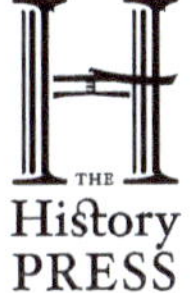

Published by The History Press
Charleston, SC
www.historypress.com

Copyright © 2018 by Duncan T. Patten
All rights reserved

First published 2018

ISBN 9781540233561

Library of Congress Control Number: 2017963925

Notice: The information in this book is true and complete to the best of our knowledge. It is offered without guarantee on the part of the author or The History Press. The author and The History Press disclaim all liability in connection with the use of this book.

All rights reserved. No part of this book may be reproduced or transmitted in any form whatsoever without prior written permission from the publisher except in the case of brief quotations embodied in critical articles and reviews.

Contents

Preface

The Gallatin Canyon has been part of my life for many years. I was first introduced to it in 1943 and 1944, when our family were guests at Elkhorn Ranch on Sage Creek. We arrived in Bozeman by train and were driven up the canyon. Although I was only eight and nine those years we were at Elkhorn, I recall many events and, with study of the canyon, am reminded of canyon activities and locations not only from that time but also from what I've read and heard about earlier times.

When I was a "dude kid," I remember occasionally driving down to Karst's Camp in mid-canyon to watch wildlife movies that Ernest Miller, founder of Elkhorn Ranch, had taken. Elkhorn had no electricity at the time, but Karst had a small hydroelectric facility nearby on Moose Creek. Electricity came to the upper canyon in 1948. In 1951, our family rented Seven Eleven Ranch in the summers from Elkhorn Ranch. Seven Eleven Ranch, a small ranch up Sage Creek, was originally a homestead and then built into a ranch for polo ponies and then became part of the Rising Sun Ranches under its builder. We rented it from 1951 through 1956, after which my family took up permanent residence at Black Butte Ranch along the Gallatin River five miles south of Elkhorn across from the northwestern corner of Yellowstone National Park.

During the summers when I was in college, 1952 through 1955, I worked at Elkhorn Ranch as a dude wrangler (a ranch hand who takes out guest rides and pack trips and, in my case, also calls square dances). At that time, Elkhorn was moving its horses, about 120 head, in the spring from winter pasture to early grass on the Flying D Ranch on Spanish Creek. Prior to Elkhorn opening in early summer, this herd was trailed at a trot the thirty-five miles up the canyon along Highway 191 from Spanish Creek to Elkhorn. The highway was not truck-friendly then, and there was little traffic, so a herd of horses moving up the canyon highway hardly disrupted traffic flow. It was during my time at Elkhorn Ranch that I got to know most of the canyon's length, as we (some crew members) in the evenings often "visited" many of the watering holes from Gallatin Gateway back to the ranch, including May Pings (now Stacy's Old Faithful) in Gallatin Gateway, Karsts in mid-canyon, Bucks T-4 near West Fork and the Corral Bar. Trips to West Yellowstone along a winding road were also common occurrences. At the time, West Yellowstone, the west entrance to Yellowstone National Park, which had a terminus of the Union Pacific Railroad, was still a very "western" town. The number of bars seemed to equal the number of stores, and there was gambling and dancing girls in many of the bars. As one might expect, four summers working at Elkhorn Ranch was a wonderful experience for a college boy.

In 1955, my parents purchased property on Monument Creek across from the northwest corner of Yellowstone National Park and Black Butte. The property was owned by Mayo Story Dean, granddaughter of Nelson Story (of *Lonesome Dove* fame and an early founder of Bozeman) and daughter of Nelson Story Jr., who had purchased several homesteads on Monument Creek. He traded some lands with the federal government in the 1920s to consolidate the property. The same year my parents purchased the Monument Creek property, I lost a brother in a small plane accident up the North Fork of the West Fork of the Gallatin in what is now the Big Sky area.

In 1957, my parents moved permanently to Montana. They named the ranch Black Butte Ranch after Black Butte, a small, picturesque mountain across the valley. I was fortunate to use the Black Butte Ranch from 1957 to 1962 as headquarters for my research for master's and doctoral degrees in ecology, studying landscape patterns in the Madison Range. Since those days, we (my family, wife and four children when young) spent most summers at Black Butte Ranch, with me continuing ecological studies in the upper Gallatin drainage and in Yellowstone National Park.

All of these early events created a love for this beautiful canyon and its history. As I talked with old-timers in the canyon over the years, the thought of creating some visual documentation and remembrance of the canyon has been with me for decades. Only time and a busy life kept me from proceeding with this project.

Eventually, Bozeman and the Gallatin Canyon area called us, and we moved permanently to Bozeman in 1995 from Arizona, where I taught at Arizona State University. We built a home on land we had purchased in 1983 just outside Bozeman city limits. Living in Bozeman for over twenty years and being involved with Montana State University as a research professor and short-term director of the Montana University System Water Center has allowed me to continue my ecological studies both in Yellowstone National Park and the Greater Yellowstone area.

This book is a culmination of my continued interest in the area and recognition that we need to understand the past to better manage the future. I am now one of the old-timers in the Gallatin Canyon and hope to pass on many of my remembrances and of those whom I have known in the canyon over the past sixty-five years or more.

Acknowledgements

I wish to acknowledge and thank the several sources of the historic photographs used in this book. Gathering many of these historic photos took several years by Heidi Clark Bellorado, a graduate student working with me at Montana State University in Bozeman. I especially thank Heidi for these efforts and for taking some of the repeat photos. The photographs used in this book come from several sources. These include the archives of several federal agencies: U.S. Geological Survey (USGS), U.S. Forest Service (USFS), U.S. National Park Service (NPS) and Yellowstone National Park (YNP). Sources of most historic photos were museums and the Montana State University Library, located in the area. These include (with their initials as used in the book): Gallatin Historic Museum (GHM), in Bozeman, Montana; Museum of the Rockies (MOR), in Bozeman, Montana; Yellowstone Historic Center (YHC), in West Yellowstone, Montana; Historic Crail Ranch Conservators (HCRC) at Big Sky; and the Montana State University Library (MSU). The archivists or collection managers of these museums have been extremely helpful in this project. These include Rachel Phillips at GHM, Steve Jackson at MOR, Kathryn McKee at YHC, Anne Marie Mistretta at Crail Ranch and Kim Scott at the MSU Library. A few photos came from private collections, including those of the Gamel family website created by Charlotte Gamel, 320 Ranch and Buck's T-4 Lodge. The sources of all photos are acknowledged in each photo caption (cited as in the above parentheses).

Chapter 1
SETTING THE SCENE

HISTORIC BACKGROUND

The "Gallatin Way" was an early promotional term applied to the road through the Gallatin Canyon from Bozeman, Montana, to the west gate of Yellowstone National Park. This route, also referred to as the West Gallatin Road, traverses the canyon southward through the northwest corner of the park on to West Yellowstone (Map 1.1). Much of its route follows the path of the West Gallatin River, called *Cut-tuh-o'-gwa* (swift water) by the Shoshone Indians. From its origins in Yellowstone National Park, the river flows north some seventy miles through the Upper Basin, much of it in Yellowstone National Park, through the middle basin near Taylor Fork, through canyons to the Lower Basin where both West Fork (now the tributary supporting much of the Big Sky Resort area) and Porcupine Creek enter. From there, the river flows north through narrow canyons most of the way before entering the Gallatin Valley (Map 1.2), a rich agricultural valley rapidly being occupied by the sprawling city of Bozeman. After leaving the Gallatin Valley, the river joins the Madison and Jefferson Rivers near Three Forks, Montana, to form the Missouri River.

The Gallatin Way has been a gateway to Yellowstone National Park for well over a century (Map 1.1). Prior to that time, and before the arrival of new occupants in the late 1800s and early 1900s, the route was inhabited by several indigenous tribes, some seasonally and others more

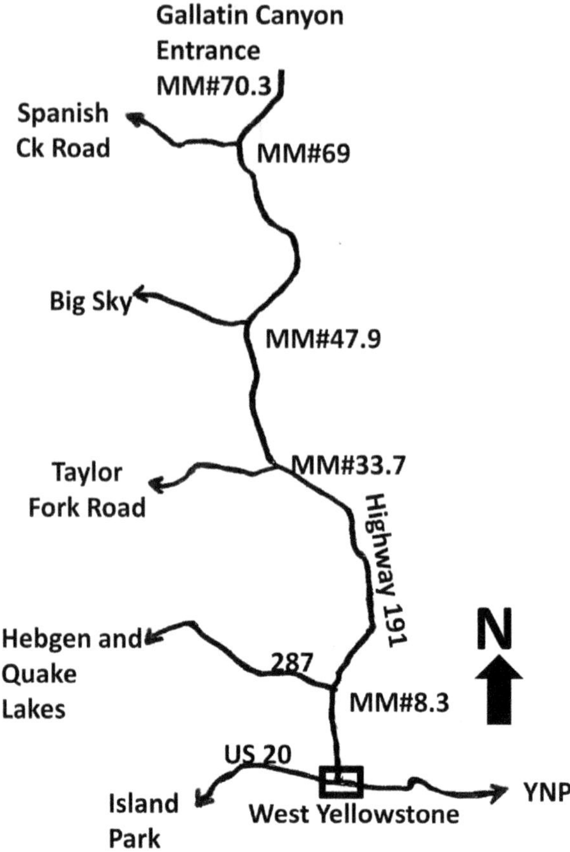

Map 1.1. The Gallatin Way, Highway 191, from the entrance of the Gallatin Canyon where one leaves the Gallatin Valley to West Yellowstone. Mile markers starting with zero in West Yellowstone indicate some major side roads.

permanently. There is also evidence at archaeological sites of indigenous occupation and/or use of the canyon during the later Paleo-Indian period (BCE 6000+/-), such as those along Storm Castle, Greek and Portal Creeks and the West Fork. There was also use into the mid-1800s by Indians called the Sheepeaters (offshoot of Bannocks), evidenced by wickiups still "standing" in northwest Yellowstone National Park along Wickiup Creek (once called Wigwam Creek) about a half mile north of Specimen Creek. As Indians abandoned the area, they were followed in the early to mid-1800s by trappers and, later in that century, by cattle ranchers, lumber companies and miners and eventually guest ranches in the early 1900s. When Ferdinand Vandeveer Hayden came through the canyon in 1872, a

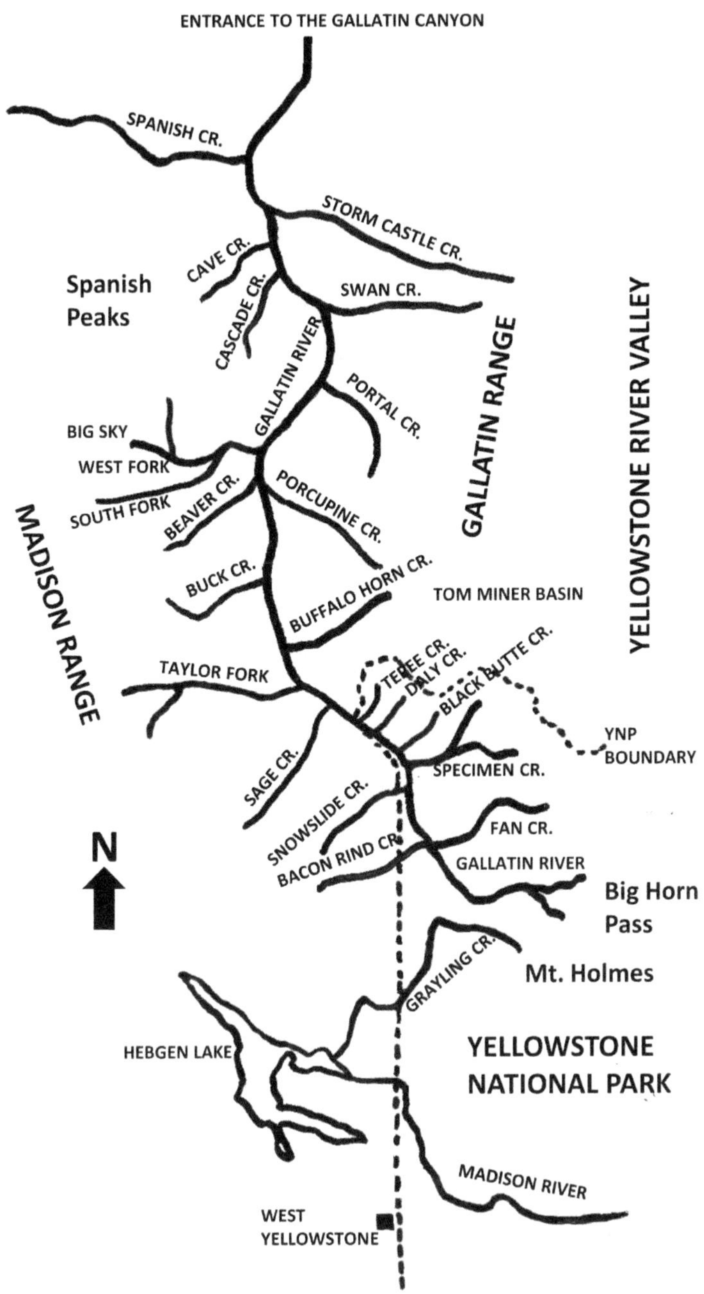

Map 1.2. Rivers along the Gallatin Way from the canyon entrance to West Yellowstone.

year after his 1871 Yellowstone Expedition, he reported that "this canyon had never been explored by any scientific party previously, and even the settlers in the open valley below knew nothing about it. A few hardy miners had ascended it in search of precious minerals." There was little success by miners in the Gallatin Canyon, although evidence of some old mine sites still remains. Trappers depleted the beaver population and moved on to more productive rivers. Cattle ranching and logging continued into the early and mid-twentieth century, when dude or guest ranches were established and more people came as visitors. Thus, as you travel the Gallatin Way leading to the west entrance of the world's first national park, think back on what it must have been like when the route in many places was no more than a wooded or rocky trail or a muddy road that was impassable much of the year or a passageway for livestock.

To give perspective to conditions through the canyon prior to road building, one only need look at photos taken by the photographer William Henry Jackson, who traveled with Hayden in 1872 (Figures 1.1 and 1.2), and read Hayden's description of travel conditions up the Gallatin in 1872. He described the canyon in his 1873 U.S. Geological Survey (USGS) report on surveys of western territories: "For a distance of ten miles we were obliged to travel with our pack-train very slowly and with great risk. In no part of the West have we found a more difficult trail, and this may account for the fact that so few persons have ascended the stream." In this 1872 expedition, Hayden traveled north from west of the Tetons into Montana Territory, passing down the Madison River to Three Forks and then to the Gallatin Valley and south through the Gallatin Canyon and back to Yellowstone National Park. In addition to Jackson's photos titled "Trail through the woods in the West Gallatin" (Figure 1.1) and "Our trail over the rocks" (Figure 1.2), several other photos from this expedition are presented in this book.

Jackson also was the photographer for the 1871 Hayden Expeditions that explored the Yellowstone region in northwestern Wyoming Territory. That expedition reported on the region's natural resource characteristics, including its unusual natural wonders. These included phenomena such as geysers, bubbling mudpots and steaming pools of water reported earlier by the mountain man John Coulter. Coulter visited the area in 1808, having parted from the second Lewis and Clark Expedition of 1804–6. This area was then often referred to as "Coulter's Hell." Reports from Hayden, Jackson's photography and the art of Thomas Moran (Moran was on the expedition as artist to capture the landscape, as photography was very new and

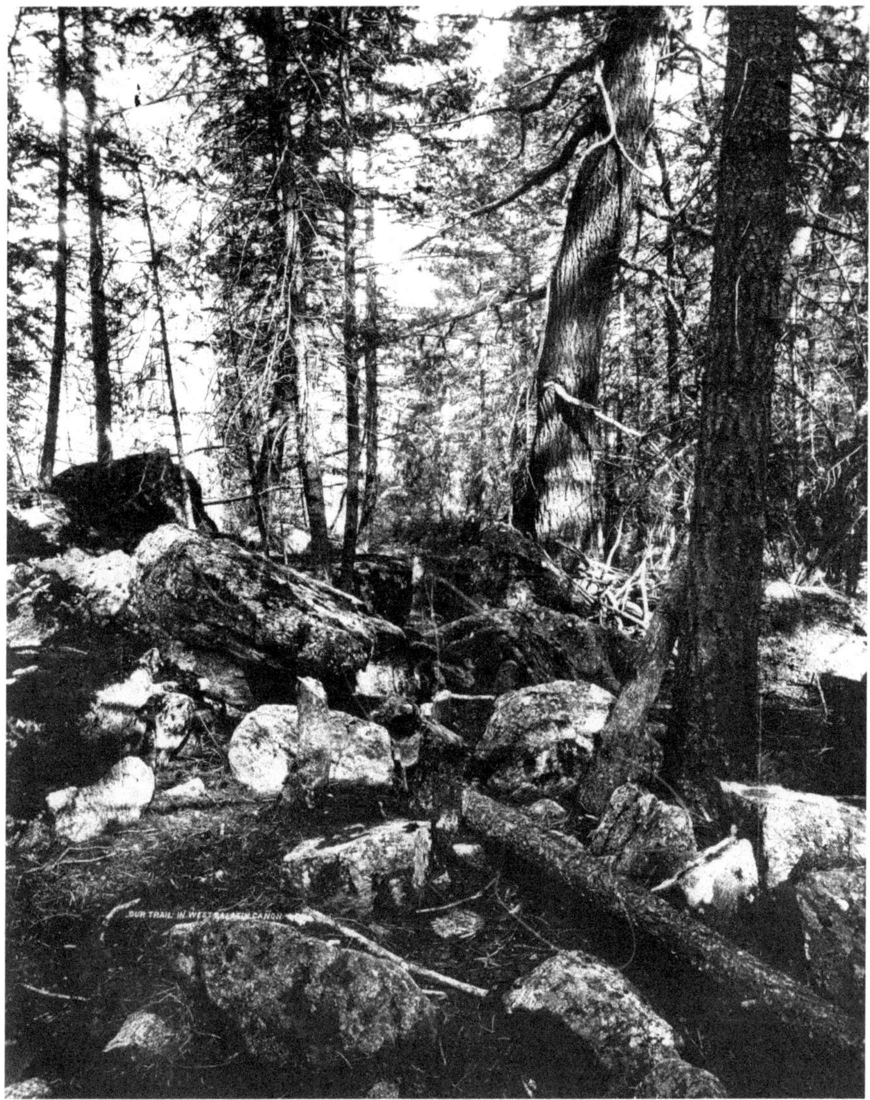

Figure 1.1 (1872). Trail through the woods of West Gallatin Canyon, location unknown. Photograph by W.H. Jackson during the 1872 Hayden Expedition. *USGS.*

uncertain) helped sway Congress in 1872 to create the world's first national park, Yellowstone National Park. President Grant signed the bill creating the park on March 1, 1872. The Yellowstone Act of 1872 designated the region as a public "pleasuring-ground," which would be preserved "from injury or spoliation, of all timber, mineral deposits, natural curiosities, or wonders

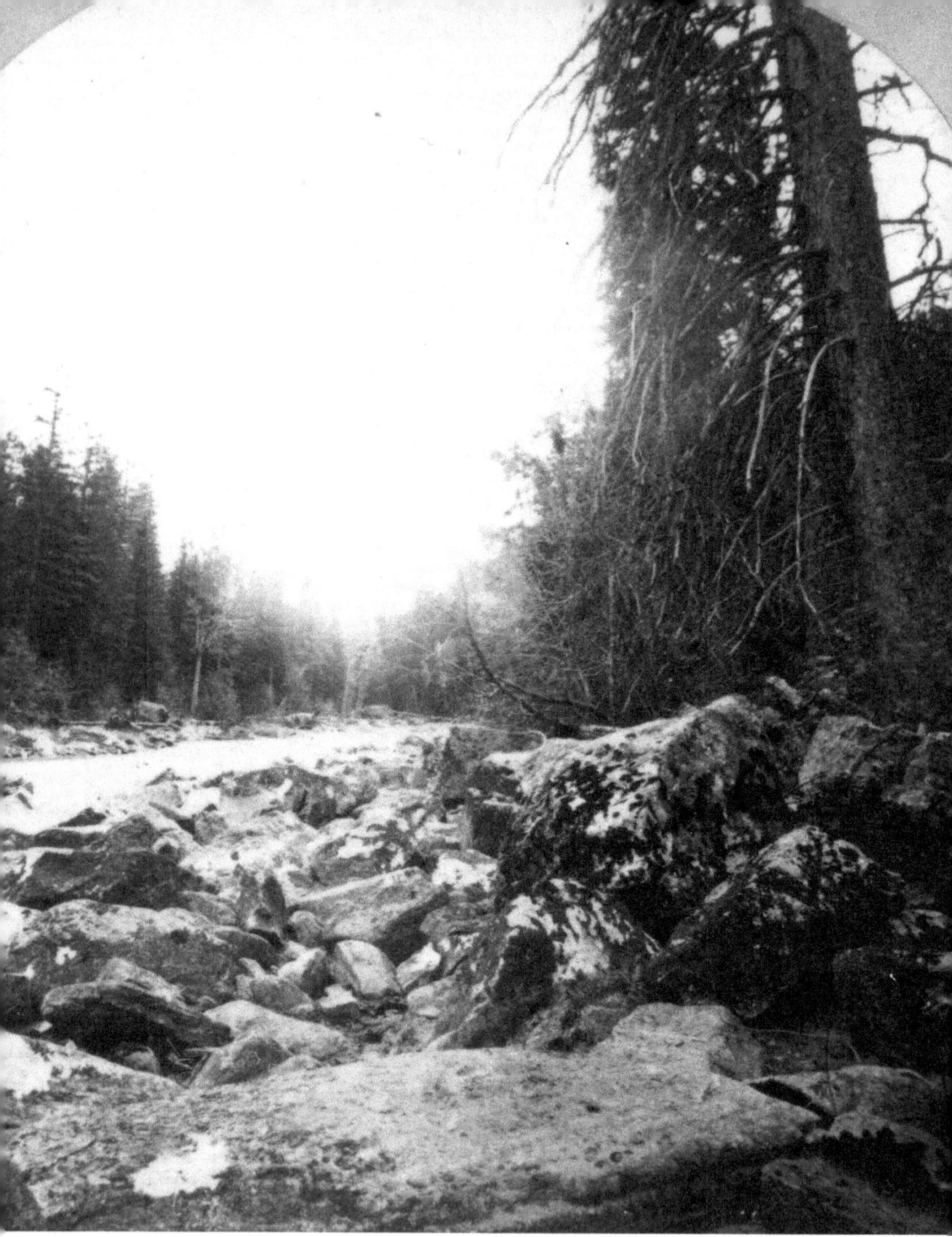

Figure 1.2 (1872). Trail over the rocks in West Gallatin Canyon, location unknown but probably in the narrow part of the canyon where there is little floodplain to walk on (original in stereo). Photograph by W.H. Jackson during the 1872 Hayden Expedition. *USGS.*

within." This surprised the country, which was accustomed to exploiting the resources of this new territory.

One early "adventurer" through the Gallatin Canyon is known to most Americans. In 1888, Theodore Roosevelt, future president of the United States, took a bear hunting trip into the canyon and beyond. His party camped the first night at Beaver Creek, a creek just south of today's Ophir School, and then the second night at Monument Creek, a creek flowing from the west into the Gallatin River near the northwestern corner of Yellowstone National Park. They then moved on to Riverside, park headquarters at that time on the Madison River just east of present-day West Yellowstone. From there, Roosevelt visited Jackson Hole for several weeks. Roosevelt had hoped to travel within Yellowstone National Park at that time. Eventually, he would travel through the park in 1903, when he was president and came to dedicate the Yellowstone National Park entrance arch in Gardiner, Montana, where he laid the cornerstone for the arch, now called Roosevelt Arch.

When Yellowstone National Park was created in 1872, there were few routes for travelers from Bozeman to the town called Yellowstone at the west entrance of the park, the town eventually becoming West Yellowstone in 1920. Also, there were no easy routes to get to the Upper Gallatin Basin, where the northwestern corner of the park was located. As there was no wagon route through Gallatin Canyon in the 1890s, the wagon route (if one could call it that) from Bozeman to the Upper Gallatin was via Trail Creek east of Bozeman to the Yellowstone River Valley, then up the Yellowstone to Tom Miner Basin. From Tom Miner, the traveler would go west over the pass into upper Buffalo Horn Creek or Tepee Creek drainages (tributaries of the Gallatin River) and then down to the Gallatin River, arriving at the Gallatin near either the location of 320 Ranch or the Tepee Creek confluence with the Gallatin River just north of the northwestern corner of Yellowstone (see Map 1.2 for the location of the various rivers). It was, however, possible to walk, move livestock or ride horses through the narrow parts of the Gallatin Canyon, as Jackson did in 1872. This entailed many crossings of the river, which, like most mountain rivers, ran high in spring from snowmelt.

The lack of easy access did not keep people from the canyon but required that those who did venture through it, or decide to develop and stay, had to be very self-sufficient. Returning to "town" was often a multiday adventure and, in some cases such as heavy winter snows, an event that was delayed until late spring or summer.

The desire of citizens in Bozeman in the early 1900s for easier access to the west gate of Yellowstone National Park and the town of Yellowstone led to eventual construction of a road through the Gallatin Canyon to the upper Gallatin, then down Grayling Creek into the Madison Valley. The history of the Gallatin Road, described later in this chapter, extends over many decades in the early to mid-twentieth century. This history describes how the road came into existence and how it was improved from a muddy track (Figures 1.3 and 1.4) to the condition of today. It is integral to understanding the expansion and development in the canyon, for without the road, and because of the road, many of today's locations would not exist.

In addition to early explorers, ranchers and developers in the canyon, the fast-flowing river (Cut-tuh-o'-gwa) enticed those who wanted to harness the river for reclamation to propose several dams along the course of the river. Initially, three damsites were proposed by the U.S. Army: one just downstream of Taylor Fork/Gallatin River confluence (MM#34), one just downstream and north of the West Fork/Gallatin River confluence (MM#48) and one near the mouth of the canyon just downstream of the Spanish Creek/Gallatin River confluence (MM#68.2). These proposals occurred under the New Deal in the 1930s, a period when dams were being

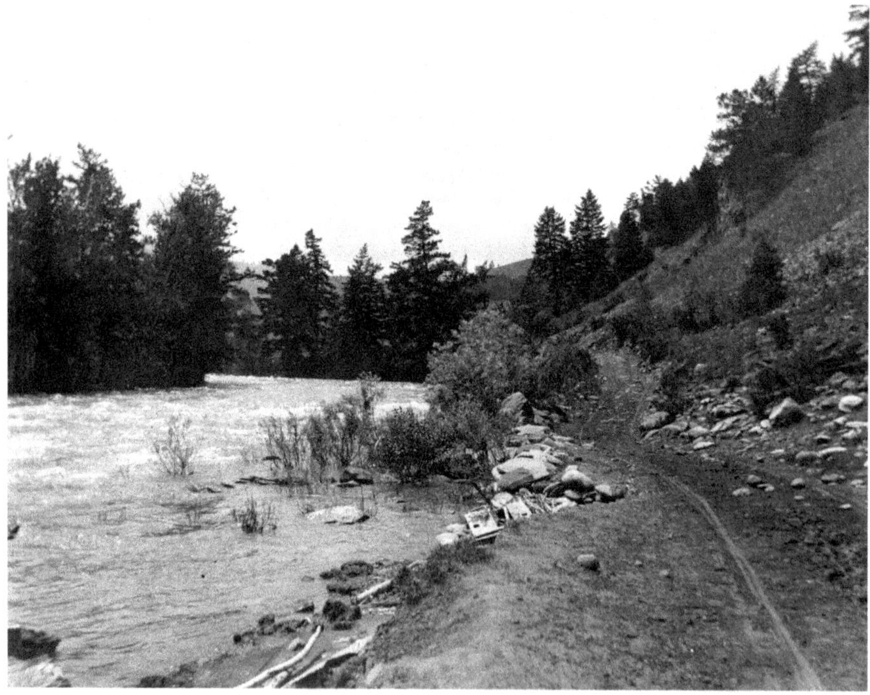

Figure 1.3 (circa 1907). Gallatin River road (location unknown) in very early conditions with little road base and no hard surface. *GHM*.

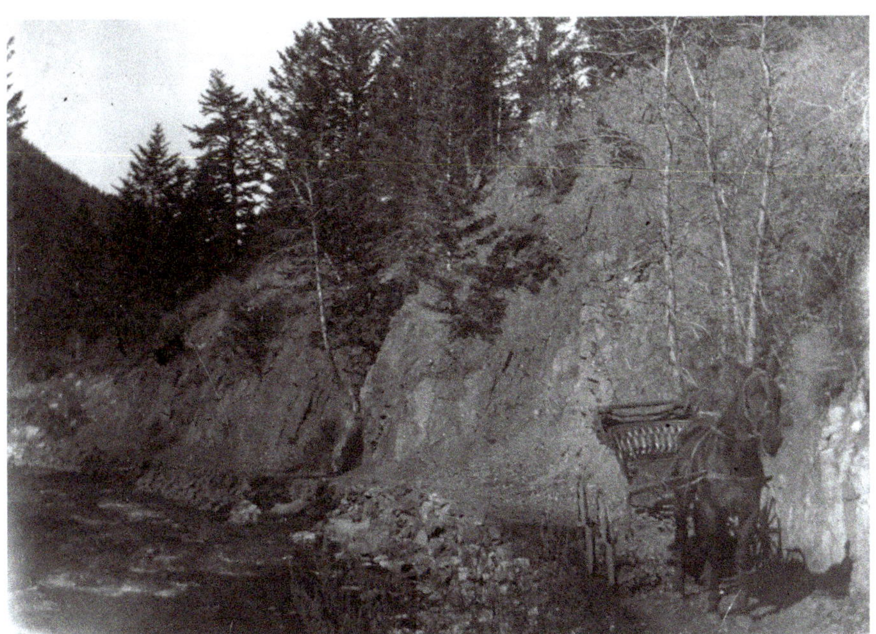

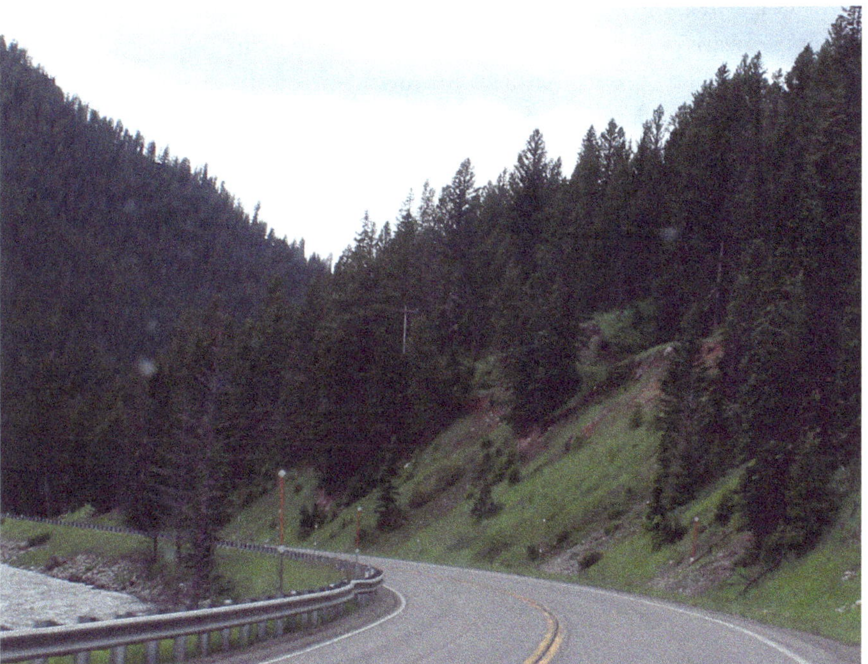

Figure 1.4. Gallatin Canyon along the Gallatin River road 1.2 miles south of Red Cliff Campground (MM#40.3).
Upper photo (1908): Horse and buggy in a location where the canyon wall was cut and fill was used to create a very narrow roadway. *GHM.*
Lower photo (2016): The highway has been placed in the river channel and the river moved to the east (left in picture). Location of upper photo is farther down the highway at the curve.

built throughout the West. In 1937, the Bureau of Reclamation approved the West Fork and Spanish Creek sites for dam building, but cost and World War II prevented any action. Proposals to dam the Gallatin River near Spanish Creek resurfaced in the 1950s, again supported by the Bureau of Reclamation. Fortunately for the Gallatin Canyon and citizens who loved it and opposed dams, proposals for dam construction never achieved sufficient appropriations or public support and eventually died. The possible construction sites for dams at various locations along the West Gallatin River are mentioned again when the area for each location is discussed.

We tend to forget how things have changed along the Gallatin Way over the last century and a half. We now readily accept our modern ways, transportation and all, and often do not realize that others have paved the way for today's occupation and enjoyment of this beautiful route through the mountains, canyons and valleys to the west gate of Yellowstone National Park. Many of the conditions along this route and their changes, especially in the Gallatin Canyon, have been described in several books and documents about the history of the area. These documents often include historic photos that offer a glimpse into the past; however, few of these documents allow us to "see and understand the changes" that have taken place along the Gallatin Way, through the canyon and beyond. These changes may open our eyes to how modernization of our travel, expansion of our occupation and losses of the near "pristine nature" of the route are part of the history of the canyon and the Gallatin Way.

As one reads this book, local people will discover many familiar sites—for example, Storm Castle peak (originally called Castle Rock or, as described in 1872 by photographer Jackson, "a limestone mountain on the east side of the canyon, lying directly upon volcanic rocks"); House Rock (a large rock in the river in mid-canyon); Karst Kamp area, adjacent to today's Park View West Development and just south of Moose Creek campground; Lone Mountain at the head of West Fork, home of the Big Sky Resort; and Black Butte, just inside the northwest corner of Yellowstone National Park. Scenes in early photos of these locations, although familiar upon first glance, appear differently than they do today upon closer inspection. The river often appears to have changed very little; however, comparisons indicate how much the river, often changing on its own, has been altered by having its channel moved to satisfy transportation and development needs. Developments have come and gone, but many locations still exist, some with newer structures and names. The Big Sky development has obviously changed the face of the canyon much more than most earlier developments. Long-term residents of the canyon and locations farther south often viewed Big Sky as a blemish on the beauty of the canyon, while others now see it as an integral part of today's canyon and the Gallatin Way. Change is normal—everything changes over time; thus, how the canyon and the Gallatin Way have changed is a lesson to recognize that we "cannot turn back the clock."

This book is organized to offer the reader the experience of entering and traveling south along the Gallatin Way through the canyon and basins from near Gallatin Gateway to West Yellowstone (Map 1.1). This organization allows today's traveler to experience the same route as people in earlier days when they went to Yellowstone National Park from Bozeman, traveling up the canyon toward the headwaters of the Gallatin River to its divide with Grayling Creek and then south down Grayling Creek to the Madison River basin, now home of Hebgen Lake behind Hebgen Dam (built in 1914), and then on to West Yellowstone (see Map 1.2 to follow the pathway of the rivers).

HISTORY OF THE GALLATIN WAY ROAD (WEST GALLATIN ROAD)

The traveler along the Gallatin Way may assume the road has been unchanged for some time, and yet, history of the Gallatin Way and Gallatin Canyon is very much aligned with the highway and its history. This highway through the Gallatin Canyon and on to West Yellowstone has seen many changes over the past century or more. This changing highway, or road in early days, reflects other changes that took place along this route (shown with photos in this book). As the road improved, more opportunities opened for development and vehicular travel. Consequently, it is important to review how this route changed over time so that changes shown in the repeat photographs can be related to access and travel conditions along the ever-changing route up the canyon through the upper basins and on to West Yellowstone. The following is a summary of the history of the Gallatin Way road, with information acquired, for example, from Montana Department of Transportation, national park road history and personal observations since the early 1950s. Where helpful, mile marker numbers (MM#) are included for reference, numbers starting in West Yellowstone and increasing going north along U.S. Highway 191.

The road up the canyon wasn't even started until the late 1890s, reaching Taylor Fork (MM#34) in August 1898 (other dates, for example 1901, have been given for completion of the first road to Taylor Fork). This road facilitated getting supplies to the railroad tie company developed by Walter Cooper, located about seven miles up Taylor Fork valley west of the "new" road. Even by this time, the main road up the Gallatin may not have been fully completed, as a bridge near Cave Creek and Cascade Creek, downstream from the present thirty-five-mile-per-hour curved bridge (MM#61.3), appears to have been only partially completed in 1899 (Figure 3.6). This bridge was completed by 1900 (Figure 3.7) (see chapter 3). The new road was wide enough for a wagon or buggy but had a dirt surface that would not hold up in inclement weather.

Imagine today what a trip up the Gallatin Canyon actually would have entailed in the early 1900s. The "road" was no more than a wide trail, a muddy wagon road. Several of the photos in this book show this road condition (e.g., Figures 1.3 and 1.4), and some of the photos were taken some years later, when some road improvement had taken place, although it may not be apparent (e.g., 1920s, Figure 8.12). In 1908, the first car was driven up the canyon to West Fork, where there were several homesteads. The car, driven by Maurice Lamme of Bozeman, had a chain drive and hard rubber tires.

In the late 1800s, there were several other early routes leading to the west entrance of Yellowstone National Park. From the Virginia City and Ennis area, travelers made their way south through the Madison Valley, arriving at Raynolds Pass. From there, they either proceeded east through the Madison River Canyon to the basin now holding Hebgen Lake, or they crossed Raynolds Pass to Henry's Lake and then went east over Targhee Pass into the Madison basin toward the west entrance. By the 1880s, stagecoaches crossed Centennial Valley and Red Rock Pass before joining the route over Targhee Pass.

In the early 1900s, people in Bozeman wanted a shorter route to Yellowstone National Park's west entrance and encouraged road construction south from Bozeman and the Gallatin Valley through the Gallatin Canyon to the park. A proposal in 1904 for a road to the park was to extend it south from Taylor Fork and place it over Big Horn Pass (Map 1.2), near the headwaters of the Gallatin River, ending it near Mammoth Hot Springs. This route followed the Bannock Indian Trail used by the Indians when they traveled back and forth from the Snake River plain (in present-day Idaho) through Yellowstone to the Absaroka Mountains. It also was occasionally used later by wagons attempting to reach Mammoth, a difficult journey over the mountains. This route was once proposed for a railroad in the early 1900s. During this period, Union Pacific was building tracks from Monida, Idaho, to the west entrance to the park and had reached the area near Big Spring in Island Park, Idaho. Eventually, the railroad would reach the west entrance in 1907 and begin service in 1908.

In October 1905, the Bozeman Chamber of Commerce sponsored a trip to take U.S. Senate members on a trip up the Gallatin Canyon to promote a stage route from Bozeman to the west gate of the park. This trip apparently did not result in funds for the road. However, in 1907, funds were made available to survey a possible road from Bozeman through the northwest corner of the park, following a similar route to the 1904 proposal. This road would start in the park from a point seven miles south of Mammoth Hot Springs on the Norris Hot Springs Road and meet the road along the Gallatin River at a point where the river crosses the park's northwestern boundary. It was determined that this route would not only be too costly to maintain but also would be open only a few summer months of the year.

Eventually, in 1910, Gallatin County commissioners received permission to build a road from Bozeman to the west entrance (now West Yellowstone) through the northwest corner of Yellowstone National Park. At that time, this would include fourteen miles in the park.

In October 1911, the road was completed from Taylor Fork (31.10 miles, with 14.00 miles in the park; in 1913, it was considered 17.86 miles in the park with forty-seven bridges; there is no explanation for the discrepancy in miles in the park). The road had sixty bridges because of the number of small creeks flowing across the path of the road and occasional wetlands. This route included a 120-foot-long bridge over Madison River about 4.00 miles north of the west entrance. Once the road was completed, the park constructed a checkpoint "soldier station" at the park line near Black Butte (there is no longer any evidence of this structure).

The initial road was constructed as a wagon road; however, once the road was completed, the Gallatin County commissioners sought permission from Yellowstone National Park to allow cars on the road. At that time, no cars had been permitted in Yellowstone National Park. The request was forwarded to the secretary of the interior. In May 1913, the secretary of the interior granted permission for cars on the Gallatin Road in Yellowstone National Park but nowhere else in the park. Road conditions did not allow car passage on this stretch of the Gallatin Road until 1914. Eventually, when roads in the main part of the park were opened to cars in 1915, the cars competed with horse-drawn conveyances, creating major issues. Shortly thereafter, horse-drawn conveyances were eliminated. This new West Gallatin Road cut the travel distance for cars from Bozeman to the west gate town of Yellowstone (now West Yellowstone) from 136 miles via the Madison to about 90 miles.

Even when the road was passable, road conditions were not easy for automobiles. In 1914, the U.S. Army Corps of Engineers described the West Gallatin Road in Yellowstone National Park as "narrow, fairly easy grades and a fairly good dirt road most of the way." However, it was miry in wet weather and was late opening in the spring of 1913 and really not passable until 1914. Some of the expense of maintenance at the time was for clearing out trees carried down across the road by snowslides.

In August 1918, at a meeting held in Bozeman between Horace Albright (then assistant director of the National Park Service) and Henry Graves (chief forester of the Forest Service), a tentative agreement was reached whereby the U.S. Forest Service (USFS) agreed to construct a road in the forest reserve along the east side of the Gallatin River in the area of Crown Butte, Lava Butte, Black Butte and Specimen Creek (MM#31.5 to MM#26.5) to the location of the Gallatin Soldier Station in the park located near Specimen Creek (built in 1910 and "accidentally" burned down in 1918) (for more on the soldier station, see chapter 9). This would be an improvement on the county road completed in 1913 that crossed the Gallatin River south of Daly Creek near MM#30 (Figure 9.2) and then, after entering the park, crossed the river to the east over a bridge located near the location of a future park cabin (see Figures 9.6 and 9.7). From there, it passed a small Soldier Check Station on the east side of the river where the road turned south farther into the park. Existence of most of these buildings is no longer evident, except the 1910 soldier station foundation farther south (Figure 9.8). In 1918 (park records indicate 1925), a ranger station, barn and other buildings were constructed on the west side of the river where the bridge crossed toward the small soldier station (these buildings were removed in 1968, as was the bridge).

As part of the 1918 agreement, the National Park Service improved the remaining portion of the road within the park. As part of this improvement, the National Park Service suggested in 1919 that the West Gallatin Road be widened and that the section from Grayling Creek to the town of Yellowstone (West Yellowstone), Montana, be rerouted within the park boundary. Congress stopped this proposal because it thought enough had been spent on Yellowstone National Park roads. The road from Grayling Creek to West

Yellowstone mostly remained outside the park, as it does today, but with major changes in routing in the 1950s and '60s, some within the park.

In 1920, Gallatin County commissioners proposed improving the Gallatin Road with gravel from Salesville (now Gallatin Gateway) to the point where the West Gallatin Road was constructed by the USFS near the present north entrance to the park (circa MM#31). In the late 1920s, there was still an effort (supported by the Chicago, Milwaukee and St. Paul Rail Road [CMStP RR]) to build a road up the Gallatin River and over Big Horn Pass at the river's headwaters. This would allow the CMStP RR to bus passengers from its Inn at Gallatin Gateway up the West Gallatin Road to Mammoth Hot Springs to compete with passengers arriving at the north entrance to Yellowstone near Gardiner via the Northern Pacific Rail Road. Yellowstone National Park discouraged this new road in order to preserve the wilderness nature of the park in that area. This proposed route continued to be considered into the 1940s.

In 1926, the park decided to improve its portion of the Gallatin Way Road by moving it mostly to the north and west of Grayling Creek and the upper Gallatin River, as it was at that time no more than a "muddy track" with many log bridges over Grayling Creek and occasional wetlands. By 1928, most of this construction was complete, including new bridges over Bacon Rind Creek and Specimen Creek. The location of this road is still evident with road cuts apparent west of the Gallatin River between Specimen and Bacon Rind Creeks (MM#26.5 to 22.7).

In 1929, President Hoover signed two bills within several days of each other, one that created Grand Teton National Park and the other that altered some of the boundaries of Yellowstone National Park. Under the second bill, Yellowstone National Park annexed an area in its northwest corner from near Tepee Creek to north of Specimen Creek and bounded on the west by the Gallatin River and on the east by the divide between Daly and Black Butte Creeks and Tom Miner Basin (Map 1.3). This allowed the Park Service to preserve the petrified forest in this area. It also put some of the road constructed by the Forest Service in 1918 into the park.

During the early to mid-1930s, the Gallatin Way Road was resurfaced and oiled, greatly improving its durability. A 1935 road map shows the entire length of the highway through the canyon to West Yellowstone with a road-oil surface. Road-oil is a very basic asphalt surface (like the blacktop once used on playgrounds), so you could technically say that the highway was paved by 1935. This paving in the 1930s may have been part of a federal make-work or CCC project during the Great Depression.

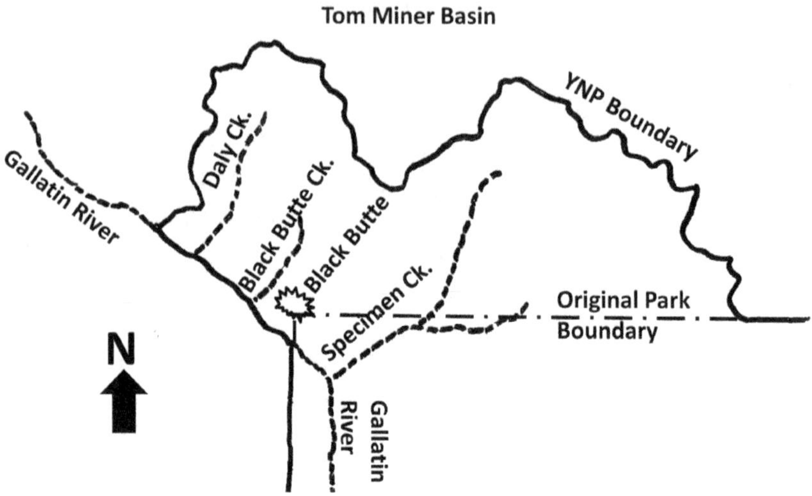

Map 1.3. Northwest corner of Yellowstone National Park, which was annexed to the park in 1929.

No major work was done on the West Gallatin Road during the late 1940s and the Second World War years.

During the 1950s, the Yellowstone National Park portion of the West Gallatin Road (the Gallatin Way) was surveyed and considered in very bad condition. This report came from a 1952 inspection of the primary roads in Yellowstone National Park that showed that the overall system was in generally good condition, with the exception of the Gallatin Road. The unstable subgrade, the less-than-desirable base and the heavy volume of truck traffic continued to plague the engineers on this section of the road. Approximately 75 percent of the 21.3 miles of road had been patched or showed distress. It was thought that at least 12.5 miles of the road would need complete reconstruction.

In 1955, the State of Montana took over maintenance of the whole West Gallatin Road, including the portion in Yellowstone National Park. Following this takeover, the state decided to greatly improve highway conditions from Bozeman to West Yellowstone, rerouting the highway along a relatively level route and building several new bridges to accompany the highway improvement. This construction was done to create safer conditions and allow more large (interstate) trucking. Thus, in the 1950s and 1960s, the Gallatin Way Road saw many changes. Where there were hills (e.g., Sagebrush Point hill, MM#59; Figure 4.3) or sharp curves (e.g., "hairpin curve along Grayling Creek near MM#16"; Figure 10.1), the highway was placed along the river or aligned in a straighter route. Filling in the river to accommodate the highway was difficult in early years. During this period, not only was fill placed in the river to widen the road but several locations had the river rerouted or "moved over" to allow highway construction where the river channel was originally located. Examples of this river rerouting occurred along the river below Sagebrush Point just downstream of Greek Creek Campground (circa MM#59; Figure 4.4), downstream of Rainbow Ranch at Halfway Point (MM#43; Figure 7.1) and the stretch of highway between Specimen Creek bridge and Bacon Rind Creek (MM#26.5 to MM#22.7), where not only was the river put in a new channel in one location but wetlands were filled in to allow for a straight highway route. In addition to rerouting Highway 191, several bridges were either replaced, removed or rebuilt.

The Gallatin Way Road continues to have regular maintenance, but the basic highway alignment remains the same as it was after the major construction period of the 1950s and '60s. Concern for the heavy volume of traffic to Big Sky from Bozeman has initiated many suggestions for widening the highway or rerouting it; however, both those efforts would require major disruption of the Gallatin Canyon, a suggestion most local citizens would discourage.

Repeat Photography for This Book

Repeat photography—the retaking of historic photos to describe changes—has been used for many decades. Locations where repeat photography has been used include general landscapes, national parks and urban areas. In some cases, it has been used to quantify changes in landscape cover to address management issues. For this book, historic photos have been acquired from many sources such as governmental archives, museum collections and personal collections. All sources are credited for each photo. To repeat a photograph, one must first identify the exact location where the historic photograph was taken. In some cases, documented for certain photos, the past location was forested or no longer achievable due to road building or destruction of the photo point, and thus the repeat photograph is taken from

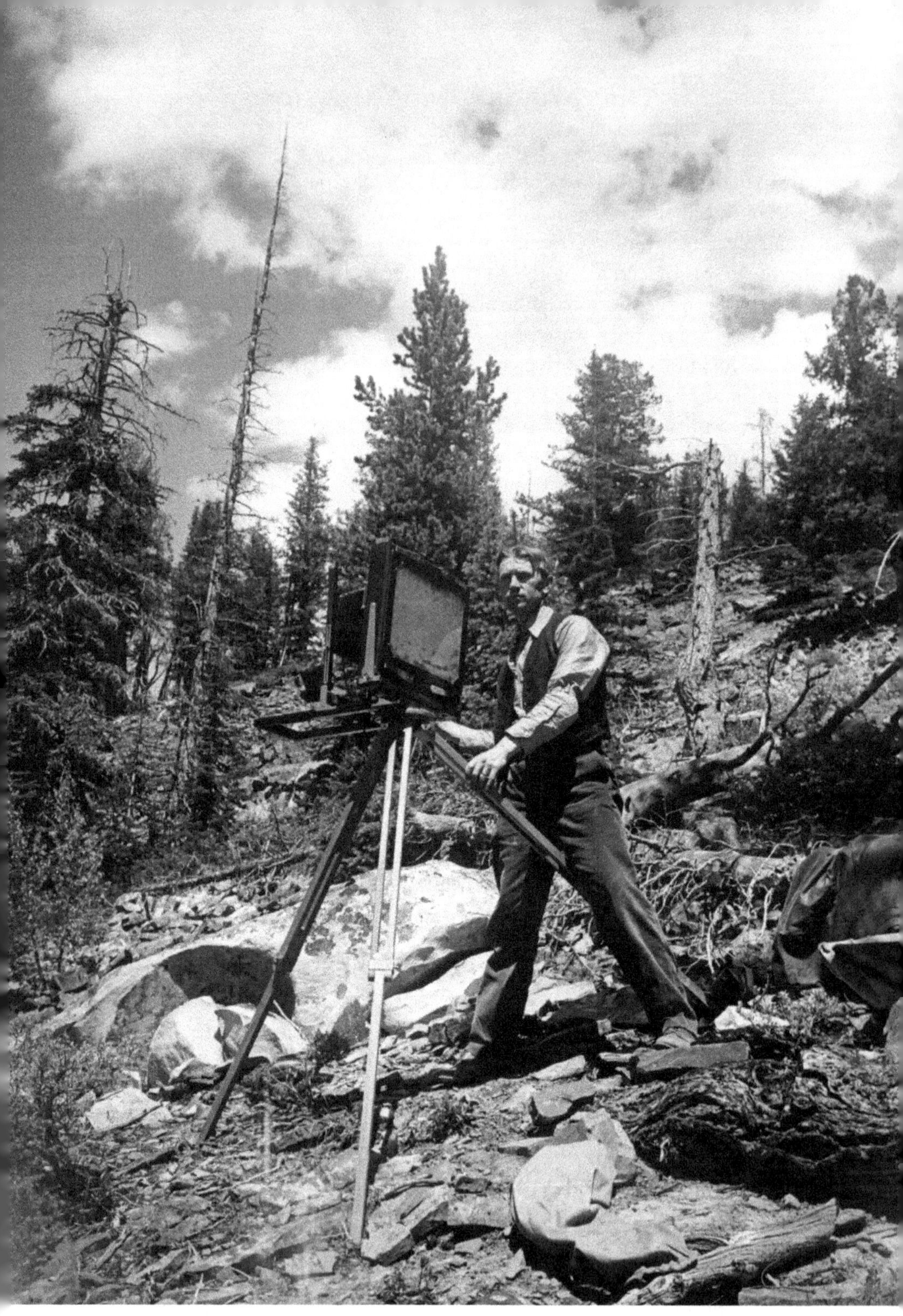

the next best location. Some repeat photos do not exactly mimic the location of the historic photo but rather show a slightly broader view.

Many early photos were taken with big boxlike (eleven by fourteen inches) cameras using glass photo plates and mounted on tripods. These were often placed in very difficult locations, as noted in the photograph of Albert Schlechten photographing from a rocky slope (Figure 1.5). In contrast, a single-lens reflex Canon EOS Rebel T3i camera was used for most of the repeat photography in this book without a tripod, as many photos were taken standing on or immediately adjacent to a very busy highway. For many repeat photos, a wide-angle lens was used because many early cameras took the equivalent of today's wide-angle photos, and to get the same width of view from the same photo point, a wide-angle lens was necessary.

Opposite page: Figure 1.5 (circa 1910). Albert Schlechten with his eleven- by fourteen-inch view camera, Gallatin Canyon, Montana. *MOR*.

Chapter 2

Entering the Gallatin Canyon

(MM#70.3 to MM#63.6)

The entrance or mouth of Gallatin Canyon is located about five miles south of Gallatin Gateway on U.S. Highway 191 and two miles downstream (north) of where Spanish Creek enters the Gallatin River. At the canyon entrance, Highway 191 crosses the Gallatin River over Harringer Bridge, constructed in 1958, allowing the highway to head south directly out of Gallatin Gateway into the canyon (Map 2.1). The location of this bridge may have been used as a ford across the river in the early years of canyon development. Prior to placement of this bridge, access to the Gallatin Canyon was via River Road (now Gallatin South Road), which enters the canyon just west of Harringer Bridge. Access to this road from Gallatin Gateway is across a bridge just west of the center of town and then south along the river to the canyon's entrance. The Harringer Bridge and new highway reduced the distance and eased travel into the canyon (Figure 2.1).

After entering the canyon, the highway continues through a narrow portion for about two miles before reaching Spanish Creek. The Spanish Creek road leads off to the right (west) before Spanish Creek while the main highway curves left and south over the Spanish Creek Bridge (Figure 2.2). This narrow part of the canyon downstream of Spanish Creek was one location proposed for a dam, once in the 1930s and again in the early 1950s. This narrow section is also the location for the USGS river monitoring gauge, which measures the amount and rate of flow of water leaving the canyon. In the early 1900s, the main road, after leaving the narrowest section of

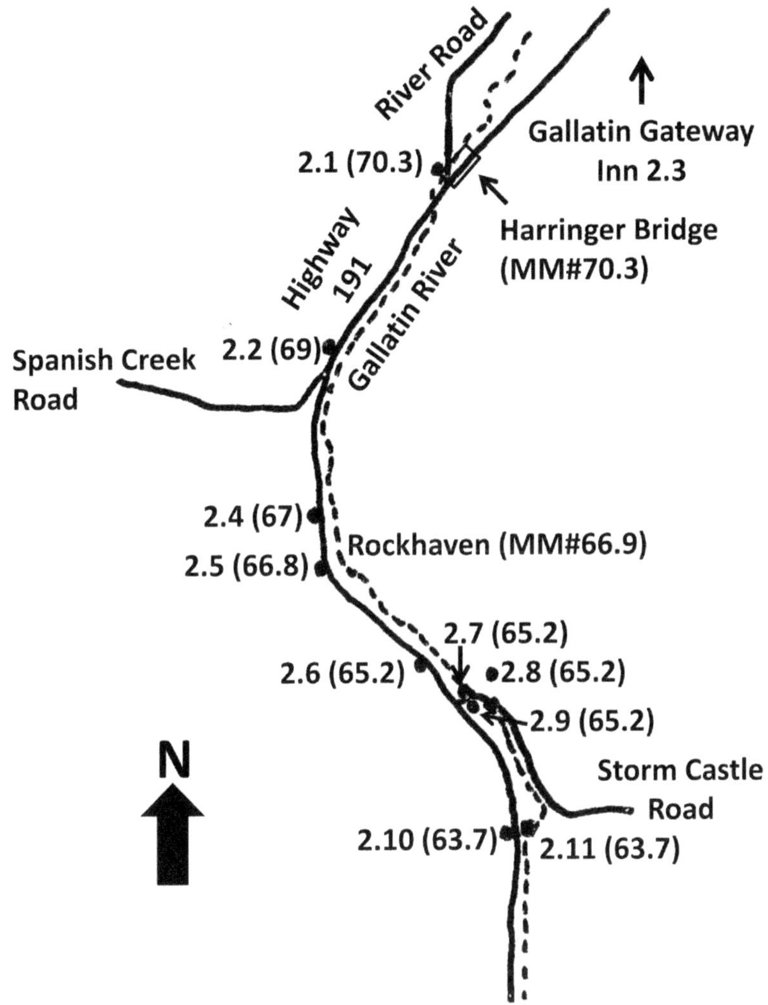

Map 2.1 Entering the canyon (MM#70.3 to #63.6). Map of photo locations along Highway 191 and the Gallatin River (mile markers in parentheses).

the canyon, went west up Spanish Creek to buildings of the Spanish Creek Ranch (Figure 2.2).

In 1892, Thomas Lemon homesteaded the land where Spanish Creek enters the Gallatin River. Lemon sold this property in 1900, including extensive acreage up Spanish Creek, to W.W. Wylie. Wylie, who had a BA and MA, came to Bozeman in 1878 to be superintendent of schools. He

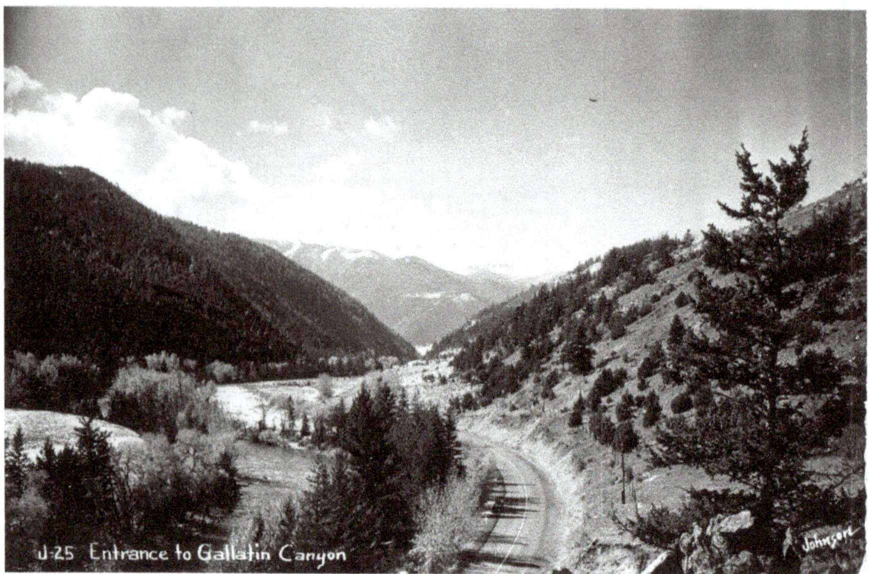

Figure 2.1. Entrance to the Gallatin Canyon just north of Spanish Creek (MM#70.3).
Above photo (circa 1930s): The road in foreground is River Road (original Highway 191), which, until 1958, was the only access route into the Gallatin Canyon. The roadway has inexpensive blacktop. *GHM.*
Below photo (2016): The River Road (now Gateway South Road) in the foreground is paved and joins Highway 191 coming in from the north (*left*) and across the Harringer Bridge built in 1958 (visible behind cottonwood, *left center*) speeding access to the canyon from the Gallatin Valley and Bozeman, Montana.

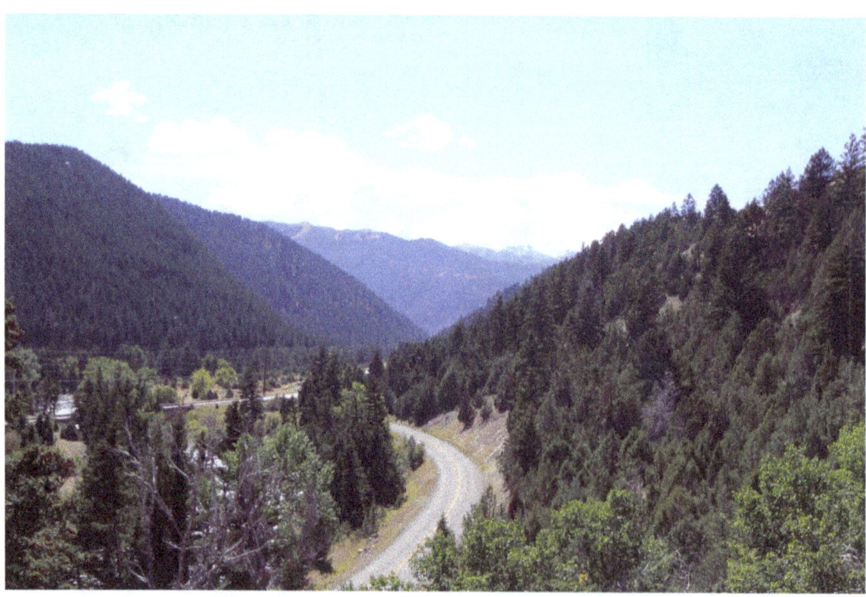

eventually became superintendent of state education. He decided to develop a tourist business in Yellowstone National Park after visiting the park in 1881. The year after that trip, he wrote the first guidebook to the park. To develop his tourist business, he formed two companies, the Wylie Transportation Company and the Wylie Way Camping Company. The first transported tourists, and the second managed many candy-striped tents used by tourists in Yellowstone National Park. He also had more than three thousand horses to transport the tourists and goods and for pack trips, so he needed pasture for wintering the horses. The property near the mouth of Spanish Creek became some of his pastureland. After giving up the Wylie companies in 1905, Wylie tried running a guest ranch at Spanish Creek, but it failed after a year. He sold all he had to Harry Childs and Charles Anceney and left Montana for California and warmer climes.

Anceney had started a small ranch up Spanish Creek in 1895, and Childs had been brought in to help finance expansion of the ranch. The land near the canyon became the Spanish Creek Ranch and the remainder to the west the Flying D Ranch. After Childs and Anceney died, Childs's son-in-law Billie Nichols took over the ranch. In 1944, he sold all of the Flying D Ranch, with the exception of the Spanish Creek Ranch along the Gallatin River, to James Irvine of California. Nichols used the Spanish Creek Ranch until he built a home nearby on the east side of the Gallatin. The land continued to change hands several times after that until Ted Turner purchased it in 1989.

The old road that passed by the ranch buildings—a few built by Childs in 1921 still remain—crossed Spanish Creek and then headed south across what is today horse pasture. At the south end of the pasture, the road went through an arch built by the Milwaukee Railroad in 1926 (see also history of Milwaukee Railroad below) and toward Sheep Rock Mountain seen across the river from the Rockhaven Camp and Retreat Center. In 1931, a bridge was built across Spanish Creek downstream from the ranch buildings, allowing rerouting of the highway. This 1931 bridge was reconstructed in 1955, when the West Gallatin Highway was improved. The highway just south of the Spanish Creek Bridge was improved again in the early twenty-first century, increasing the radius of the curve.

A 1905 trip to promote a canyon road organized by Bozeman Chamber of Commerce (see chapter 1) included the state's two senators. The party had two wagons: one for food and baggage and one for "refreshments." The first night of the trip, the party camped at Spanish Creek, where tables with white linen were set up, and everyone ate and drank heartily. This party

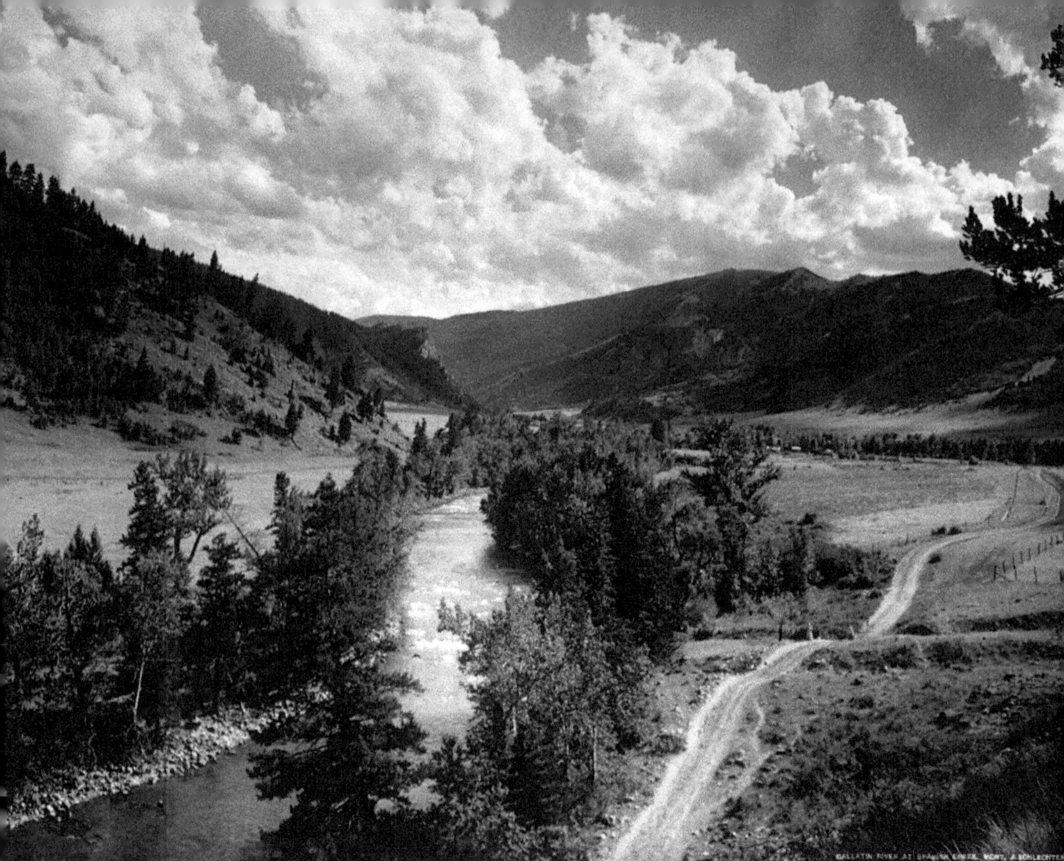

Figure 2.2. Road along the West Gallatin River south of the entrance to the canyon just before crossing Spanish Creek (MM# 69).
Left photo (1900–5): The early road into the canyon was a single-track dirt road following the natural contours. *MOR.*
Right photo (2016): Highway 191 showing turnoff into Spanish Creek following early road alignment with main highway turning left. (Original photo location was inaccessible.)

gradually became disorganized, and only a few made the full trip through the Gallatin Canyon to the upper basin of the Gallatin River.

Access to Yellowstone National Park, aside from locals wanting a road to the west entrance, was also promoted by several railroads that had extended west as a destination for vacations, sightseeing and enjoyment. Three railroads developed facilities or routes to encourage visitors to the park. Tracks up the Yellowstone River Valley were first completed from Livingston to Cinnabar in 1883 by the Rocky Mountain Railroad of Montana and leased as a branch line to the Northern Pacific Railroad, which eventually extended the rail in 1903 to Gardiner, Montana, where it had built a depot. In 1907, the Union Pacific placed tracks from Monida, Idaho, to the west entrance to the park, eventually to be West Yellowstone, beginning rail service in 1908. Oregon Short Line, a subsidiary of Union Pacific, managed

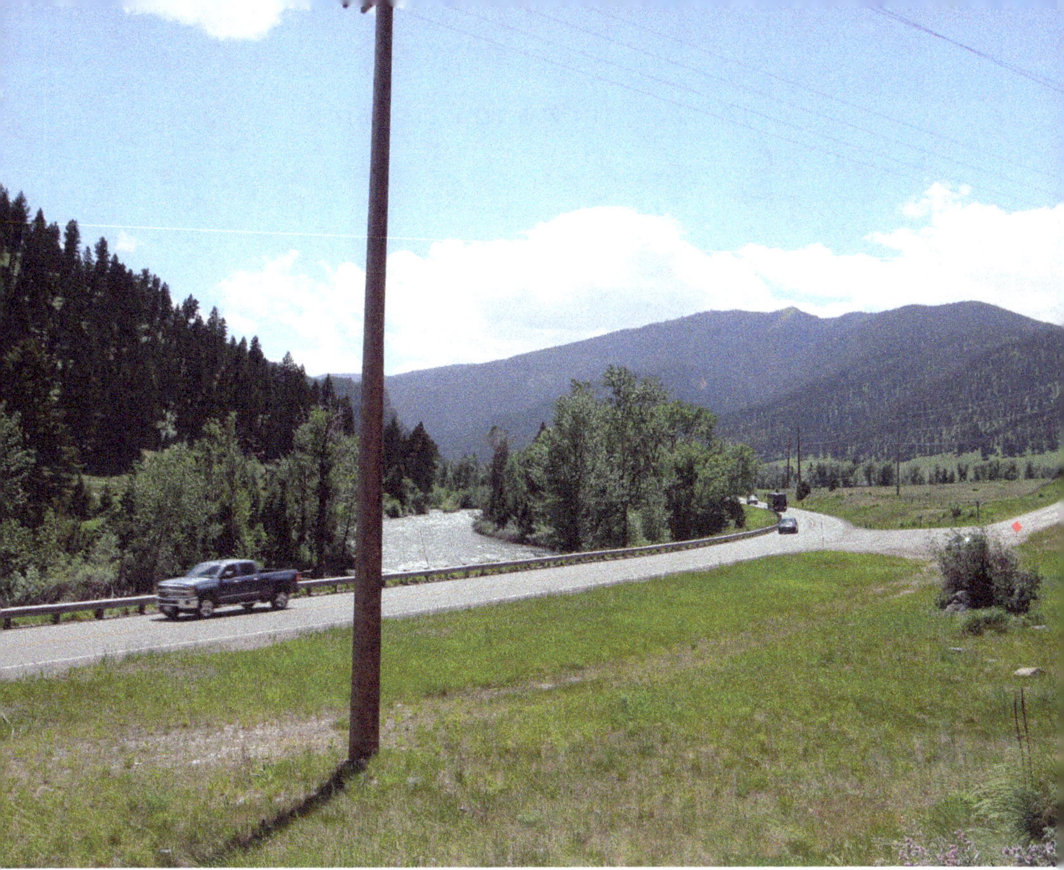

this line. The Burlington Northern had tracks to Cody, Wyoming, which provided access to the east entrance of Yellowstone.

To compete with the other railroads, in 1926 the Chicago, Milwaukee and St. Paul Rail Road (renamed Chicago, Milwaukee, St. Paul and Pacific Rail Road in 1927 after coming out of bankruptcy, and also known as the Milwaukee Railroad), promoted the Gallatin Canyon as a "Gateway to Yellowstone." The president of the Milwaukee Railroad, Henry Scandrett, knew the canyon, as his family were faithful early guests in the early 1920s at Elkhorn Ranch (MM#33.1) along the upper West Gallatin. In 1925, the railroad built an electric spur line from Three Forks to Salesville, Montana. It also convinced locals to rename the town Gallatin Gateway after building the Gallatin Gateway Inn in 1927 (completed in four months) at the end of its spur line (Figure 2.3). As part of its promotion, in 1926, the railroad had constructed an arch over the highway (Figure 2.4) just north of present-day Rockhaven Camp and Retreat Center across the Gallatin River from Sheep Rock Mountain (MM#67). The railroad's arch was removed in the 1950s with the widening and improvement of the highway.

The Milwaukee Railroad's promotion was based on sending bus trips up the Gallatin Way through the Gallatin Canyon to Yellowstone National

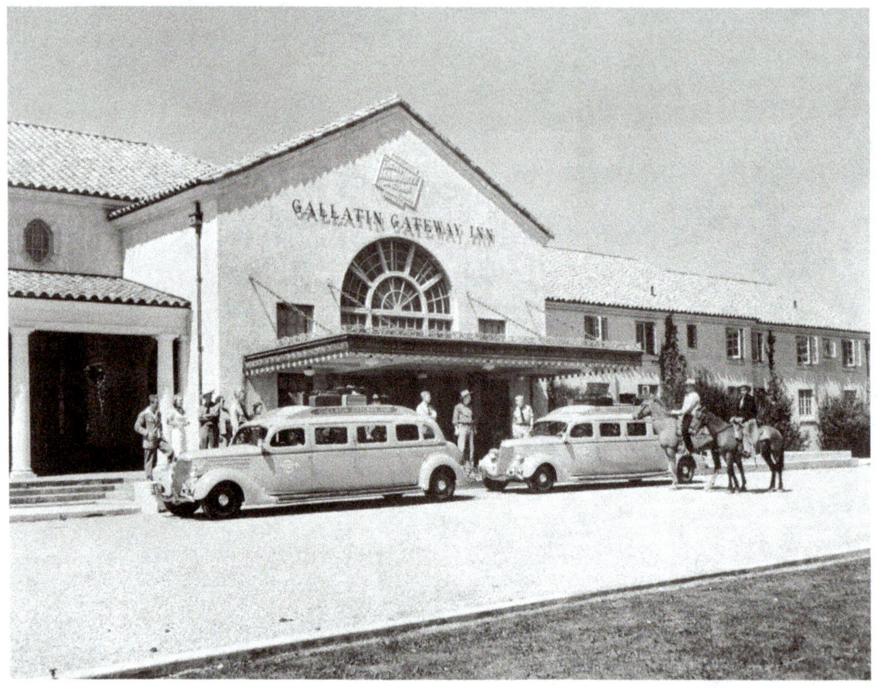

Figure 2.3. Gallatin Gateway Inn. Constructed by the Milwaukee Railroad in 1927 and considered one of the Historic Inns of America.
Above photo (circa 1930): Buses belonging to the Gallatin Gateway Inn used to take visitors through the Gallatin Canyon to the west entrance of Yellowstone National Park. *MOR*.
Below photo (2016): Gallatin Gateway Inn seems unchanged. It ceased operations in 2013.

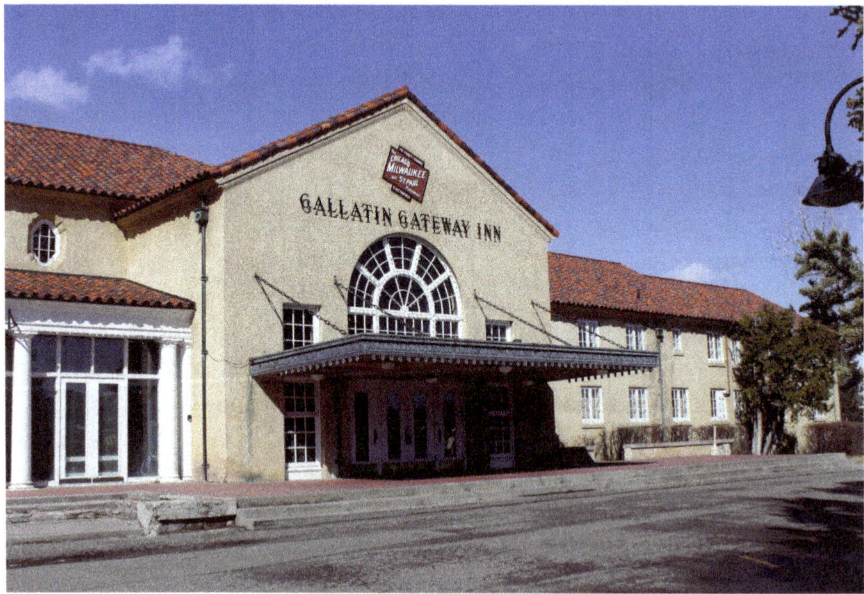

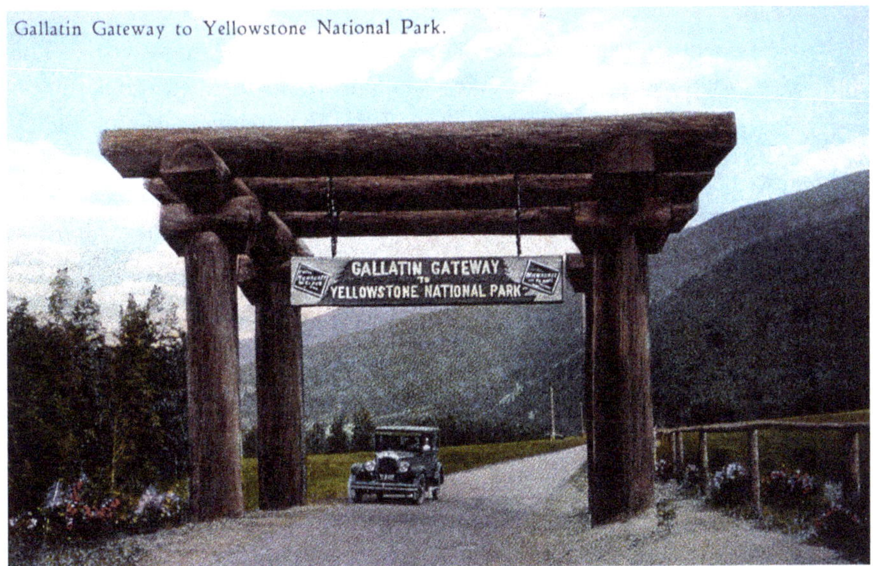

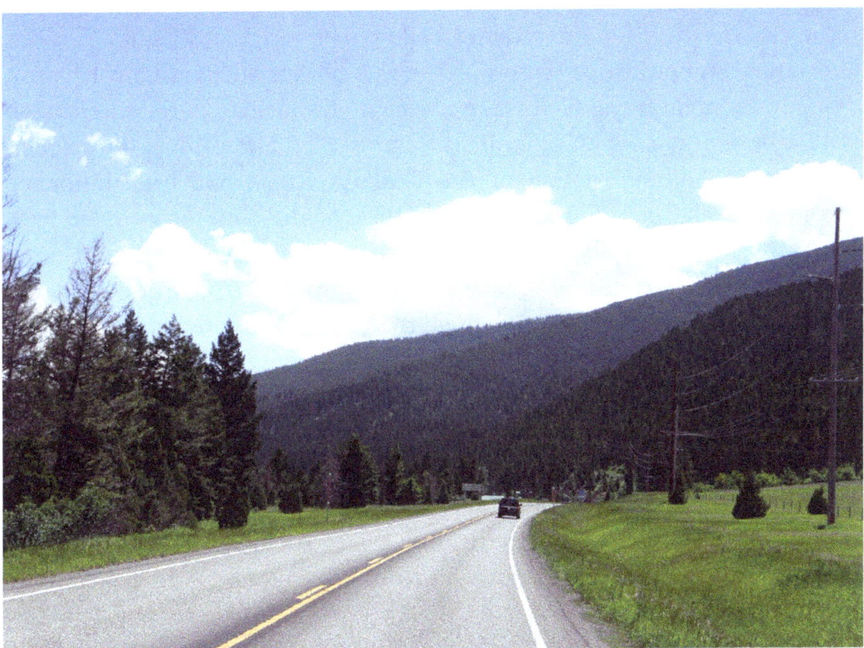

Figure 2.4. Archway location along the road from Gallatin Gateway to Yellowstone National Park. About a half mile north of Rockhaven and a mile south of Spanish Creek (MM#67).
Upper photo (circa 1927–30): This arch was constructed by the Milwaukee Railroad in 1926 only a short distance into the Gallatin Canyon. Tinted photo of arch. *NPS.*
Lower photo (2016): Present location of the arch along Gallatin Way showing improved and widened road, which prevented continued use of arch.

Park's west entrance from its newly constructed Gallatin Gateway Inn. The highway headed south along the West Gallatin River through the arch and past the location of Rockhaven (Figure 2.5). This location was originally homesteaded as the Sheep Rock Ranch in 1886 by Earl Benham's father. Earl Benham, a midwesterner born in Wichita, Kansas, in 1885, eventually homesteaded farther up the canyon. From near Rockhaven, the highway meanders south toward a wide section of the canyon near where Hellroaring Creek crosses the road, often referred to as Beckman Flat or, historically, Hellroaring Flat (MM#64), and then on through the narrow part of the canyon. As more people used cars to travel to Yellowstone National Park, traveling to the Gallatin Gateway Inn by rail and then bussing up the canyon lost its attraction, and the Milwaukee Railroad sold the Gallatin Gateway Inn in 1951 and discontinued its rail service to the inn.

Several miles south of Rockhaven, after passing several private residences and the INN on the Gallatin (originally called Castle Rock Inn), the road straightens (Figure 2.6). Through this straight stretch, there is a turn off to the east over a bridge to Storm Castle Creek (originally Squaw Creek). This large cement bridge (Figure 2.7) was built over the Gallatin River in 1935–36 by men at the CCC camp, which was located across the bridge in an area that is now an open field (Figure 2.8). The bridge, built across a relatively confined section of the Gallatin River, had little influence on the river channel (Figure 2.9). In 1935, at the time of construction, the CCC camp held about 180 men. The camp housed men (and boys) during the Depression in a "make-jobs" program. Teams from the camp improved trails in the area and helped the USFS with forest management. The camp closed in the late 1930s and was removed. In the 1950s, the Upper Gallatin USFS Ranger Station was located here, which repeated history, as in 1906, Rhesis Fransheim, the first forest ranger in the canyon, built the first Forest Service station at this location. He then built an overnight station at Cinnamon Creek in 1907 and moved his headquarters to Cinnamon in 1908. He served until 1912. Today, all management of the USFS Upper Gallatin area comes from Bozeman or West Yellowstone USFS headquarters, and the area now houses some USFS quarters and a helipad. After crossing the bridge to the east, the gravel road continues south and then up Storm Castle Creek.

South of the Storm Castle Bridge, the river leaves the highway and traverses under large limestone cliffs. This stretch of the river was used for fly-fishing scenes in the movie *A River Runs Through It*. The river channel returns to near the highway at the south end of Beckman Flats, where

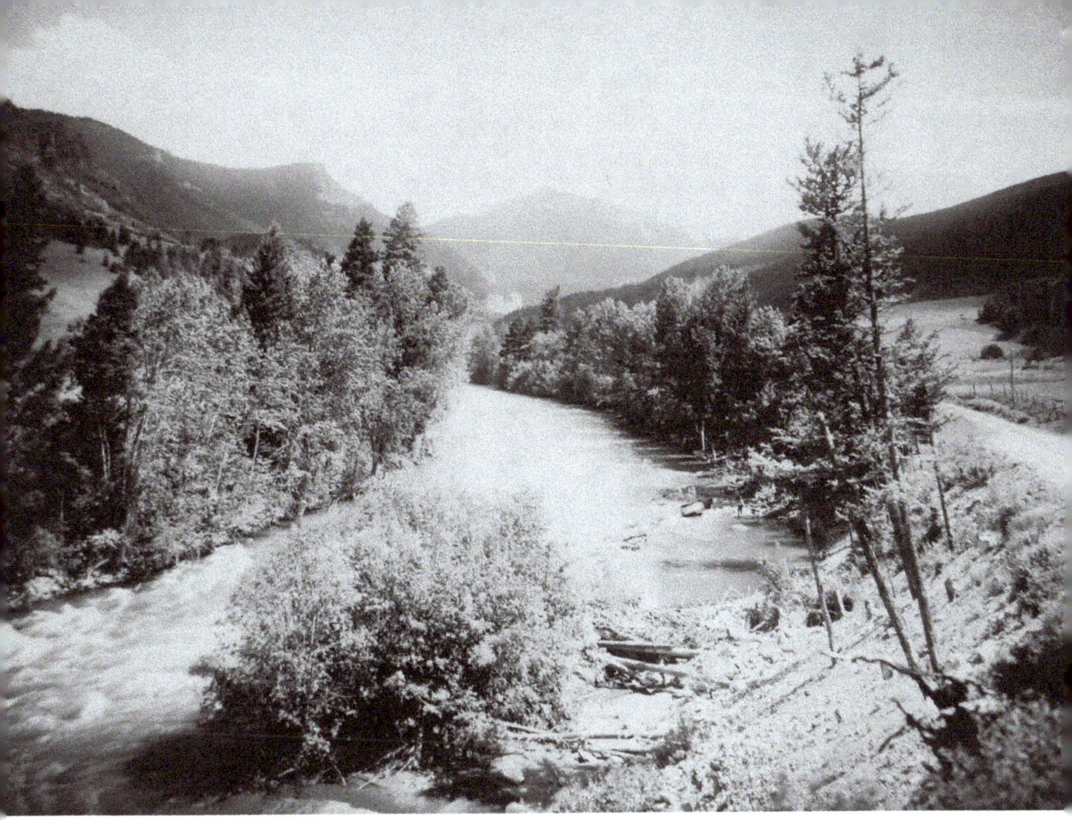

Figure 2.5. Curve along Highway 191 just south of Rockhaven (MM#66.8).
Above photo (1905–15): Old highway showing closeness of road to river. *MOR.*
Below photo (2012): Highway curve showing new placement of highway away from river channel.

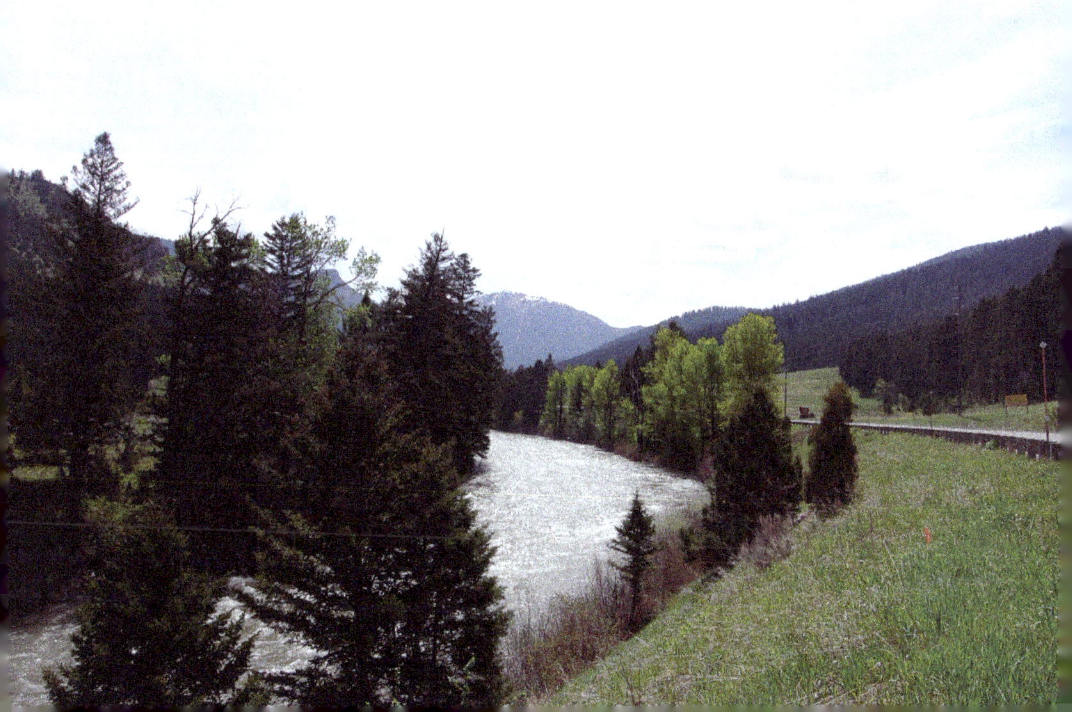

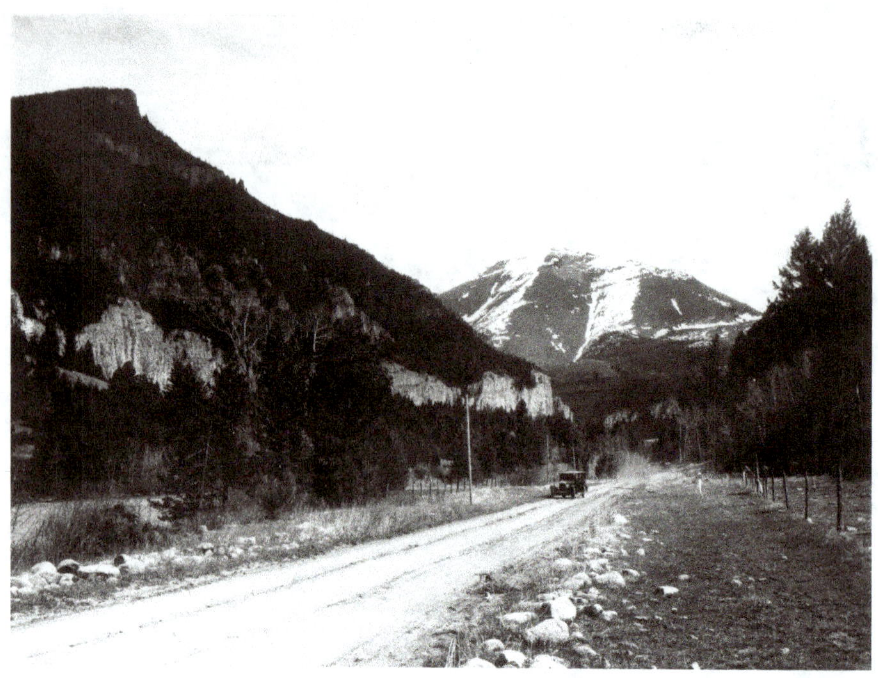

Figure 2.6. Highway south of the INN on the Gallatin heading south toward Beckman Flat near the Storm Castle turnoff (circa MM#65.2). Garnet peak is in background, which has Old Baldy Lookout on top. The edge of Storm Castle Mountain (aka Castle Rock) is on the left.
Above photo (1920s): A slightly improved gravel roadway. *GHM*.
Below photo (2016): Greatly improved highway leading up to the turn lane into Storm Castle Creek. Note that the avalanche shoots on Garnet, very apparent in the winter upper photo, are mostly healed.

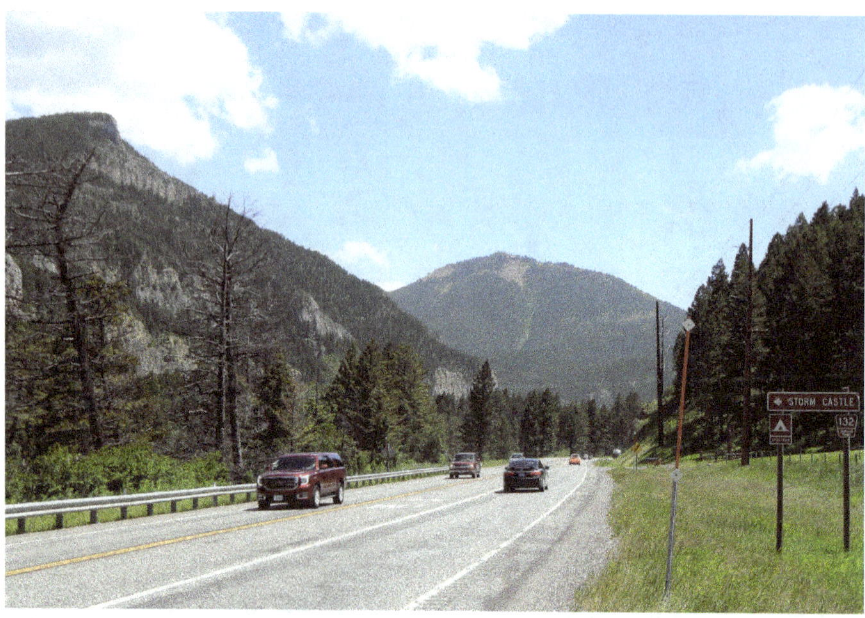

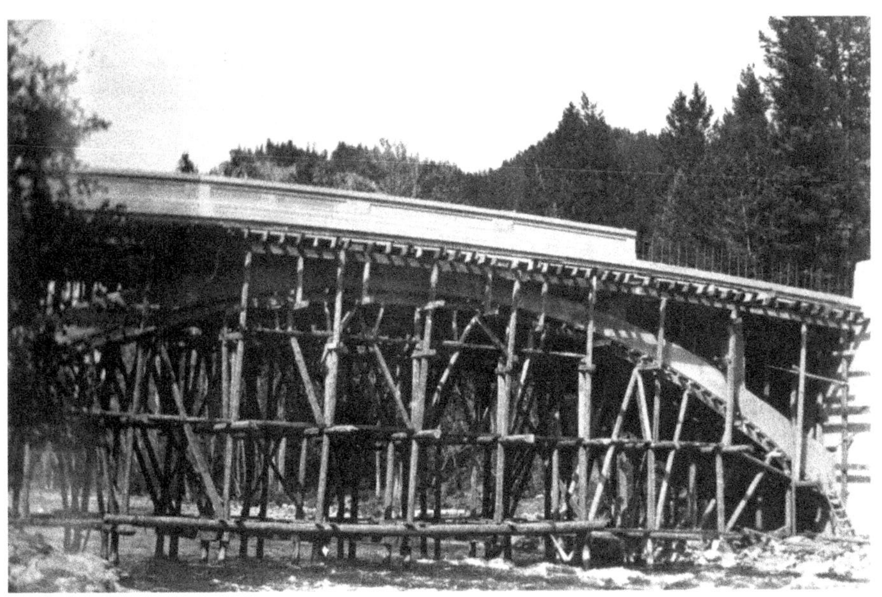

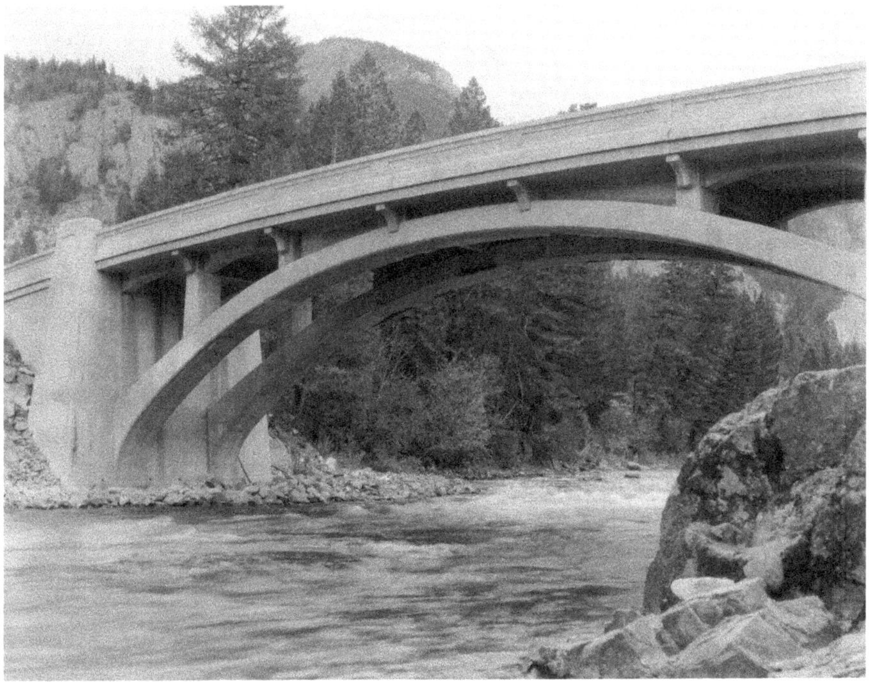

Figure 2.7. Bridge over the Gallatin River (MM#65.2) to Storm Castle (Castle Rock) and Storm Castle Creek (Squaw Creek).
Upper photo (early 1930s): Construction of the bridge by the CCC that went to the CCC camp (Figure 2.8) when it was being developed. *GHM.*
Lower photo (1936): This bridge, essentially unchanged today, now is commonly used to reach trails and cabins up Storm Castle Creek. *MOR.*

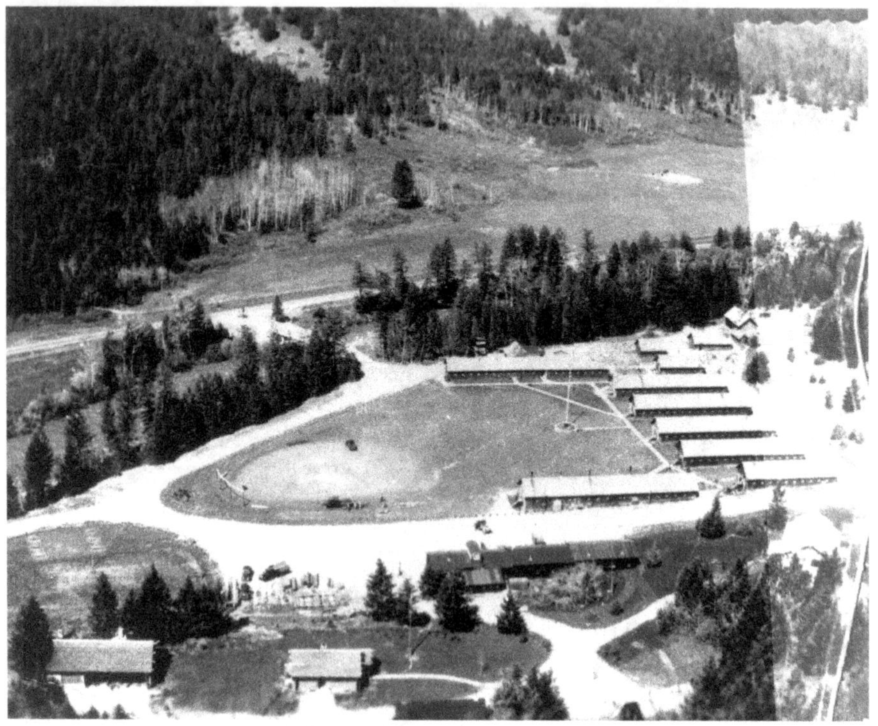

Figure 2.8. Squaw Creek Civilian Conservation Corps Camp #54 showing many buildings housing up to 180 men (MM#65.2). (1936). Squaw Creek has been renamed Storm Castle Creek. *GHM.*
The repeat photo location is forested and unattainable.

Montana Whitewater presently (as of 2018) has headquarters. Beckman Flats is named after J.E. Beckman, who in 1953 bought land in the area homesteaded by George Dier in 1912. In the late 1950s, perhaps into the 1970s, when passing through Beckman Flat, I often observed an elderly man sitting in front of an old homestead cabin smoking and watching cars go by. This old cabin still exists. Was this Dier's cabin that Beckman used? No records for the cabin exist today.

One can appreciate that Hayden's 1872 expedition south through the canyon may have rested at this broad grassy area while scouting for a route south through the narrowing canyon. Jackson, Hayden's photographer, photographed Storm Castle peak from this location (Figure 2.10). Also, early photos looking downstream near the south end of the flats show a bridge across the Gallatin that no longer exists (Figure 2.11). This bridge may have been one of several routes for trails up the canyon in the late 1800s

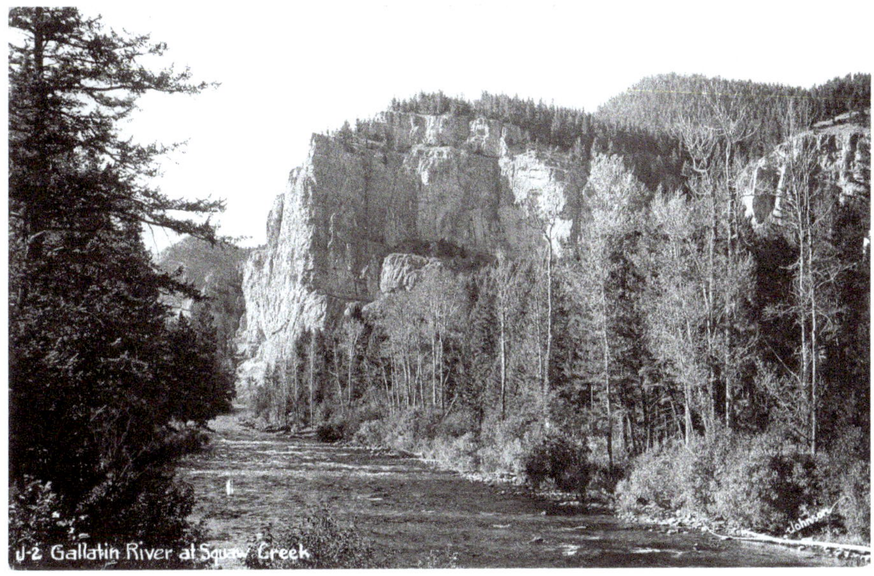

Figure 2.9. The view downstream from the Storm Castle (Squaw Creek) Bridge (MM#65.2).
Above photo (mid-1930s): View with stands of cottonwood along right bank and dense riparian vegetation. *GHM.*
Below photo (2013): Little has changed along this reach of river, although the right bank vegetation appears to contain more conifers.

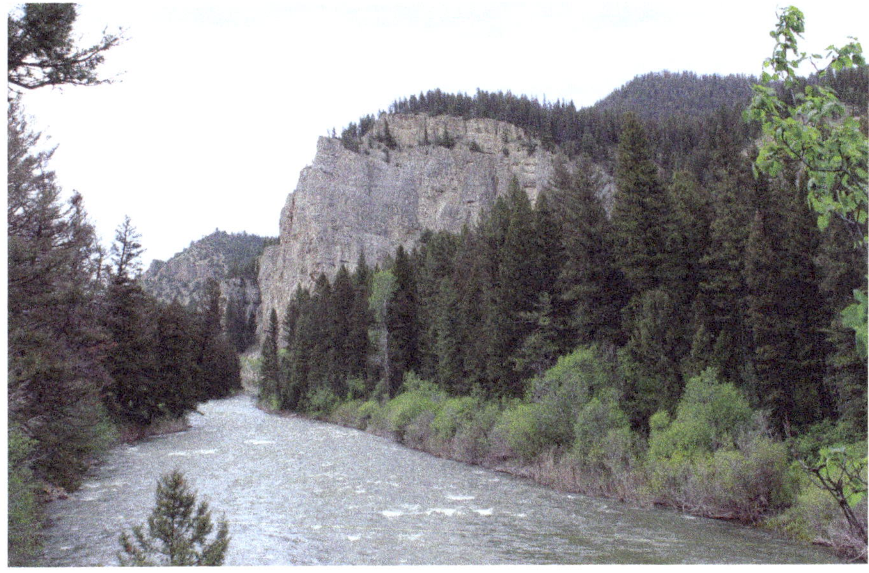

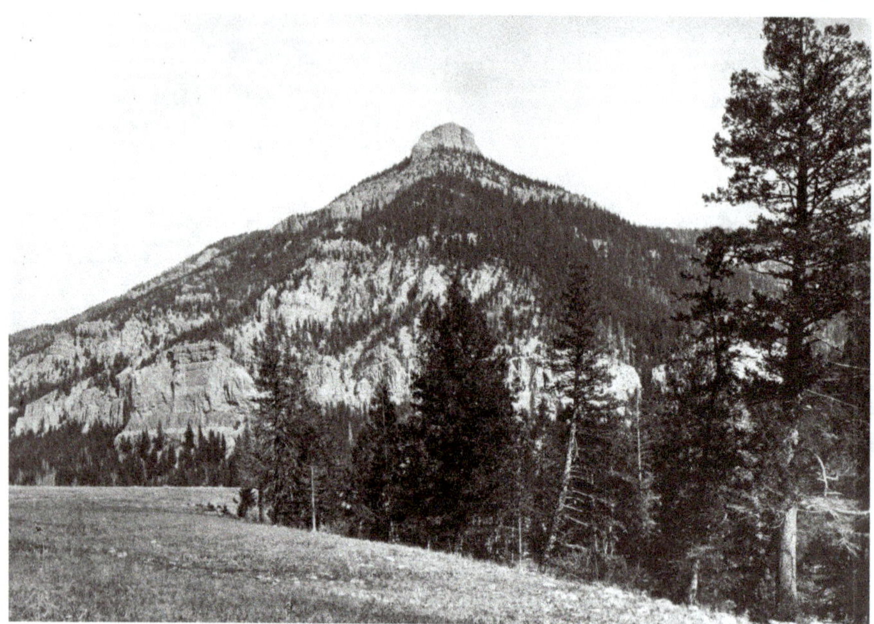

Figure 2.10. Storm Castle (originally Castle Rock) in the Gallatin Canyon photographed at southern end of area called Beckman Flat. (MM#63.7)
Above photo (1872): View of Storm Castle taken before there were any buildings or roads. Photograph by W.H. Jackson during the 1872 Hayden Expedition. *USGS.*
Below photo (2016): Storm Castle with buildings, roads and power poles in the Beckman Flat area.

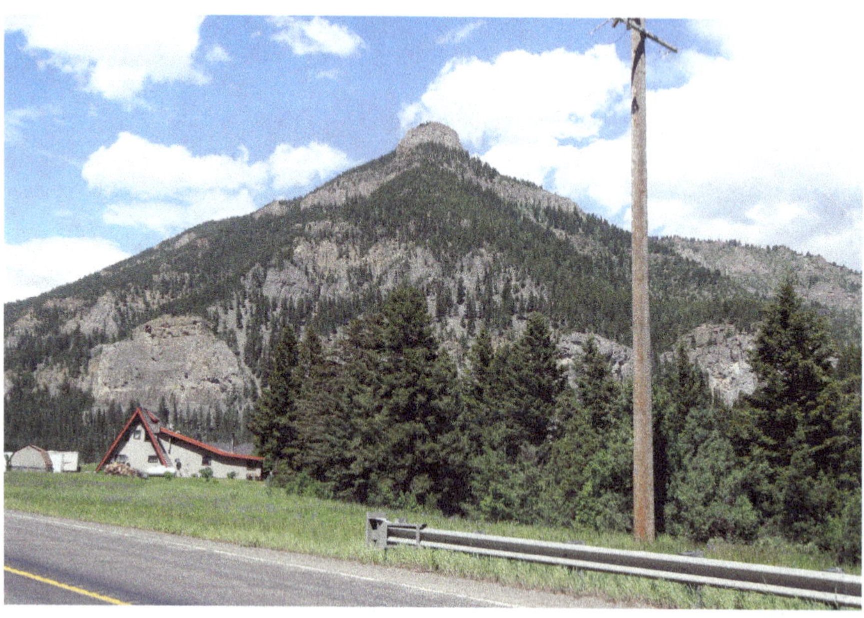

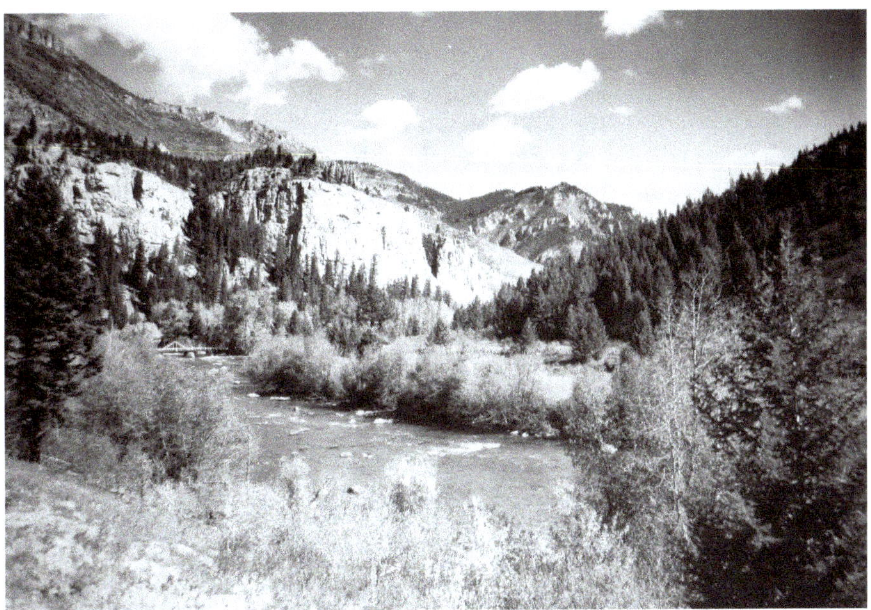

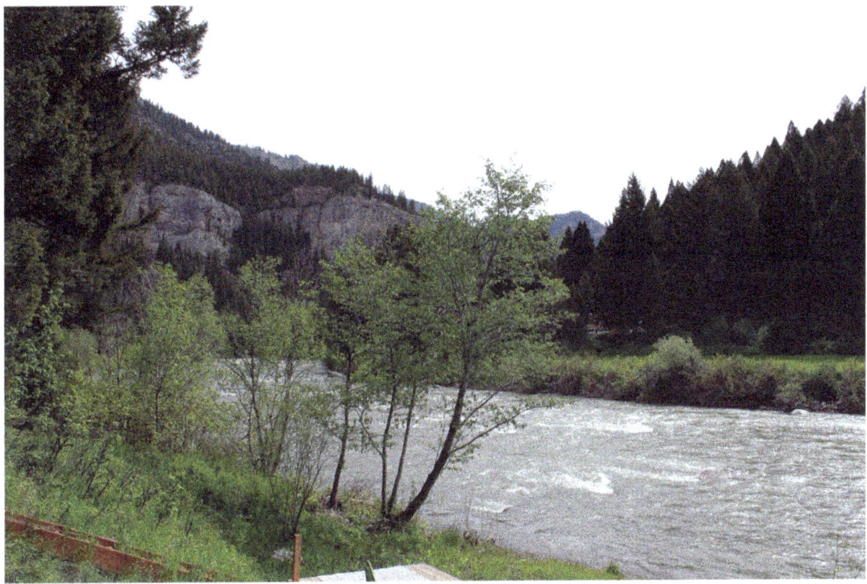

Figure 2.11. Looking downstream on the Gallatin River into Storm Castle Creek Canyon (originally Squaw Creek Canyon) and the confluence of the Gallatin River and Storm Castle Creek. Photo point near MM#63.7.
Upper photo (circa 1915–20): Stream side has no evidence of dwellings, and a bridge is visible crossing the Gallatin River downstream from photo point. Use of this bridge is uncertain but may have allowed access to the east side of the Gallatin River and up Squaw Creek in the early 1900s. *MOR.*
Lower photo (2013): Photo taken on the edge of the river near a private deck belonging to one of several dwellings along the south end of Beckman Flat. The wooden bridge has been removed, and the streamside vegetation appears sparser.

or perhaps a point to cross the Gallatin River to head east up Storm Castle Creek (then Squaw Creek) Canyon before the 1935 bridge at Storm Castle was constructed. Past this point, the canyon narrows and the river becomes an extensive whitewater reach.

The Hellroaring Creek area also had an early logging camp. English-born Zachariah Sales (founder of Salesville, now Gallatin Gateway) migrated to the Gallatin Valley in 1865 and developed a sawmill near Salesville in the early 1900s. To supply logs for the mill, he established logging camps in the canyon at Hellroaring Creek, Greek Creek and Taylor Fork, floating logs down the river from these locations to the mill. It is uncertain how Sales's Taylor Fork logging camp relates to Cooper's early 1900s logging camps up Taylor Fork.

Chapter 3

The Narrow Section of the Canyon

(MM#63.6 to MM#61)

Starting from where the river channel returns to near the road on the south end of Beckman Flat (MM#63.6) upstream for about three miles, the canyon is narrow and the river runs with many white-water reaches, a stretch of the Gallatin River very popular with kayakers and raft trips (Map 3.1). In the late 1800s, prior to road building, the narrowness of this reach of canyon limited passage by anything larger than a horse and rider or a person on foot. Even for this type of travel, the rocky cliffs, extensive rock slides and scree slopes extending to the river edge made traversing difficult, as attested by Jackson's photo shown earlier (Figure 1.2) that he titled "Our Trail Over the Rocks." As the road was developed, harsh road conditions persisted, and travel continued to be difficult. Because of the beauty of the narrow canyon, several photogenic locations are located along this stretch of river. Storm Castle (aka Castle Rock) was a magnet for early photographs as well as recent ones. Well before a road was built through this section of the canyon, photographs were taken of Castle Rock. Jackson in 1872 took several from different locations, one shown earlier from Beckman Flat (Figure 2.10) and one from near the river, a very early photo of Storm Castle with the river (Figure 3.1). As the road was constructed and gradually improved (see road history in chapter 1), more photographers took photos that often included Storm Castle. These include photos with a muddy track with horse and buggy (1906), a dirt road with a Model A–type car (1923), a newly paved road (1936) and a recent photo. Together, they show the gradual improvement

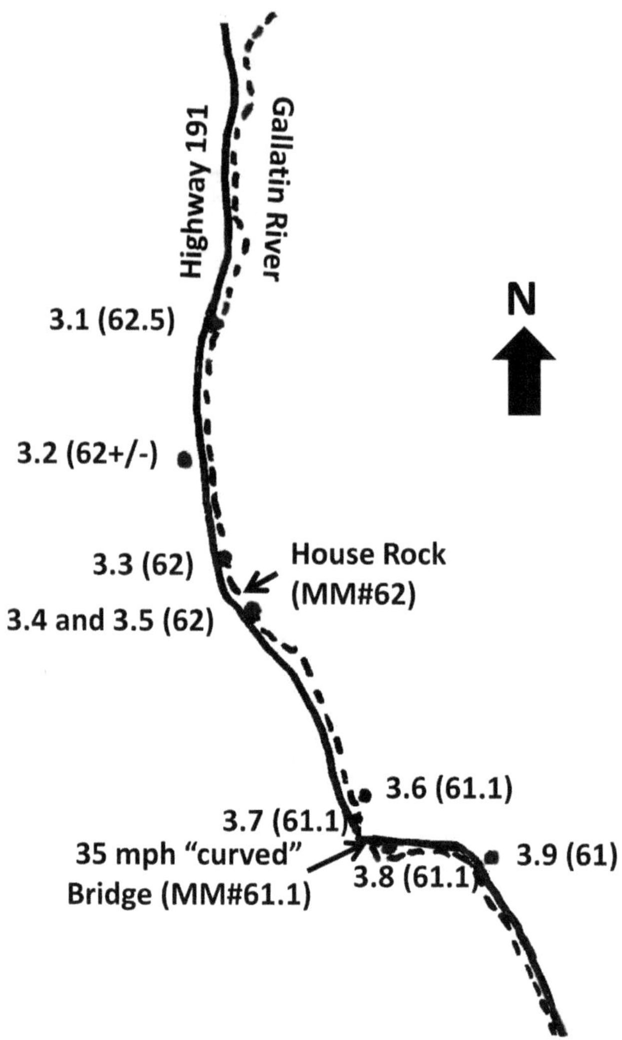

Map 3.1. The Canyon Narrows (MM#63 to 60.5). Map of photo locations along Highway 191 and the Gallatin River (mile markers in parentheses).

of travel conditions through this narrow part of the canyon (Figure 3.2). In many of the early photos here, and in the widening canyon to the south, stands of burned trees are evident, a result of an extensive fire in 1881 that burned for forty miles through most of this part of the canyon. The fire started on the Gallatin/Madison divide.

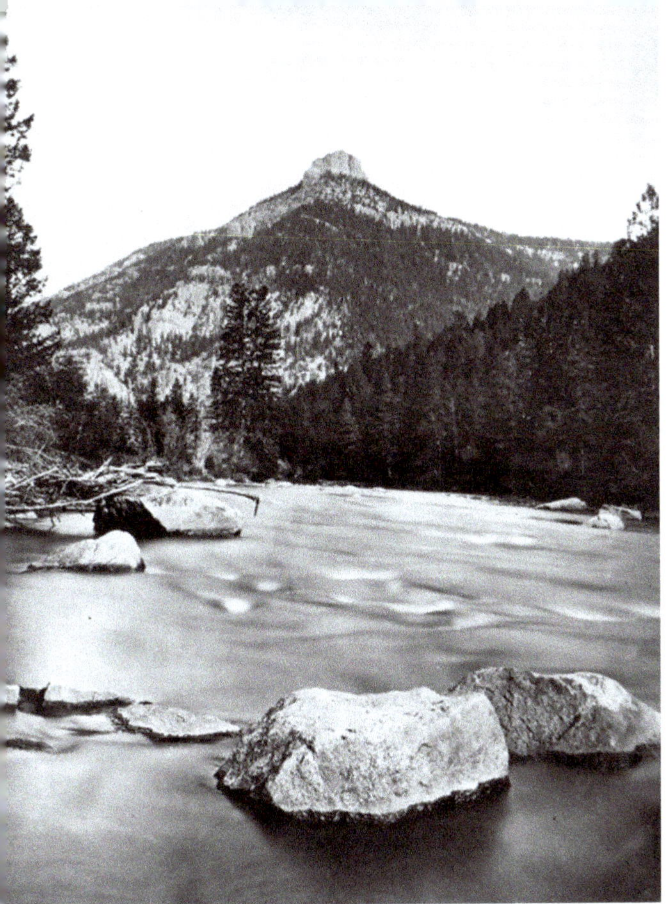

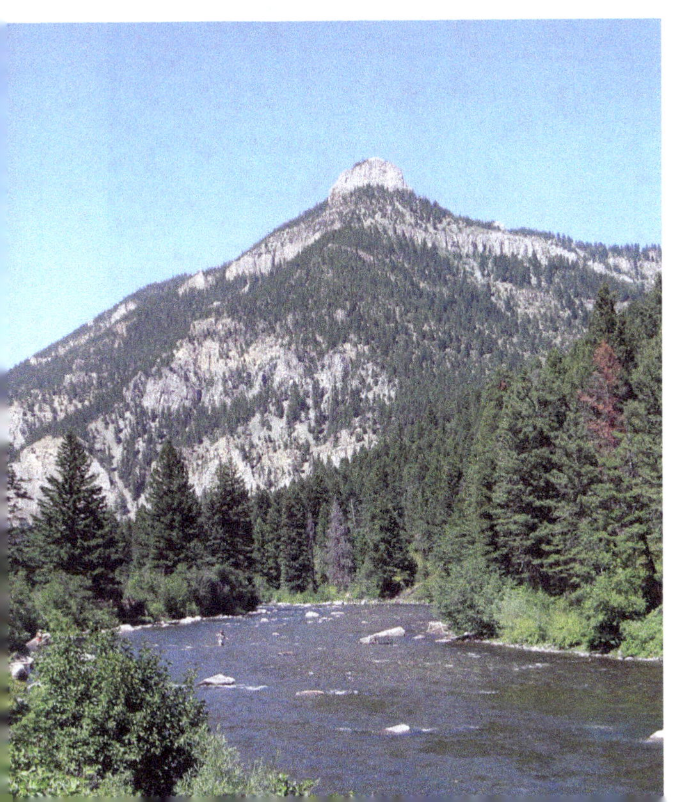

Figure 3.1. Photo of Storm Castle (Castle Rock) as seen from near the Gallatin River looking downstream. (MM#62.5).
Upper photo (1872): A very early photo showing blurred water from slow camera speed and a wide channel. Photograph by W.H. Jackson during the 1872 Hayden Expedition. *USGS.*
Lower photo (2016): The extensive highway improvement in the 1950s not only elevated the highway above the river but also greatly encroached on the river (edge of highway embankment on left covered with vegetation), creating a narrower channel than in 1872.

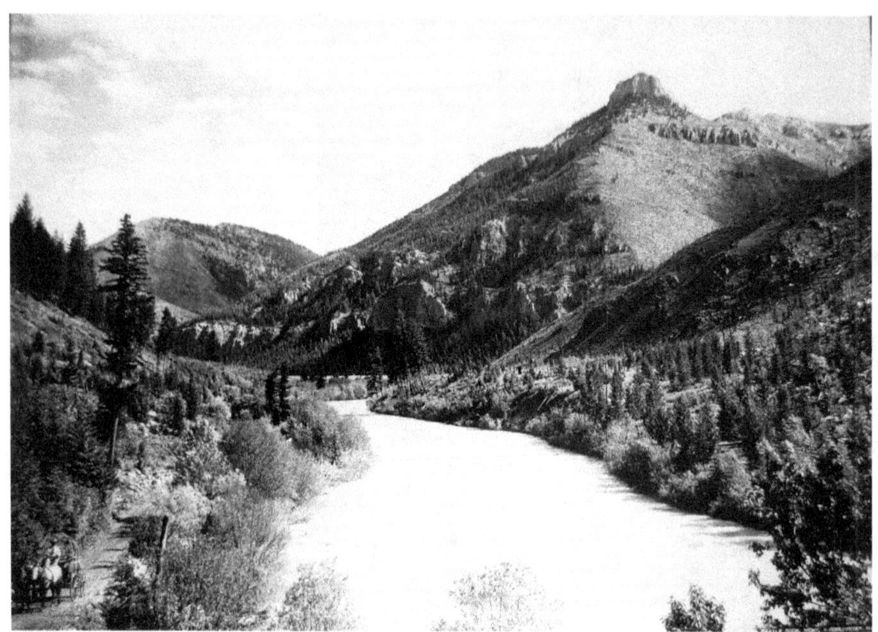

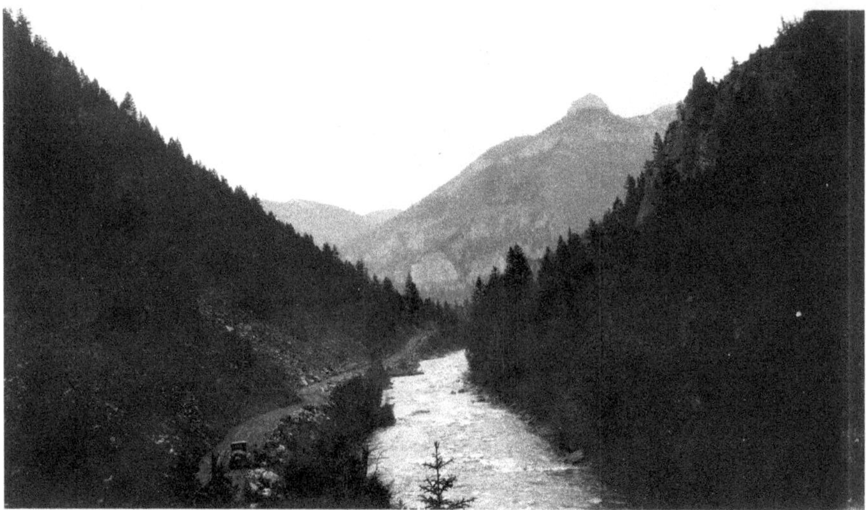

Figure 3.2. Storm Castle (Castle Rock) looking north along the Gallatin River and the parallel roadway. (MM#62+/-). Photo points are not all the same location.
Upper photo (1906): Horse and buggy on dirt roadway. Road construction did not affect the riverside vegetation. *MOR.*
Lower photo (1923): Model A–type auto on slightly improved roadway. Riverside vegetation still more or less intact. *USGS.*
Opposite page, upper photo (August 1936): Roadway greatly improved with "hard surface." Road fill has eliminated much of the riverside vegetation. *MOR.*
Opposite page, lower photo (2012): Highway greatly improved and more elevated above river, with little riverside vegetation remaining. The trees block view of highway, requiring photo from higher vantage point.

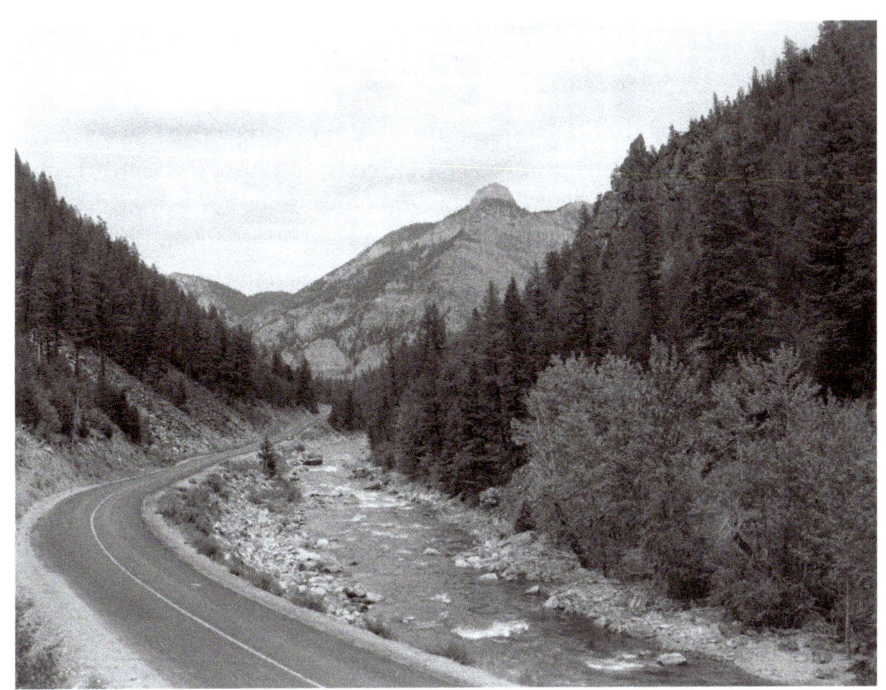

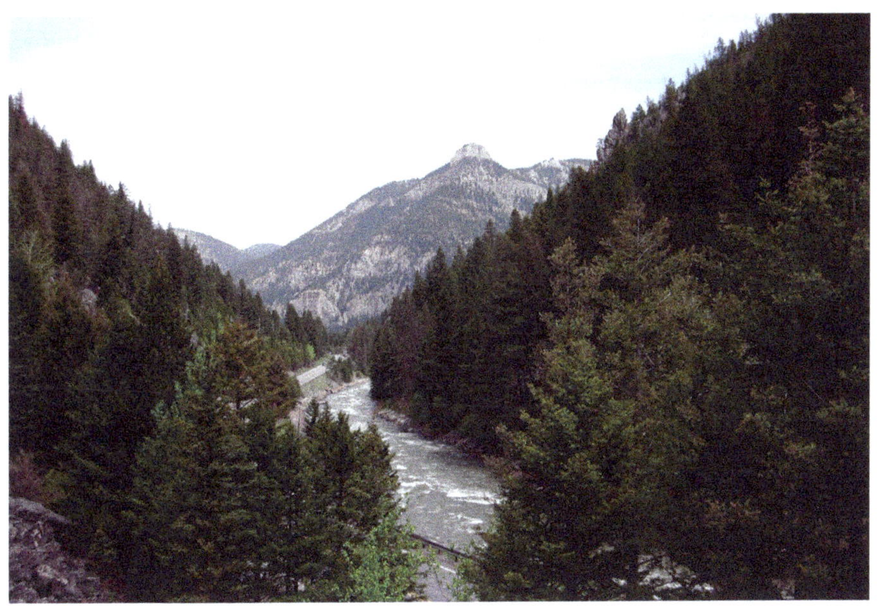

In the middle of the narrow portion of the canyon near Cave Creek, a small stream that now flows under the highway through a culvert, and downstream of present-day thirty-five-mile-per-hour curved bridge lies House Rock (MM#62), a big rock set in the middle of the river. For present-day whitewater enthusiasts, this rock creates a challenge and thus is a prime location for photographs of river runners passing the rock (Figure 3.3). The historic photo of this photo pair shows the old trail bridge discussed later. Many photos of House Rock have also been taken from upstream (some shown later). When the Gallatin River flows at near maximum stage (height), water flows over the top of House Rock, an event that occurs very seldom (1997 at a peak of 9,170 cfs being the last year in the past several decades when there was significant overtopping of the rock, although 2011 at 8,410 cfs came close). Timing, discharge and duration of high flows will change in the future with climate change and warming, peak flows coming earlier and maybe not as high. Near the highway pullouts for House Rock and close to Cave Creek are several cabins. Permits for these cabins (summer homes) were first issued by the U.S. Forest Service in 1914. Several of the early photos down the canyon appear to have been taken from near these cabins. Today, the view is blocked by trees that grew in after the 1881 fire. Very few people realize that Cave Creek even exists, but it often was a popular location for activities in the canyon over the years.

The location of House Rock in the middle of the river allowed early travelers and those moving livestock through the canyon to use a pole bridge constructed across the Gallatin River, with House Rock as the center support (Figures 3.3 and 3.4). Several photos of this wood bridge show changes in rock locations in the river over time (Figure 3.5), either a result of high water moving rocks near House Rock or highway improvement changing river rock locations as the widened highway may have encroached on the river. Some locals claim that House Rock moved downstream during the long duration high spring flows of 1974 (peak of 9,100 cfs), and perhaps it moved again during the 1997 peak. The last time the flows exceeded 8,000 cfs before 1974 was in 1892 with a peak of 8,060 cfs.

The uncertainty of the bridge over House Rock and the need for greater stability for crossing the river as the West Gallatin Road was being constructed in the late 1800s and early 1900s required a larger and better constructed bridge. This new bridge located about a half mile upstream of House Rock was completed in the late 1890s (1898–99) (Figures 3.6 and 3.7), about the time the road was being extended up the West Gallatin drainage as far as Taylor Fork (mm# 34+/-). Sometime in the early 1900s, probably

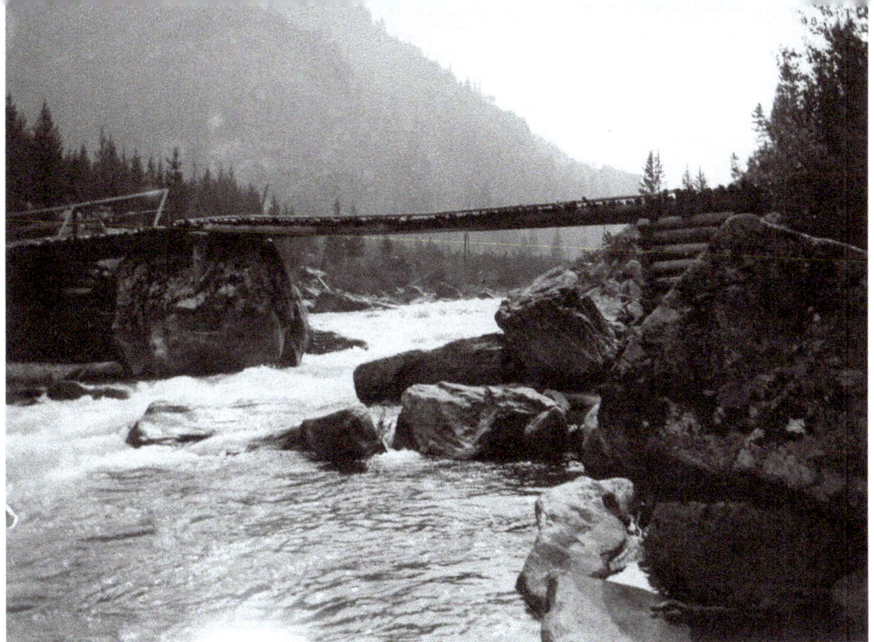

Figure 3.3. House Rock in the left center of the photo at MM#62 in the Gallatin River. This location is toward the end of the so-called mad mile, a term used by kayakers and rafters. Views are upstream.
Above photo (circa 1905): The date, although unknown, is based on lack of bridge railing on west (right) end of foot and livestock bridge. House Rock, in midstream, was used to support the bridge in the late 1800s and early 1900s. The right-side abutment was a log crib filled with rocks, a common form of bridge abutment at the time. *MSU.*
Below photo (July 2013): House Rock no longer holds a livestock bridge. Highway U.S. 191 was greatly improved with fill placed in the river and along the bank where the west bridge abutment once stood. Several large rocks in the river downstream of House Rock appear to have been eliminated, perhaps by high flows, while others on the right bank in historic photo may have been built into the roadbed.

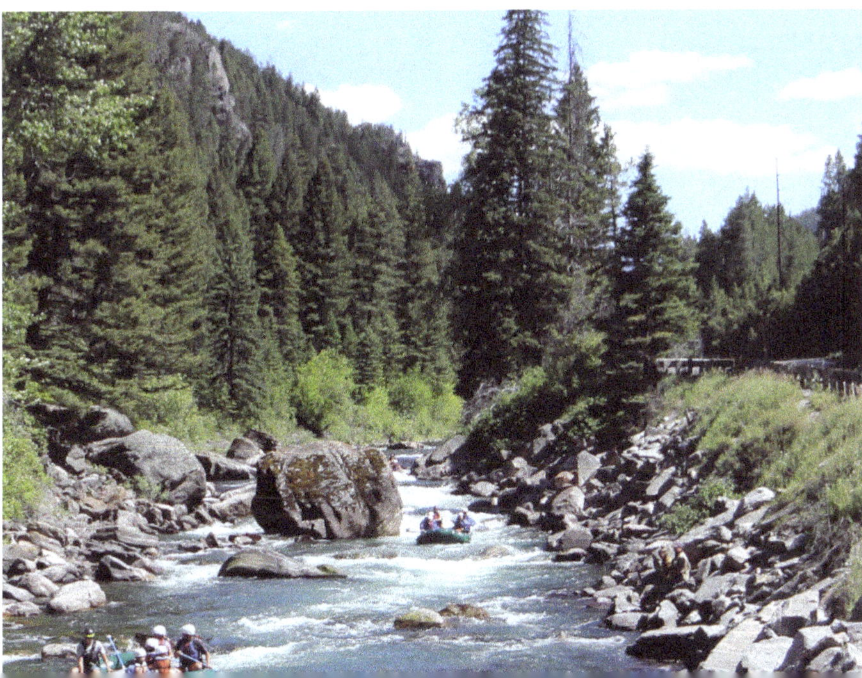

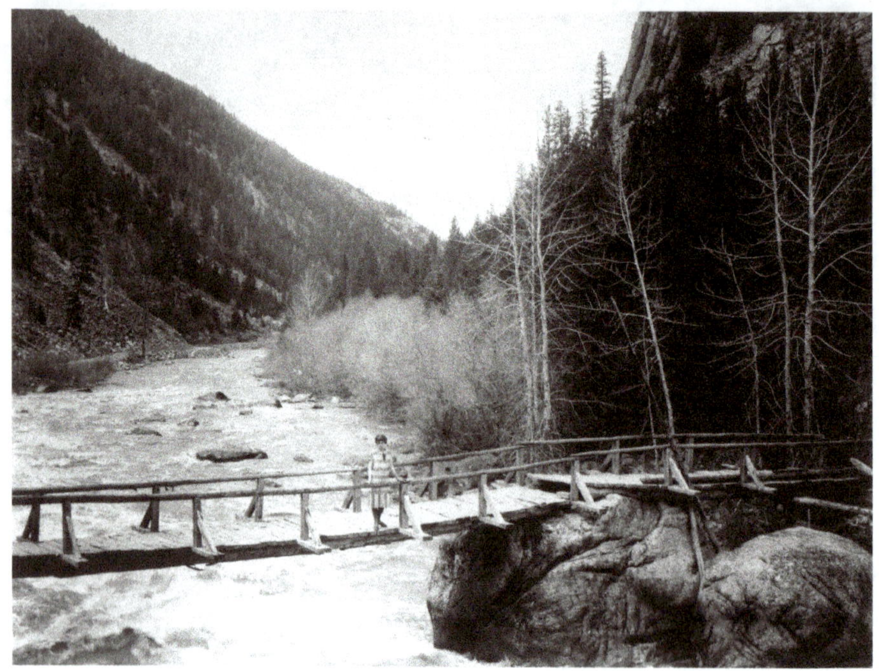

Figure 3.4. House Rock near highway MM#62 on the Gallatin River looking downstream. *Above photo* (circa 1900): Old trail stock bridge over House Rock showing Isabella Karst Durnam (granddaughter of Pete Karst) posing on the bridge. Note full railing compared to Figure 3.3. *GHM.*
Below photo (June 2013): House Rock stands alone in the middle of the river, challenging river runners. Note a missing large rock upstream of House Rock.

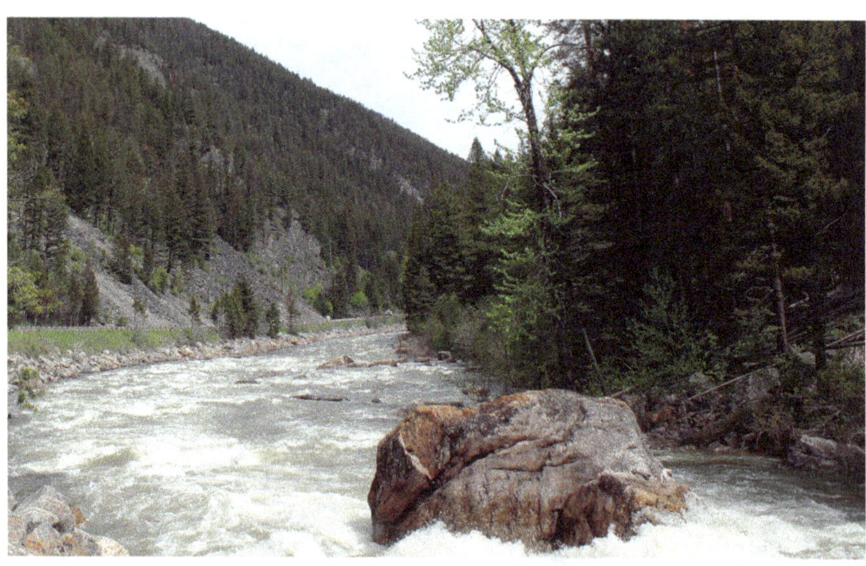

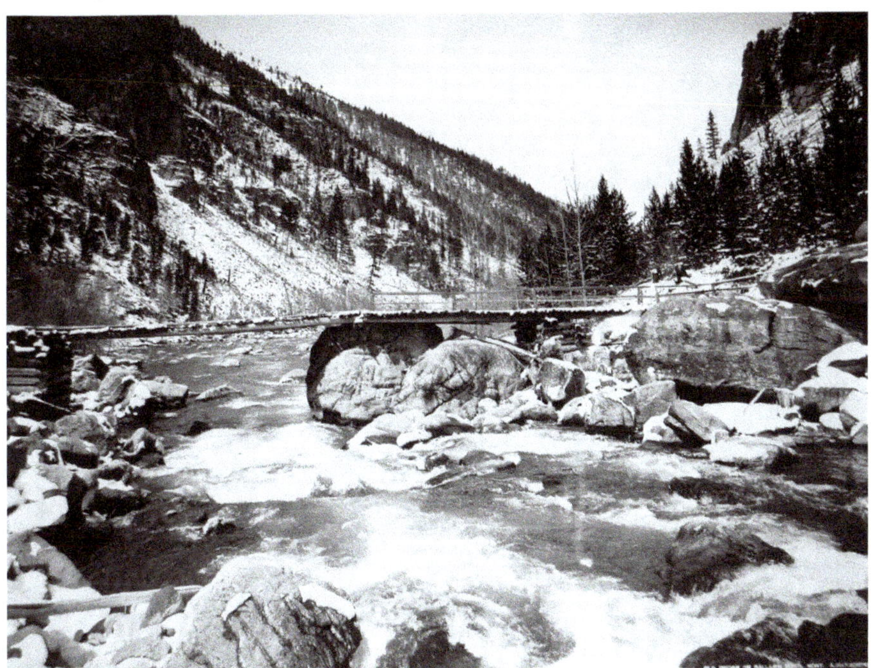

Figure 3.5. House Rock in Gallatin River looking downstream (MM#62).
Above photo (circa 1910): Trail bridge extends from log cradle on left side to very large rock on right side using House Rock for middle pier. *MOR.*
Below photo (2013): All evidence of the trail bridge is gone, and the number of rocks in the river appears to be reduced. The position of House Rock appears to be farther downstream relative to the large rock on right, and the large rock upstream of House Rock appears to have gone.

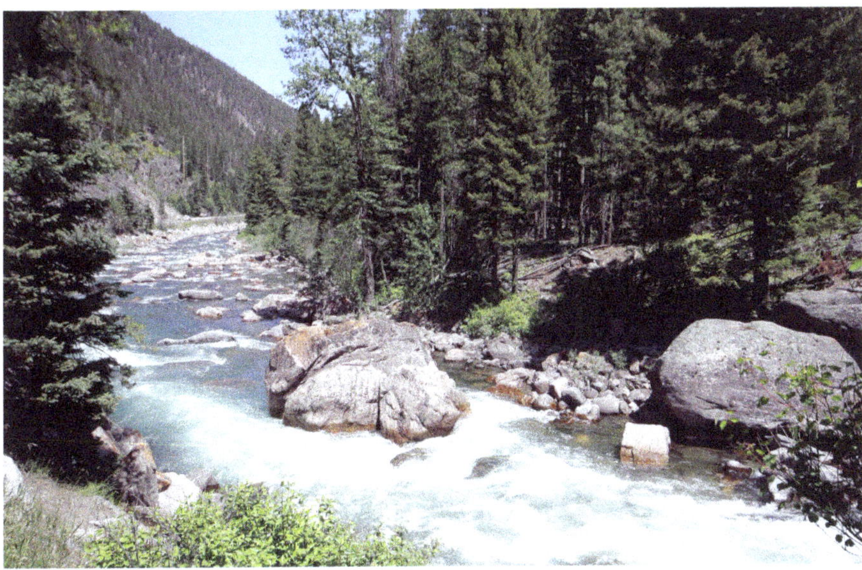

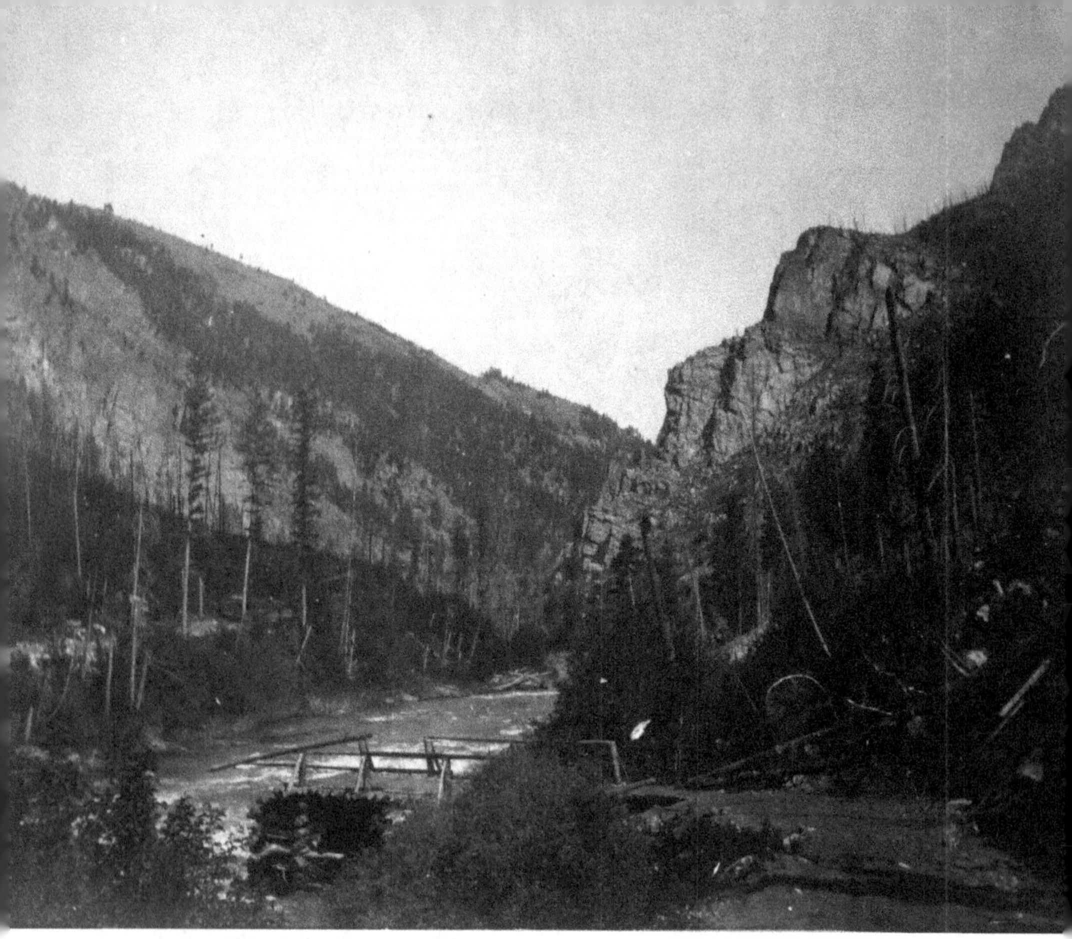

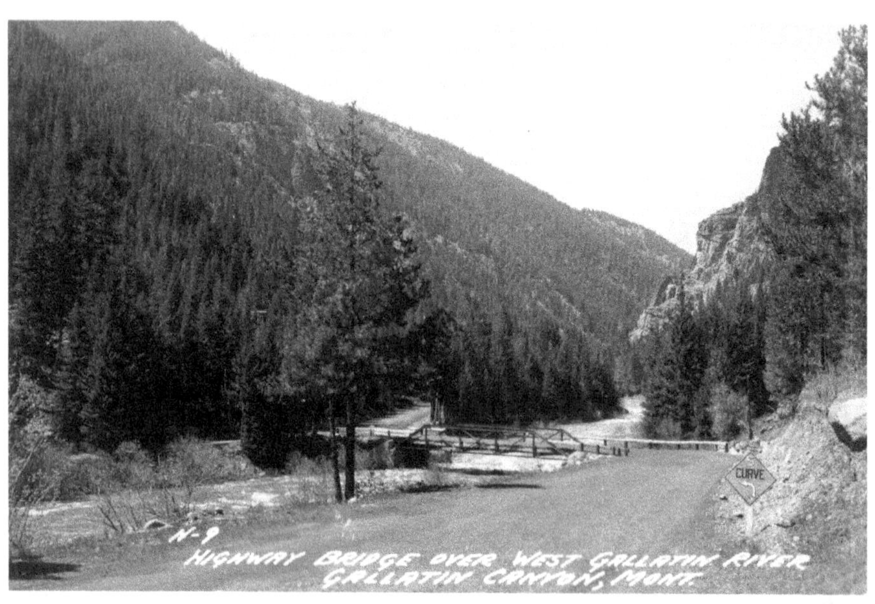
CURVE
N-9
HIGHWAY BRIDGE OVER WEST GALLATIN RIVER
GALLATIN CANYON, MONT.

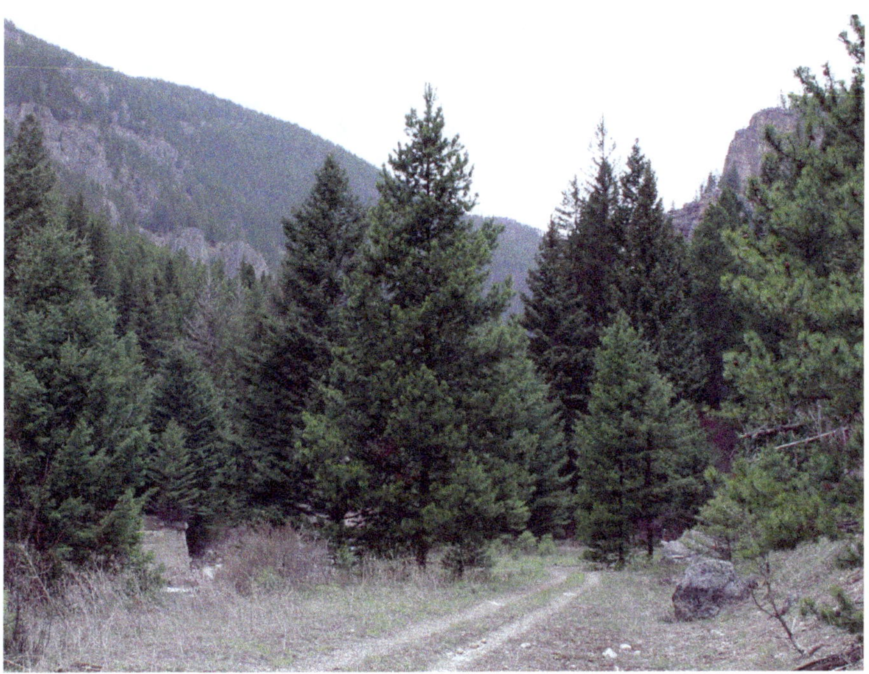

Figure 3.6. Location of the early bridge over the Gallatin River just downstream of present location of curved bridge (thirty-five-mile-per-hour bridge) (MM#61.2).
Opposite page, upper photo (1899): Incomplete abutment of the first bridge at this location. *MSU.*
Opposite page, lower photo (circa 1952): Highway bridge with steel truss construction in early 1950s before it was removed to be replaced by the thirty-five-mile-per-hour curved bridge upstream. The roadway on the opposite side of the river continued south toward what is now the Lava Lake parking and roadway to Cascade Creek cabins. This road became the approach from the north to the thirty-five-mile-per-hour curved bridge built in 1950. *GHM.*
Above photo (2012): Remains of approach roadway to old bridge showing remaining cement abutment.

about when the highway was "paved" in the 1930s, the abutments for this 1898 bridge were improved from log cradle to cement, and the bridge structure was improved to a steel truss bridge (Figure 3.6). These cement abutments are still visible today (Figures 3.6 and 3.7). The improved steel 1898 bridge continued to be used into the 1950s. It was adequate for horse and buggies, cars and small trucks from early to mid-twentieth century, but as the highway became a major transportation route, not only to the west entrance of Yellowstone National Park but also for large interstate trucks, an improved bridge was built several hundred feet upstream of the 1898 bridge. This bridge, often referred to as thirty-five-mile-per-hour bridge based on its speed limit, or curved bridge based on its structure, was constructed in

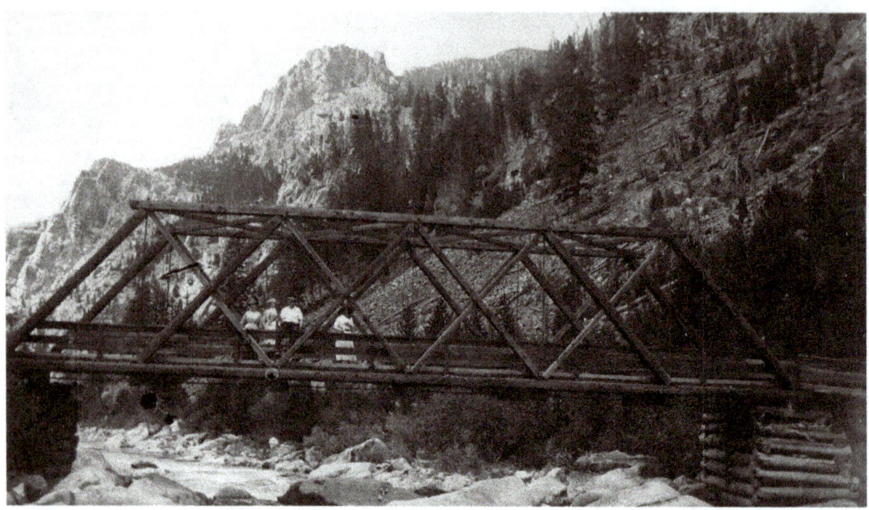

Figure 3.7. The 1898–99 bridge location about a half mile downstream from present day thirty-five-mile-per-hour (curved) bridge (MM#61.2).
Above photo (early 1900s): The 1898–99 bridge showing log cradle abutment and wooden truss structure. Decades later, the abutments were changed to cement and the bridge to a steel truss bridge (see Figure 3.6). *GHM.*
Below photo (2016): The location of the original late 1800s bridge showing cement abutments that replaced the log cradle abutments of the early bridge.

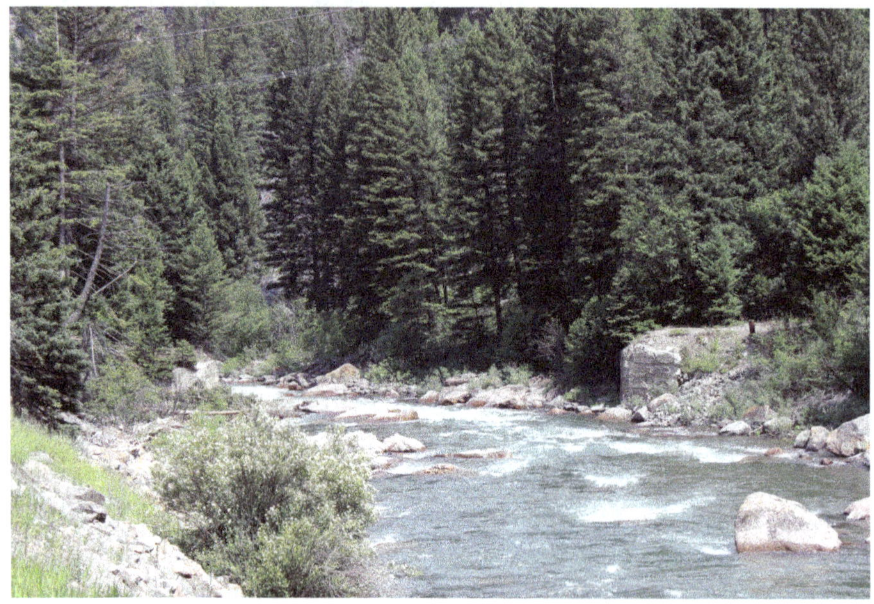

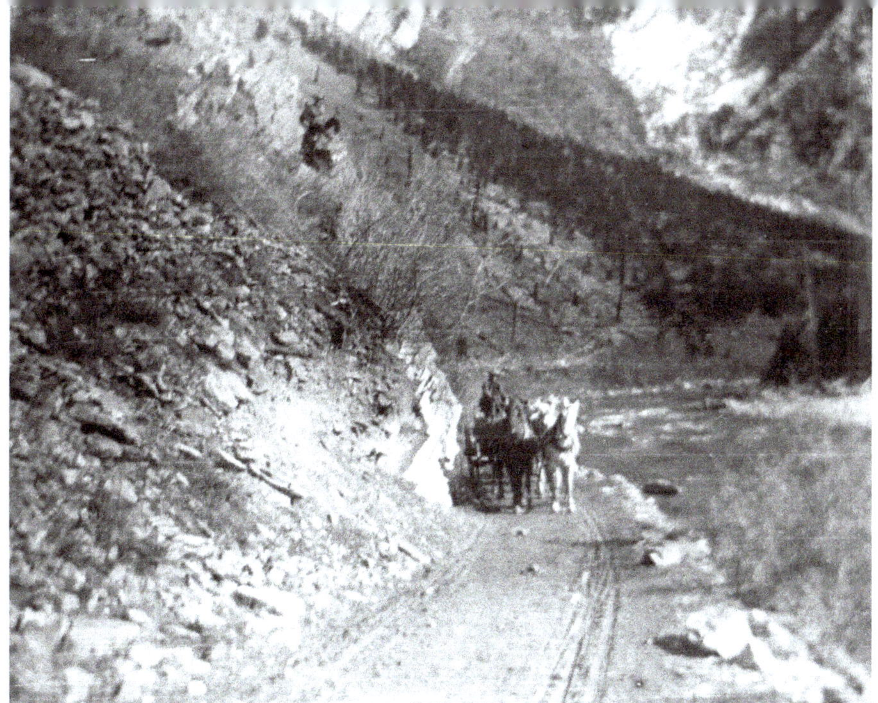

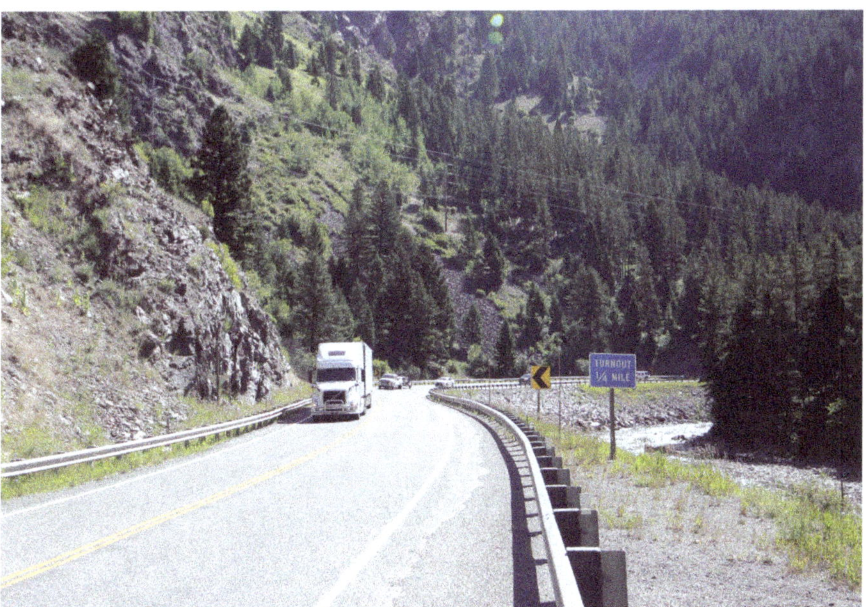

Figure 3.8. Stretch of highway along the Gallatin River just south (upstream) of present-day thirty-five-mile-per-hour curved bridge (MM#61.1).
Upper photo (circa 1900): Horse and wagon traversing narrow early roadway that was placed only a few feet above water level. The roadway was about to take the curve to the 1898 bridge (see Figure 3.9). *GHM*.
Lower photo (2016): The same stretch of highway greatly improved, elevated above the river, which has been filled in along the edge to accommodate highway construction. The rock wall near the vehicles has been carved farther away.

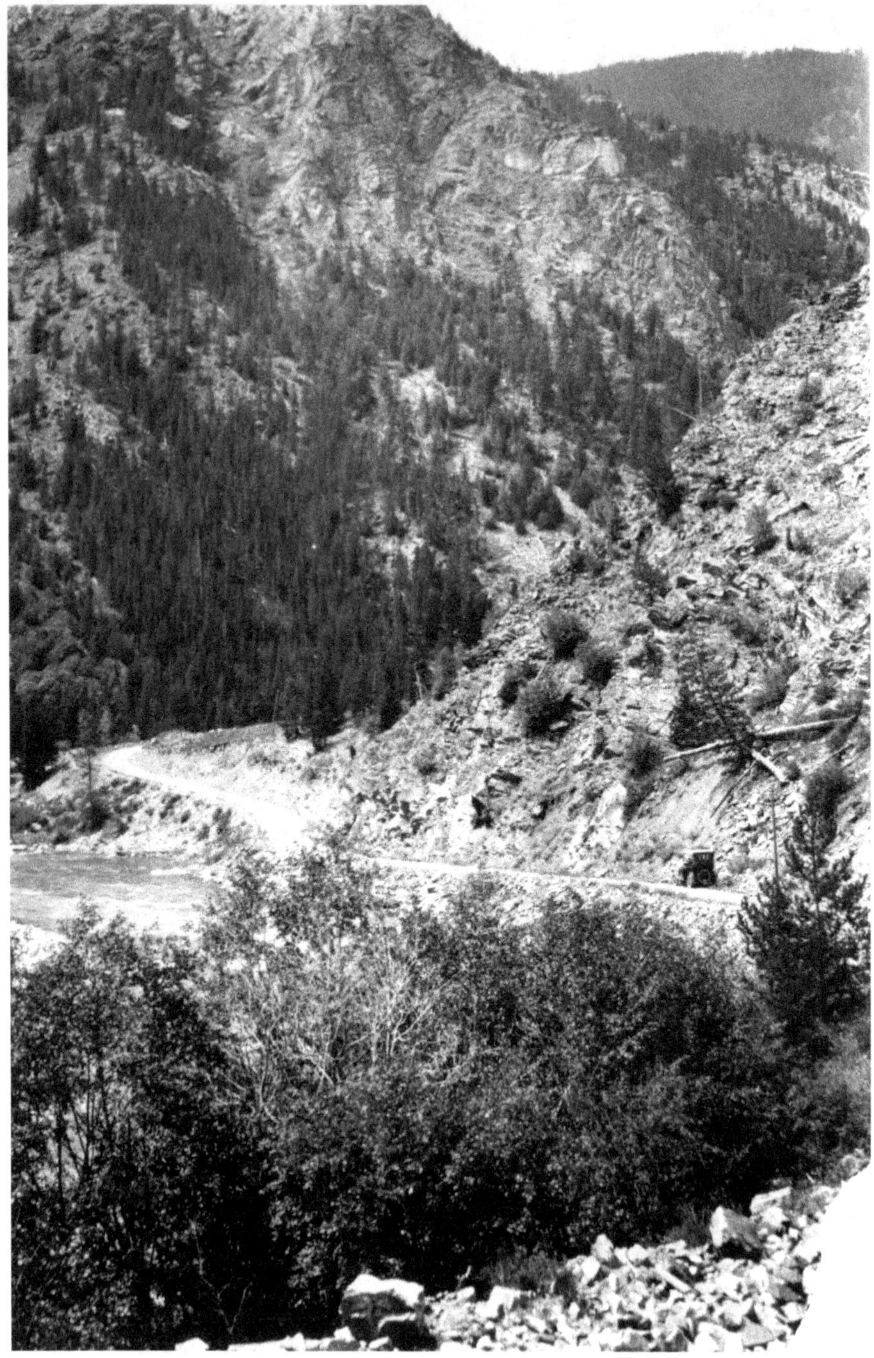

Figure 3.9. Approach to thirty-five-mile-per-hour curved bridge from the south looking downstream (MM#61).
Left photo (circa 1920s): Original 1898 Gallatin Canyon roadway curve south of present-day thirty-five-mile-per-hour curved bridge. Roadway in distance goes over the hill toward bridge built in 1898–99. Horse and buggy in Figure 3.8 was about where the car is located. *GHM.*

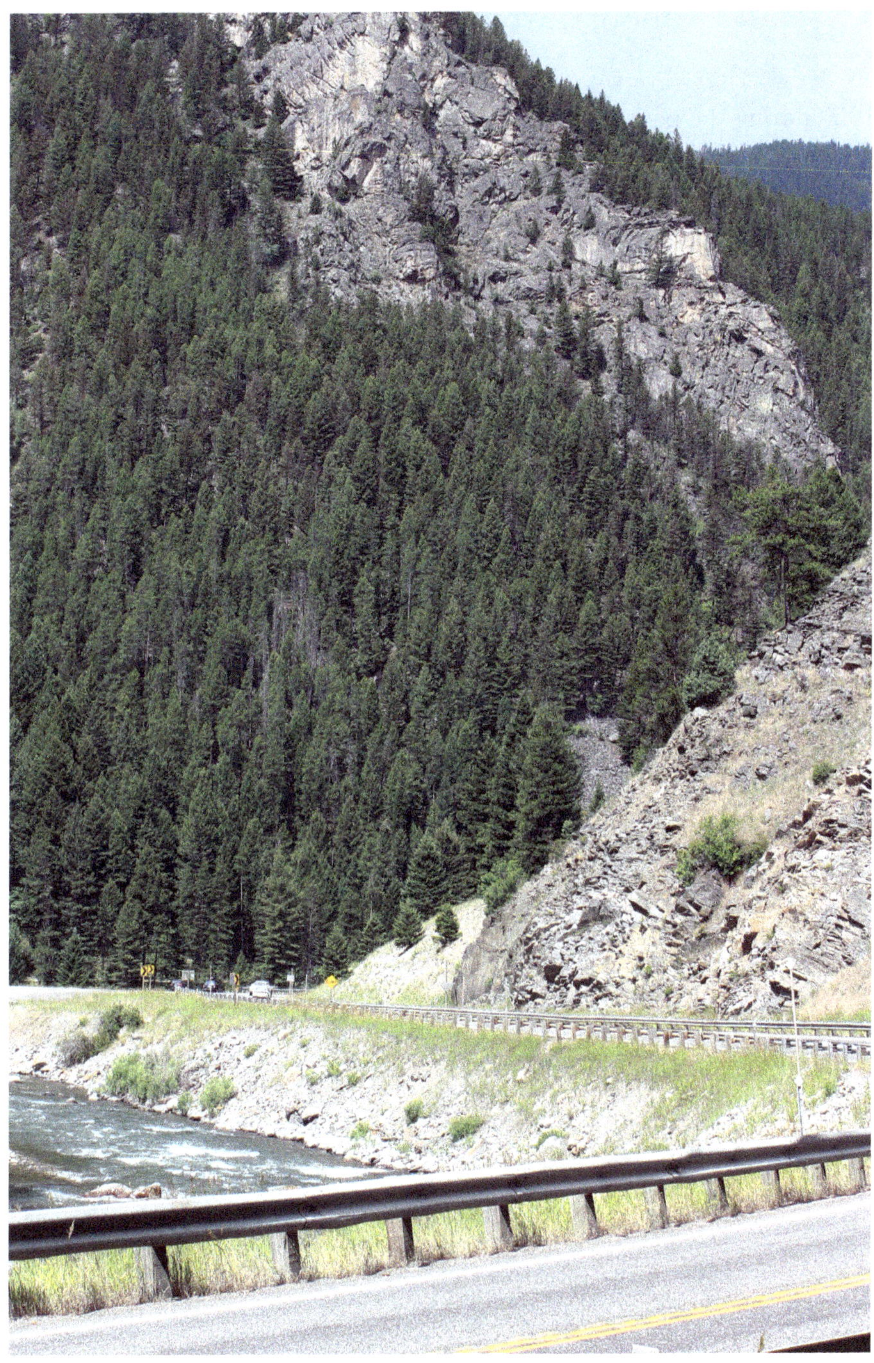

Right photo (2017): Highway greatly improved with railings and elevated above the river, which has been filled in along the bank. Cutoff to the old bridge was graded out when the thirty-five-mile-per-hour curved bridge was constructed.

1950 during the period of major improvement of the West Gallatin Road (Highway 191). Upstream of the 1898 bridge and today's curved bridge, the highway "clung" to the east side of the canyon, as it does today (Figure 3.8). An early photo of the approach to the 1898 bridge location, taken in the 1920s or 1930s, shows the location in the distance where the new curved bridge was to be built in 1950 (Figure 3.9).

Chapter 4

The Canyon Widens

(MM#61 to #57)

As one travels south and upstream from the curved or thirty-five-mile-per-hour bridge (MM#61.3), the Gallatin Canyon begins to widen in several locations (Map 4.1). Where it widens, there was room for early development, whether it be campgrounds, cabins, ranches or resorts. Many of these developments continue today.

Immediately upstream of the thirty-five-mile-per-hour bridge on the west side of the river (MM#61), accessible by a road from the highway north of the bridge used for parking for the Lava Lake trail, are long-established cabins along Cascade Creek. U.S. Forest Service permits for these cabins date to 1927 (Figure 4.1). Cascade Creek flows from the west and parallels a very popular trail to Lava Lake.

Continuing south (upstream), the road closely follows the Gallatin River channel. Although the road did not always follow the channel, where it did, and where improvements in highway elevation and roadbed took place in the 1950s and 1960s, the width of the highway increased. This required removal of much of the roadside vegetation where the highway was near the river, allowing room for safety railings along the edge of the highway, as seen in the photo of a highway curve at MM#60 (Figure 4.2).

At MM#59.5, the highway once left the valley bottom and went up and over the side hill east of the river. This section of highway over the hill was called Sagebrush Point because of a small outcrop near the high point of the hill. Like much of the early road, the stretch over the hill was at first just a muddy or dirt track, but over time, it was greatly improved (Figure 4.3). With

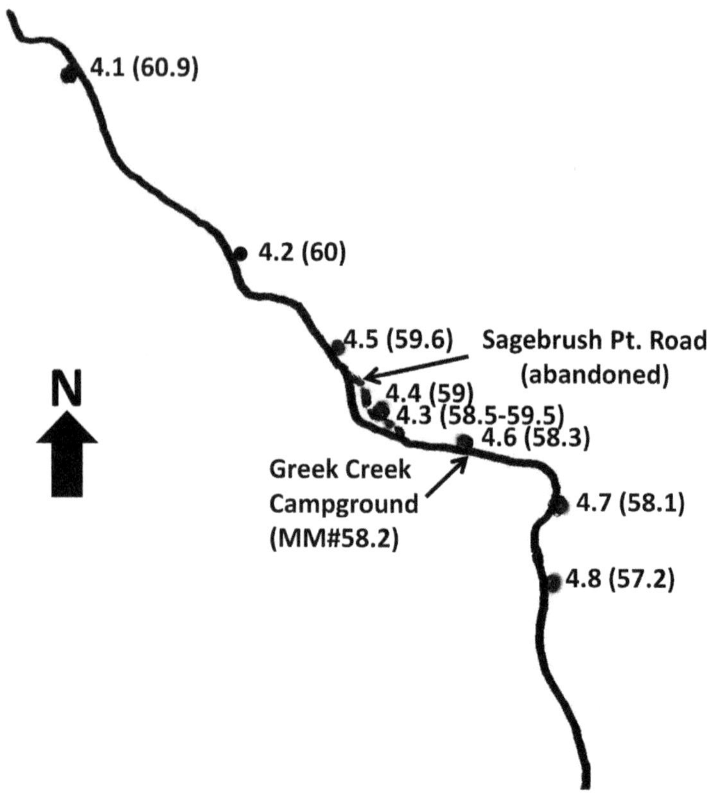

Map 4.1. Canyon Widens (MM#61 to MM#57). Map of photo locations along Highway 191 (Gallatin River closely parallels highway and is not on map) (mile markers in parentheses).

improvements in the Gallatin highway in the 1950s–60s, Sagebrush Point Hill was abandoned, and much of the highway was built in the river channel after the far bank was cut away to allow moving the river to the west of its original alignment (Figure 4.4). Cut banks on the west side of the river in several places are evidence of this highway "improvement." Heading south, the old Sagebrush Point road returns to along the river at MM#58.6, less than a half mile north of Greek Creek Campground (MM#58.2). The south end of the Sagebrush Point road where it returned to the present highway level was removed during the 2014 widening of the highway just north of the campground.

Just before the old Sagebrush Point road leaves the bottom of the valley heading south uphill, on the east side of the highway at MM#59.6, there is

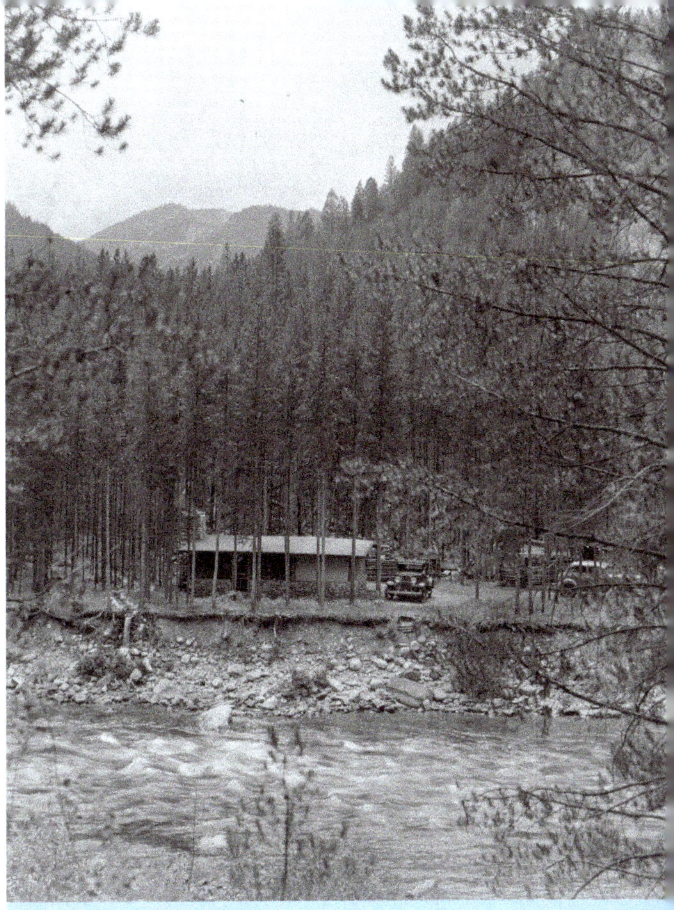

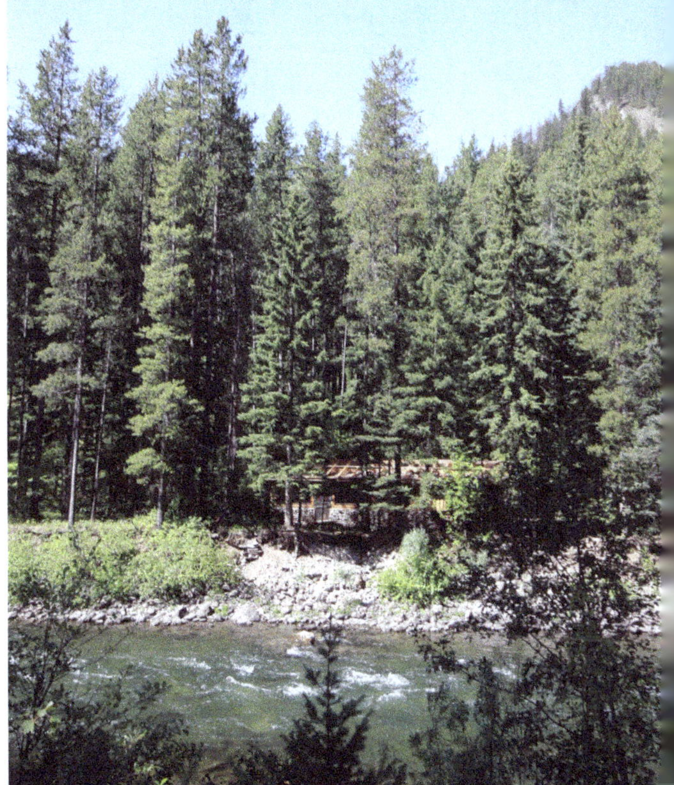

Figure 4.1. Cascade Creek summer cabins established in 1927 on U.S. Forest Service land on the west side of the Gallatin River south of the 1898 bridge (MM#61). *Upper photo* (1936): Cabin sits on edge of the river immediately above a river cut bank. The auto dates the photo. *MOR*. *Lower photo* (2016): The same cabin is visible, and it appears that it is being renovated. Little has changed relative to the bank erosion except some vegetation has grown on sections of the bank and the forest has grown higher around the cabin.

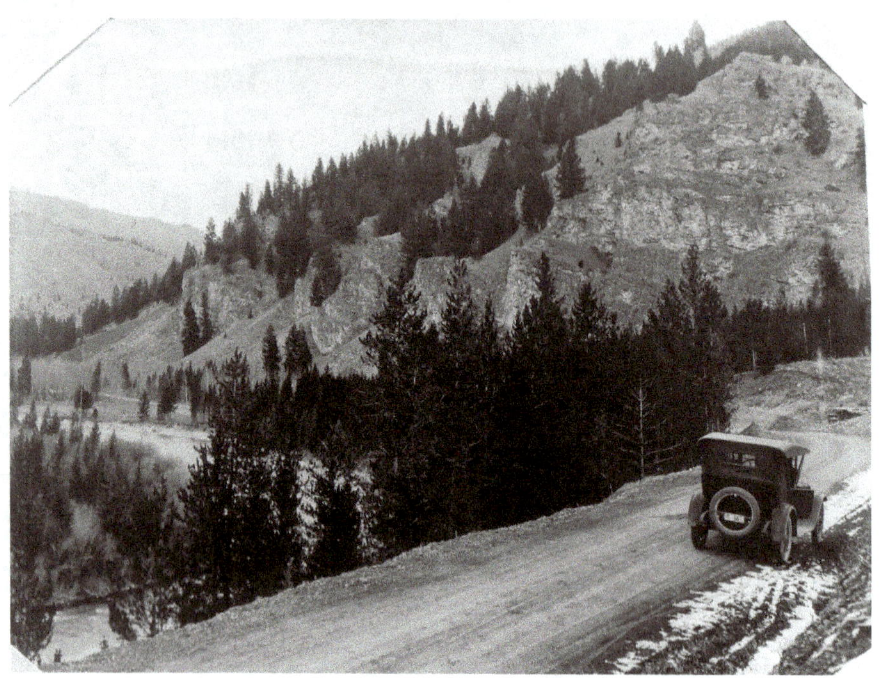

Figure 4.2. Highway curve at MM#60 just north of Kitchen Rock looking north downstream.
Above photo (1923): Improved dirt/gravel roadway shows no muddy condition, which would occur in winter if the roadway had not been graveled in 1920s. The road is narrow enough to maintain the trees along the river. *MOR.*
Below photo (2016): The modern highway has a broad base with railings eliminating trees that grew along the river in the early years.

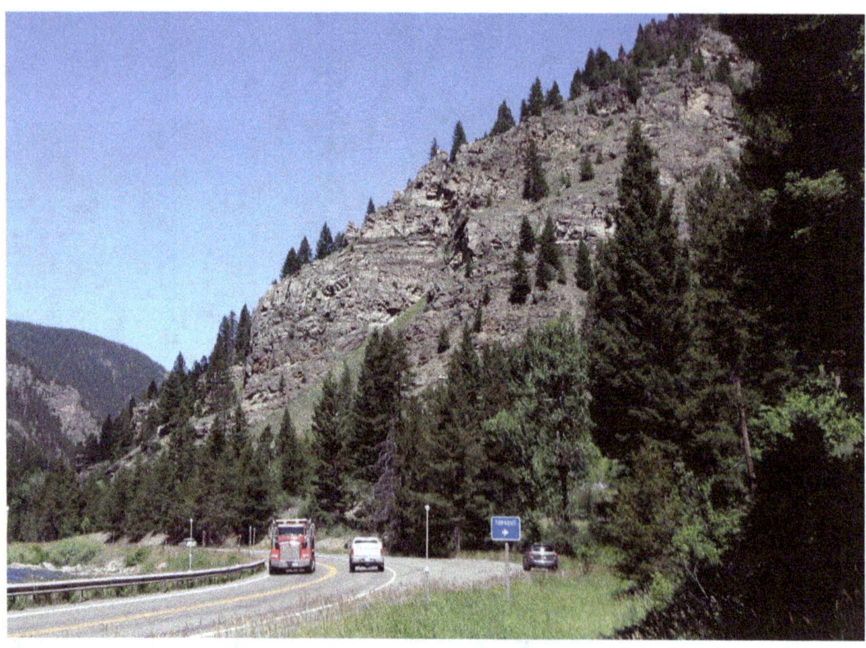

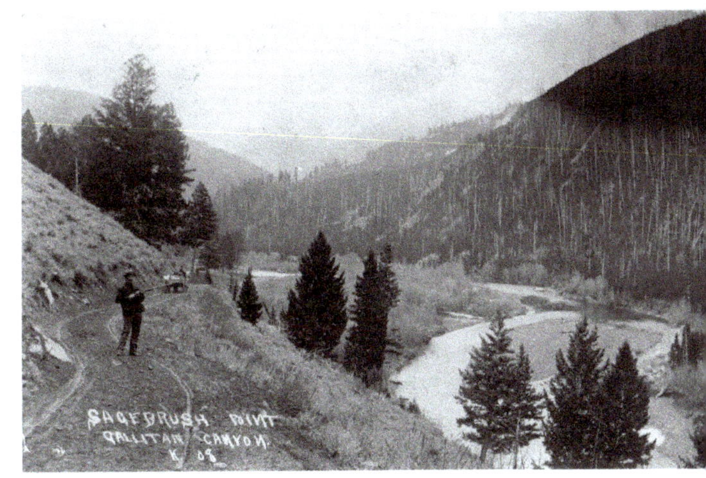

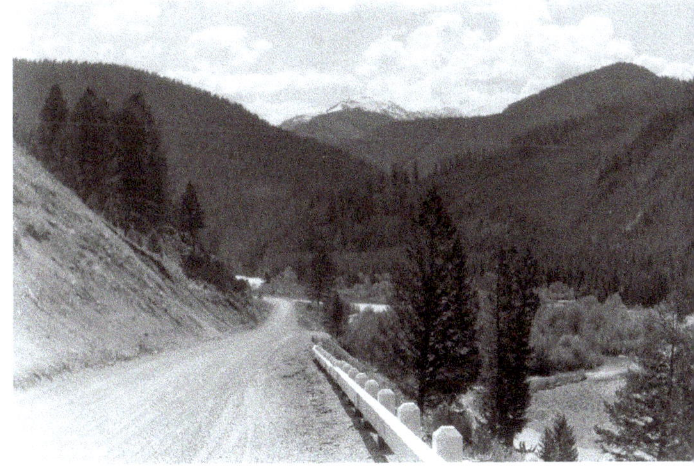

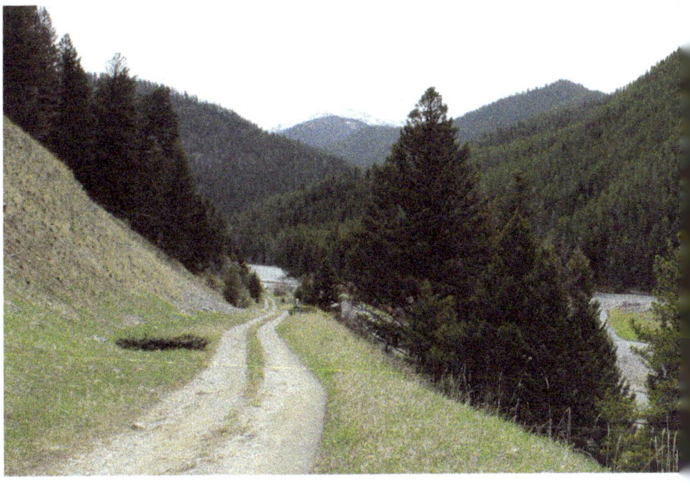

Figure 4.3. Sagebrush Point road (MM#58.5 to 59.5) on the south side of the hill looking south showing improvements over time and present abandoned roadway. The present highway is along the river down the hill from this roadway (see Figure 4.4).
Upper photo (1908): Sagebrush Point roadway in the very early days of the Gallatin Way Road to West Yellowstone. *GHM.*
Middle photo (1930s): Roadway with improved base and guardrails, which are found along many points of the road at this time. Photo appears to predate "paving" in the mid-1930s. *GHM.*
Lower photo (June 2013): Abandoned roadway, which occasionally had some use by off-road vehicles. By 2016, the roadway, used during power line improvement, had been cut off from the highway and dirt barriers were placed across the road.

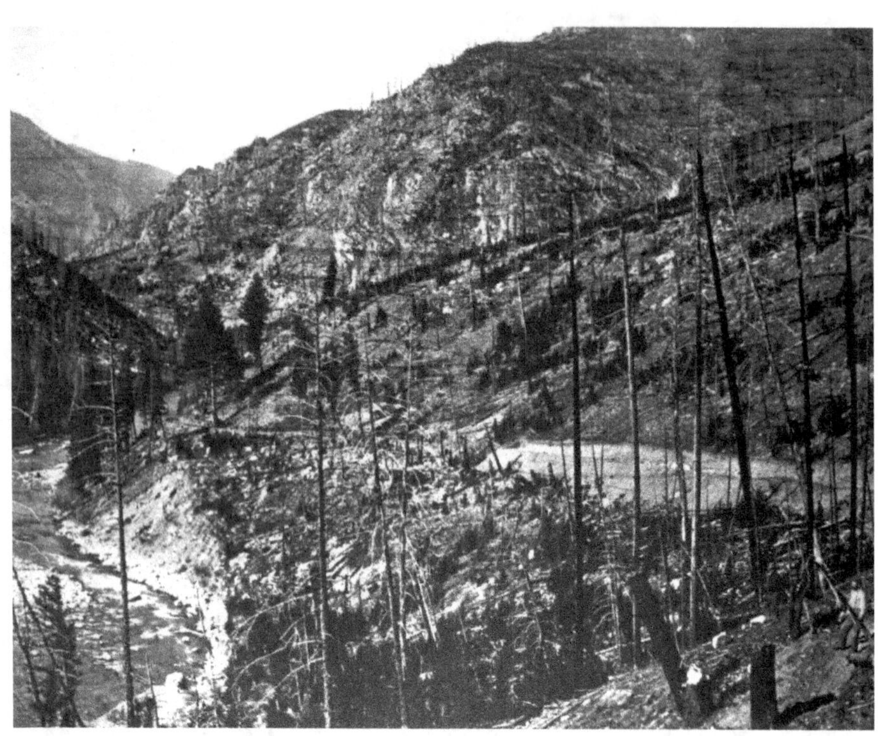

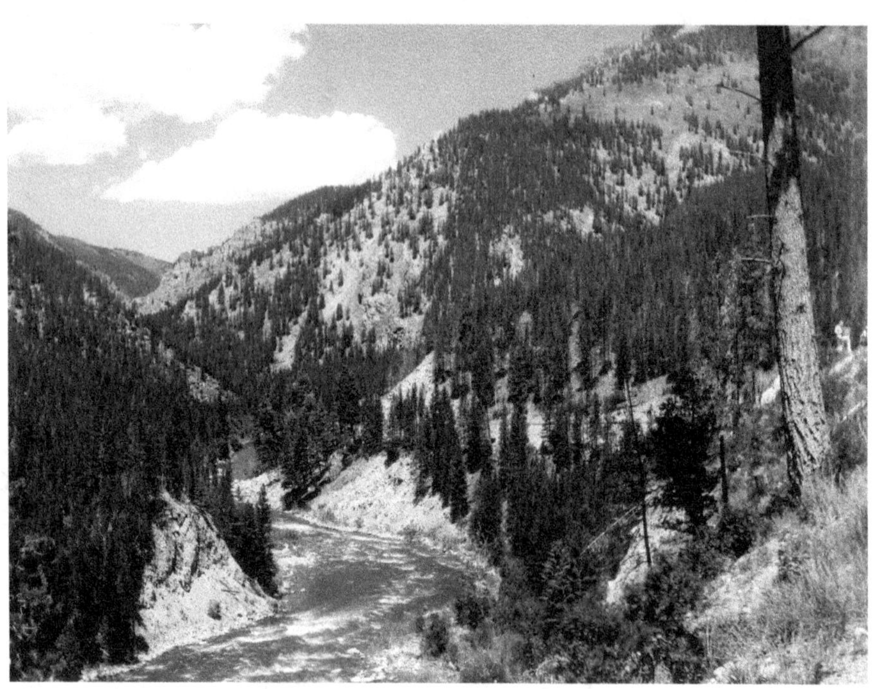

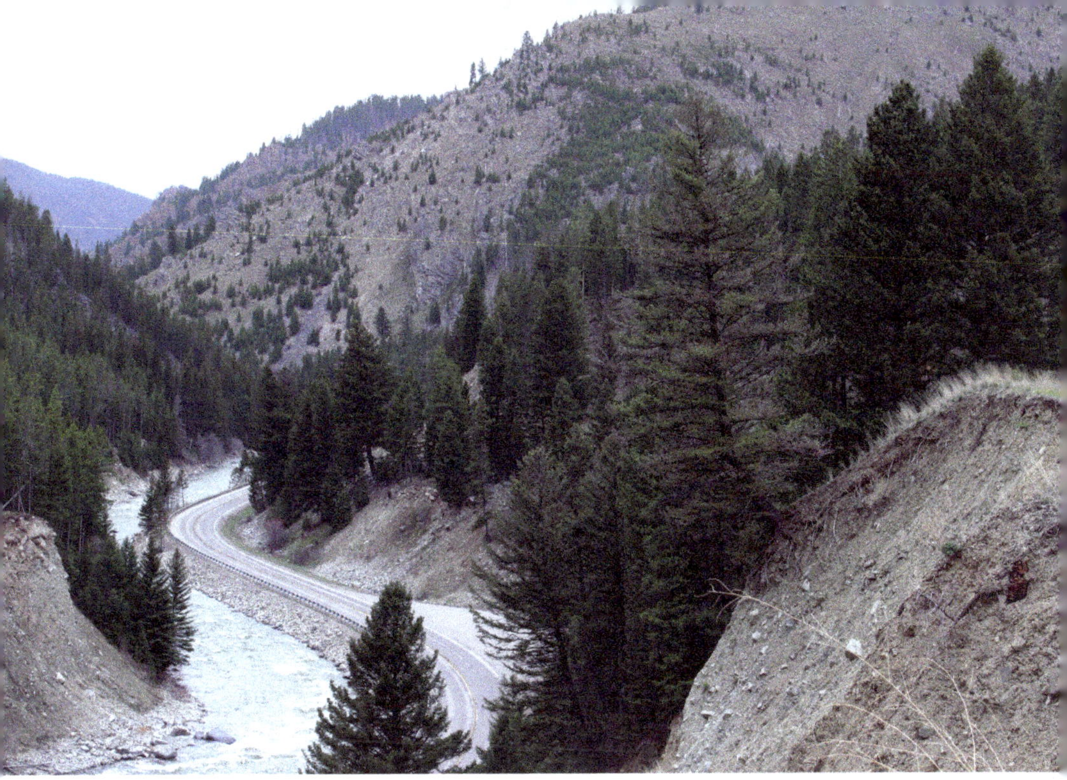

Figure 4.4. View of the Gallatin River from Sagebrush Point roadway looking north (MM#59.0).
Opposite page, upper photo (circa 1900): View shows major destruction from the 1881 forest fire. *GHM.*
Opposite page, lower photo (1930s): View shows forest recovery after forty years. *GHM.*
Above photo (2013): View shows highway placed in the river channel and left side riverbanks scoured to allow the river to "move over." Sagebrush Point roadway is eroding (lower right), making it no longer passable for vehicles, and the forest appears to be dying back from earlier recovery.

a pull-off at the location of a large rock called Kitchen Rock (Figure 4.5). Geologically, this rock is unusual for the area because it is a Proterozoic rock, meaning it is 540 million to 2.5 billion years old, whereas much of the canyon has limestone cliffs from the Madison Formation, which was laid down during the Mississippian period of the Paleozoic era (around 350 million years ago). Kitchen Rock got its name because in the early twentieth century, this was a stopping point for travelers going up the canyon, where they cooked meals on their way toward the west gate of Yellowstone National Park. One wonders whether the steep uphill of the Sagebrush Point road required a rest of horses (and people) or potential overheating of autos or buses, and thus time for a lunch break. Apparently, early autos often backed up the hill in very low gear to prevent overheating. Today, one can still see the dark soot stains at the base of Kitchen Rock from the many fires that burned at this location. Improvement of the

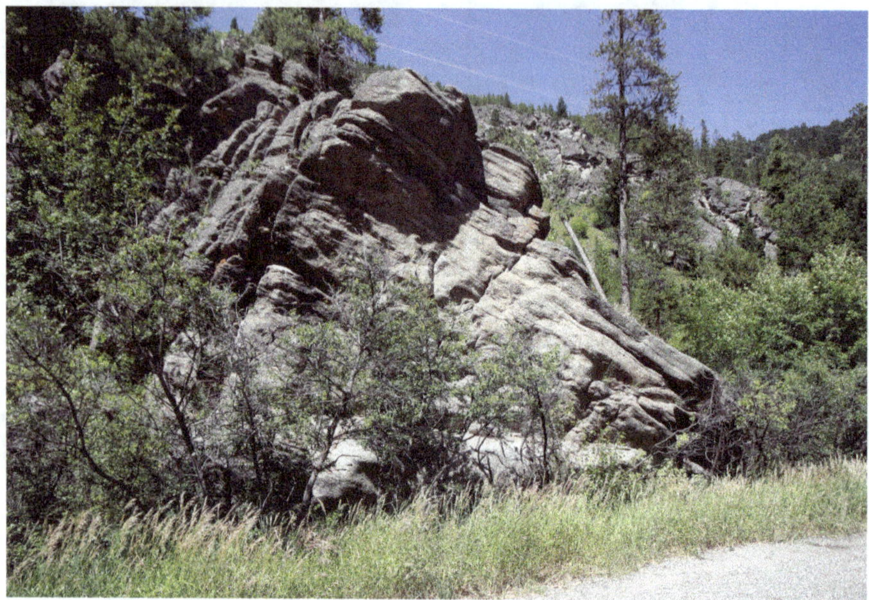

Figure 4.5. Kitchen Rock (MM#59.6). Although the highway has been built up at this point, it is still possible to look at the lower part of the rock behind the grassy roadway edge and see the area stained by smoke from the many fires that burned at the rock's base. These fires were to cook meals for early travelers heading to West Yellowstone and the park, thus the name of the rock.

highway at this point has elevated the roadbed, and the darkened base of Kitchen Rock is now several feet below the pull-off and highway level but still visible in a hole in the fill at the rock's base.

To the east and south, up the mountain above Greek Creek Campground, are Greek Creek cabins. In the late 1880s, Albert Greek built a cabin in this area near a small creek, now called Greek Creek. The Greek Creek area was also a location of one of Zachariah Sales's lumber camps, established in the early 1900s. Greek Creek Campground was built in the 1950s in what may have been a highwater floodplain. Prior to development of the campground and improvement of the highway, the road, basically a muddy track in its early days (circa late 1800s to early 1900s), passed uphill to the east of the present campground with access to the cabins and then dropped back toward the river to the north and south of the cabins (Figure 4.6). The uphill location of this road, as well as the cabins, may have been to avoid occasional flooding in the lower floodplain, where the present campground is located, as the river in the old photo appears to pass through or very near to the campground location. It is uncertain whether

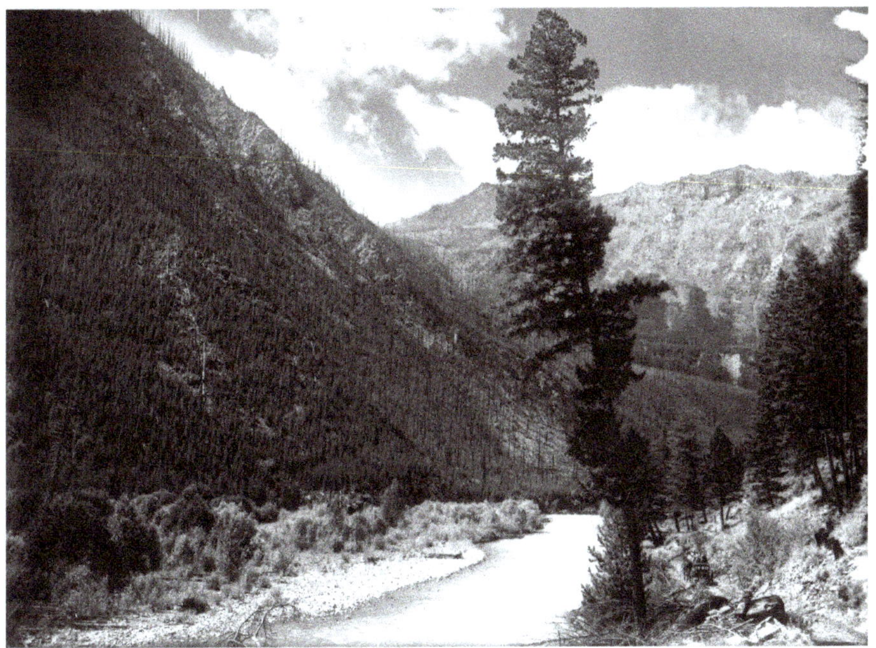

Figure 4.6. Roadway just north of Greek Creek Campground (MM#58.3).
Above photo (circa 1898): Horse and buggy, Michener Team, headed north on a very poor roadway just north of present-day Greek Creek campground and cabins area (team on the roadway is in the lower right corner of photo). *GHM.*
Below photo (2016): The new highway north of Greek Creek Campground passes an outcrop of rock that was cut back in 2014 to allow widening of the road. Note how much the channel of the river has migrated away from the highway and campground area, perhaps allowing development of the campground, which initially would have been in the floodplain, requiring the old roadway to pass above the floodplain.

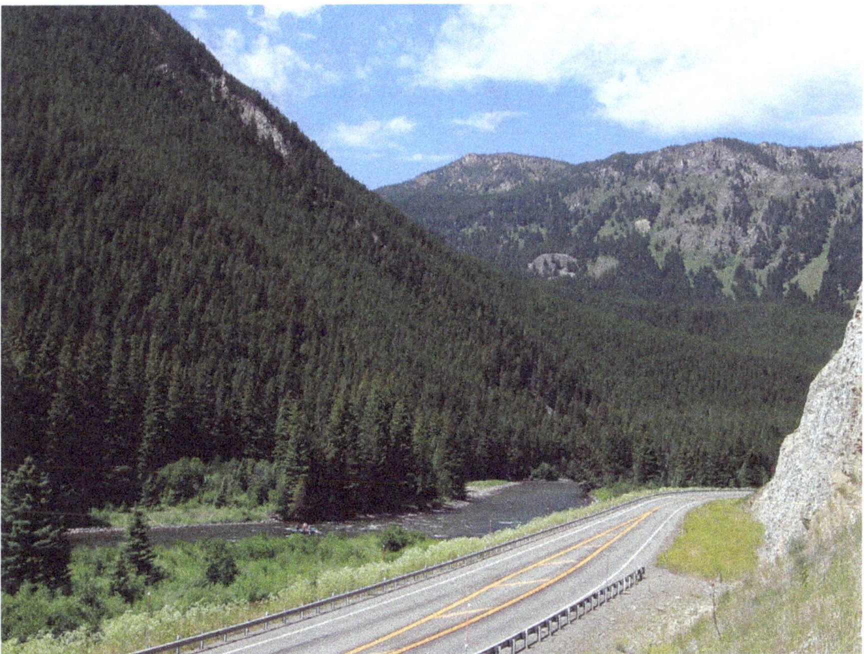

the river changed course, which is obvious for the downstream section seen in Figure 4.6, or there was some filling of the floodplain, allowing campground development. In 2014, a highway turn lane was constructed for Greek Creek Campground, requiring removal of a large portion of the cliffs to the north of the campground (seen in photo comparison Figure 4.6). This dramatic change in canyon appearance was also done at the cliffs near Red Cliff Campground (shown later farther upstream).

As discussed earlier, the canyon was often used for moving livestock from the Gallatin Valley to summer pasture in West Fork or Taylor Fork or to guest ranches farther south. This was a long trek, taking all of a day if not more. Eventual highway improvement and development of Big Sky created more traffic, making it difficult to move livestock along the highway (Figure 4.7). Better and larger trucks and stock trailers now allow rapid transport of livestock throughout the area.

About one mile south of Greek Creek Campground is the access road to Swan Creek Campground (MM#57.3). The highway bridge over Swan Creek has been modified several times over the years. Initially, it was a small bridge sufficient for single cars (Figure 4.8). It was expanded during the road improvement period of the 1950s and '60s, and then when turn lanes were developed for many intersections in the canyon in the 2012–14 period, the bridge was enlarged and greatly improved again and a canyon wall was carved back, allowing for development of turn lanes into Swan Creek. Swan Creek campground, about half a mile up the Swan Creek road, is only open in the summer. There also are several seasonal residences along the Swan Creek road, many dating prior to World War II. The Swan Creek road continues for several miles up into the Gallatin Range, making access to hiking the high country more available in this area.

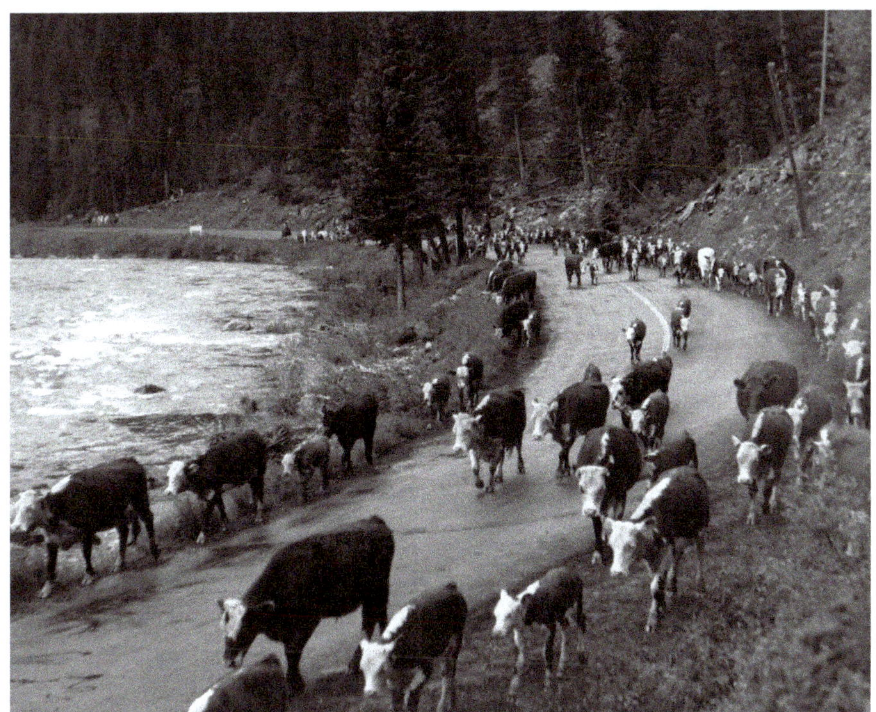

Figure 4.7. Sharp ninety-degree curve in Highway 191 just south of Greek Creek Campground (MM#58.1).
Above photo (circa 1950): Cattle drive along this stretch of the highway. *320 Ranch.*
Below photo (2016): Greatly improved highway with guardrails where the road encroaches on the river. High-volume traffic of cars and trucks no longer allows any stock drives along the road.

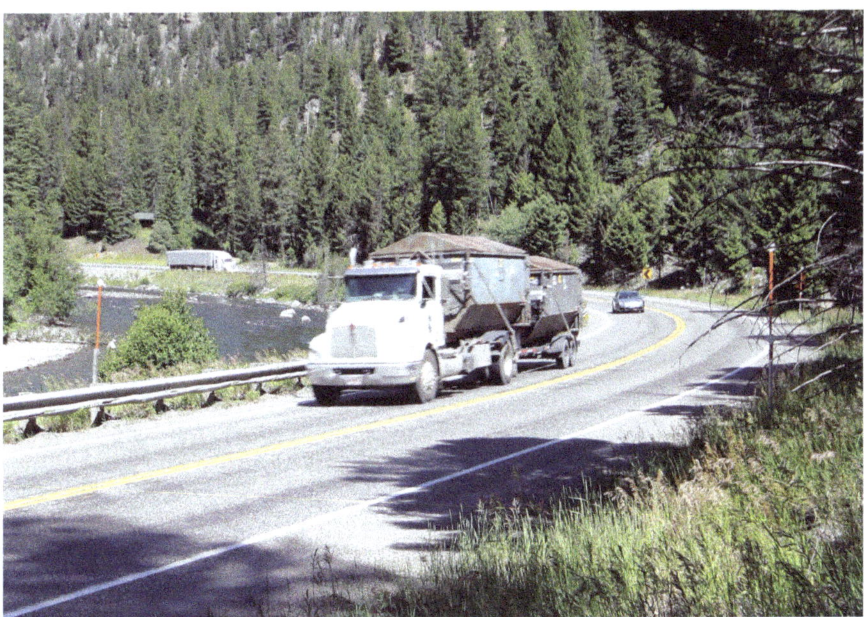

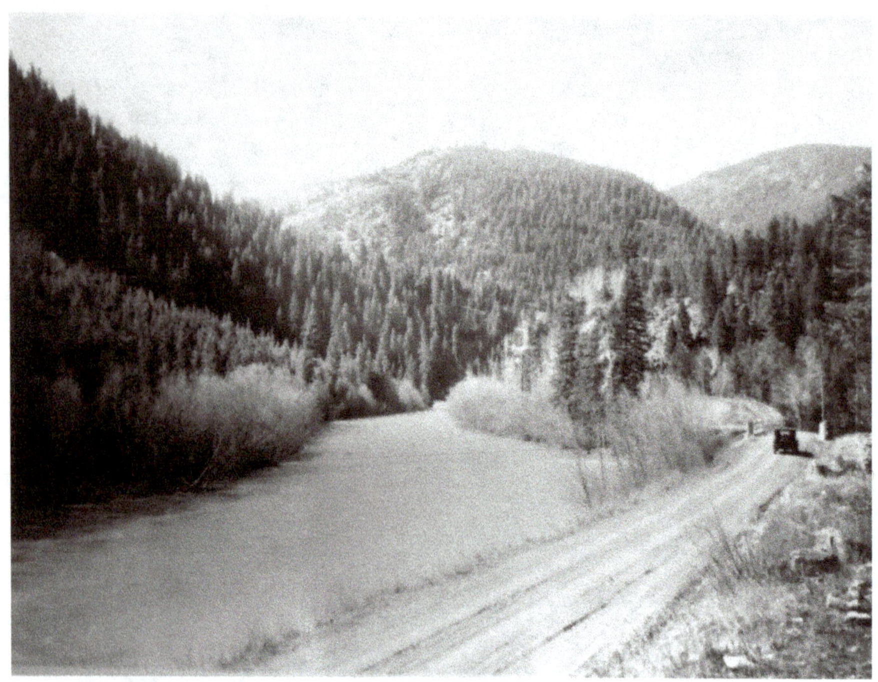

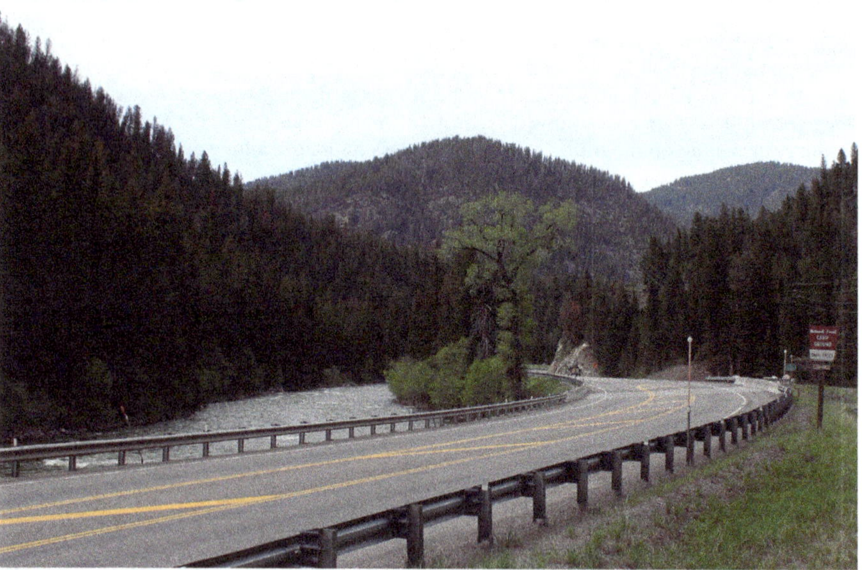

Figure 4.8. Highway heading north toward the bridge over Swan Creek (MM#57.2).
Upper photo (1929): The small bridge in the background appears to have cement sidings, but it is just over one vehicle wide. The roadway is graveled at this point in time. *MOR.*
Lower photo (July 2016): Bridge over Swan Creek was widened and moved toward the river in 2012–14. Turn lanes on the highway were constructed allowing access into Swan Creek. The earlier highway passed through where the white cross is located to the right of the present roadway.

Chapter 5

Karst Kamp to the Green Bridge

(MM#56 to MM#51.5)

Moving up the canyon from Swan Creek (Map 5.1), one arrives at Moose Creek Campground (MM#56), a reach of the canyon sufficiently wide to allow several campsites along the Gallatin River. The campground is named for the small creek crossing the road just south of the campground. In earlier years, there was a small bridge across the creek, which has been replaced with a large culvert (Figure 5.1) (MM#55.8). The early photo shows an area north of the creek that eventually became the campground.

Upstream from Moose Creek is the location of Karst Kamp (MM#55+). Karst Kamp (originally called Karst Cold Springs Resort) may be one of the best-known early developments in the Gallatin Canyon. Much has been written about Pete Karst and the development of this establishment in the middle of the Gallatin Canyon. However, for this story and appreciation of old photos, following is some reminder of the old days when Pete Karst in 1902–3 began the construction of one of very few developments in the canyon that welcomed travelers and/or guests from outside the territory.

Pete Karst arrived in the Gallatin Canyon area in 1898. He purchased the mid-canyon location from Charlie Oliver in 1903, and there he developed his resort, having originally gone into partnership with Oliver in 1902 and then bought him out. Two events helped Karst prosper in the canyon. Walter Cooper hired him to carry mail, freight and passengers up the Gallatin twice weekly to the Cooper Tie Camp at Taylor Fork. To help in moving materials up the canyon, he bought this mid-canyon property. The need for

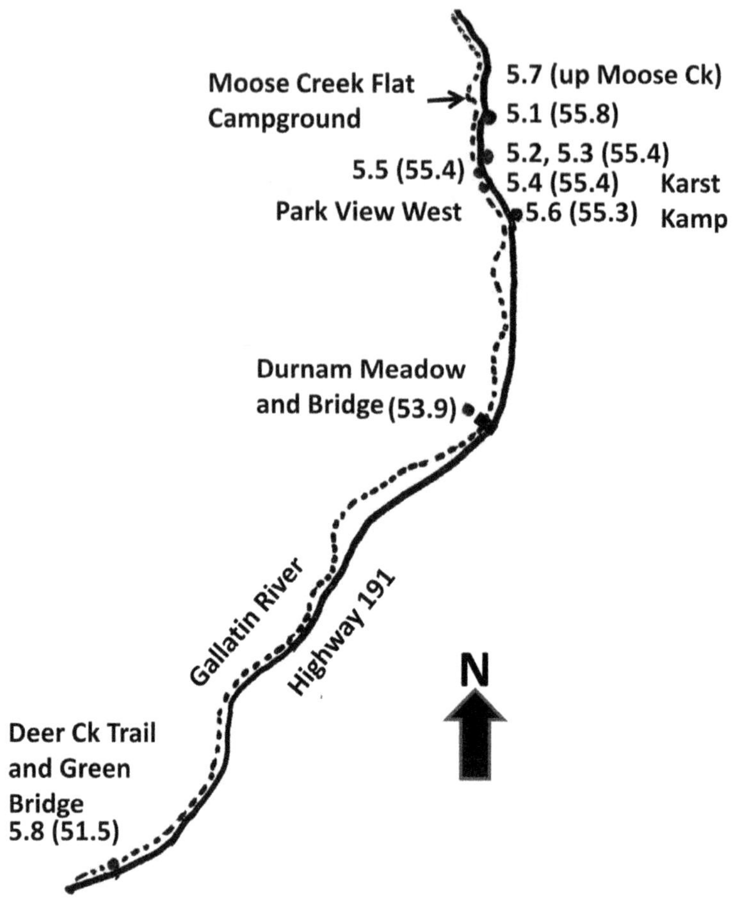

Map 5.1. Karst Kamp to the Green Bridge (MM#56 to MM#51). Map of photo locations along Highway 191 and the Gallatin River (mile markers in parentheses).

materials for the tie camp also created a demand for a better "road" up the canyon, and around 1898 or slightly later, a wagon road was built as far as Taylor Fork. It would be several years (1914) before the road extended south through Yellowstone National Park to the west entrance to the park at what would become West Yellowstone.

In the early decades of the twentieth century, at his mid-canyon location, Karst built an extensive arrangement of cabins, dance hall, bar and restaurant (Figures 5.2, 5.3 and 5.4). The main buildings included a huge dining room famous for great food, a coffee shop, gas pumps,

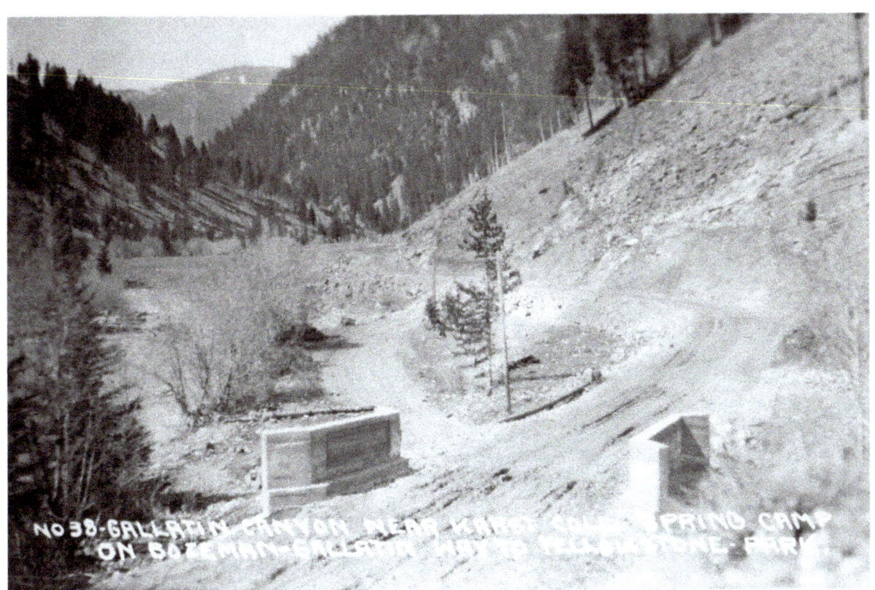

Figure 5.1. Location where Moose Creek passes under Highway 191 just north of Karst Kamp and south of Moose Creek campground (MM#55.8).
Above photo (1921–22): Small single-lane concrete bridge passing over Moose Creek. *MOR.*
Below photo (2016): Moose Creek Bridge was converted to a culvert under an improved highway. Gallatin Highway in the 1920s was often a muddy track, as seen in the early photo. Moose Creek campground can be seen in background with a few RVs.

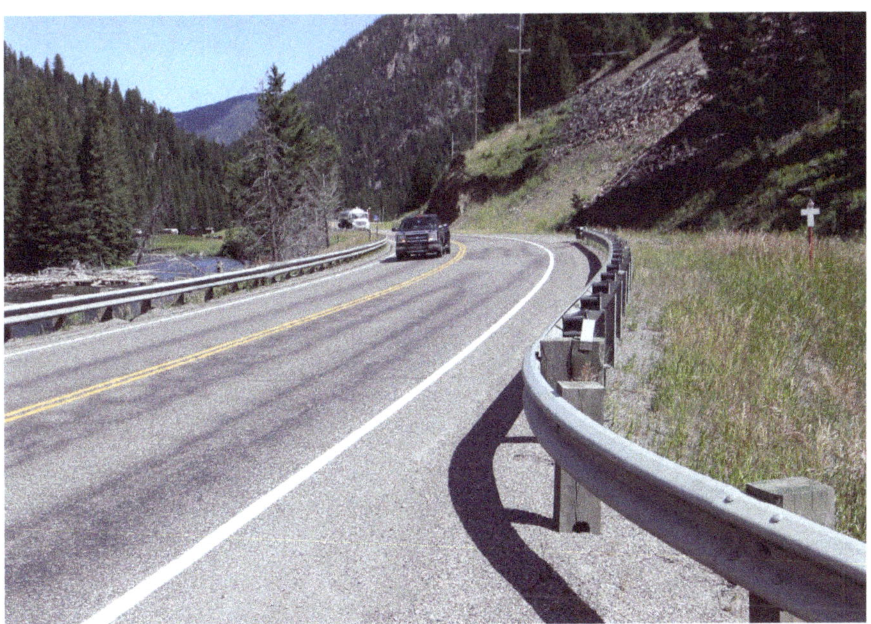

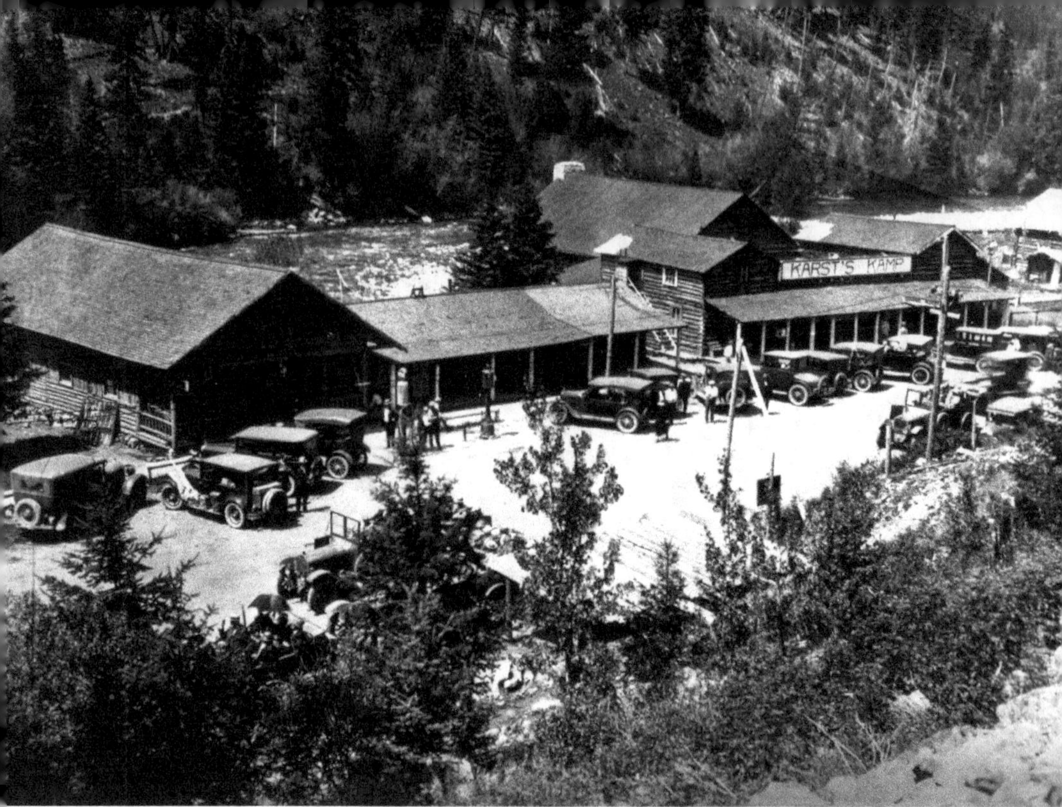

Figure 5.2. Karst Kamp (Karst Cold Springs Resort) at mid-canyon (circa 1932) (MM#55.4).
The photo, which postdates Figure 5.3, shows Karst at the height of its activities. The tall building with a chimney in the upper center was the dance hall (see Figure 5.5). Karst was a primary stop for anyone traveling the Gallatin Road. *GHM.*
Repeat photo location was forested and unattainable.

(*opposite page*) Figure 5.3. Karst Kamp (Karst Cold Springs Resort) (MM#55.4).
Upper photo (circa 1910): Karst Kamp showing early buildings of the resort, which appear to be to the far right in the 1920s photo. *GHM.*
Middle photo (late 1920s): Karst Kamp showing the store, covered gas pump and other main buildings of the resort. *GHM.*
Lower photo (2016): Location now owned by Montana Whitewater is used for an outbuilding and a firewood yard. Highway 191 passes by this area.

a general store for groceries and gifts, a summer and winter bar and a big dance hall, built in 1925, with a great view on the edge of the river (Figure 5.5). A still provided alcoholic beverages during Prohibition. Some historians claim that Karst also had a brothel to serve the miners at his asbestos mine. The many cabins (about twenty-six) extended along the road between the roadway and river (Figure 5.6). In order to process logs for all these buildings, he built a sawmill up Moose Creek (Figure 5.7), which was accessible across from Moose Creek flat, today's campground (MM#56). Karst also constructed a small golf course for his stepson-

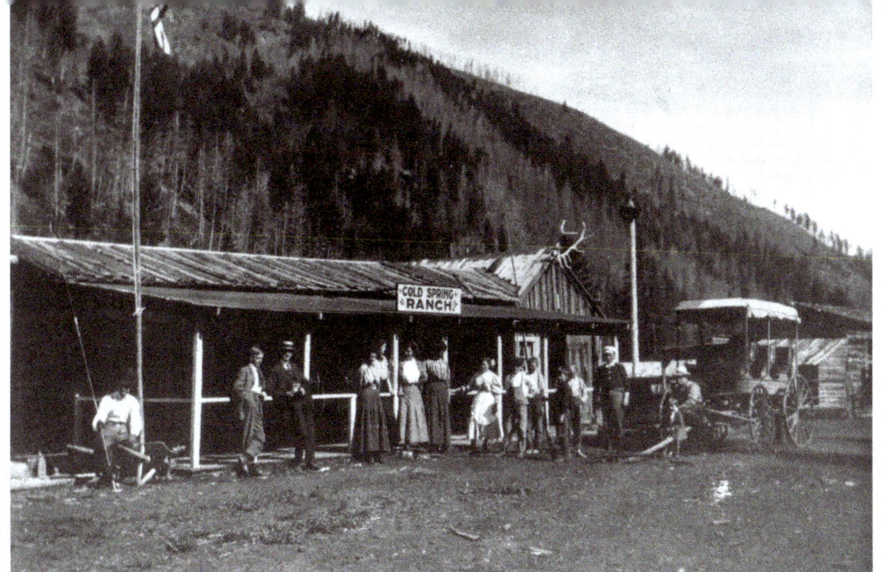
COLD SPRING
RANCH

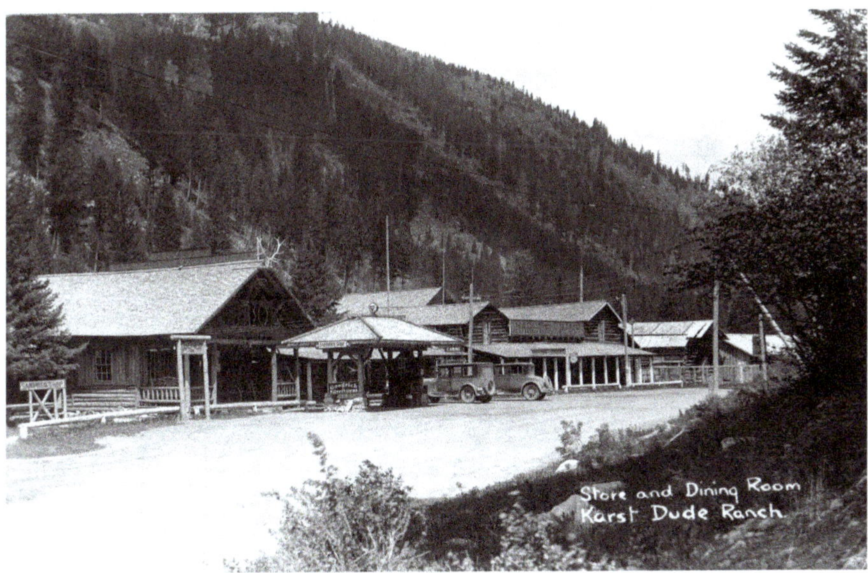
Store and Dining Room
Karst Dude Ranch

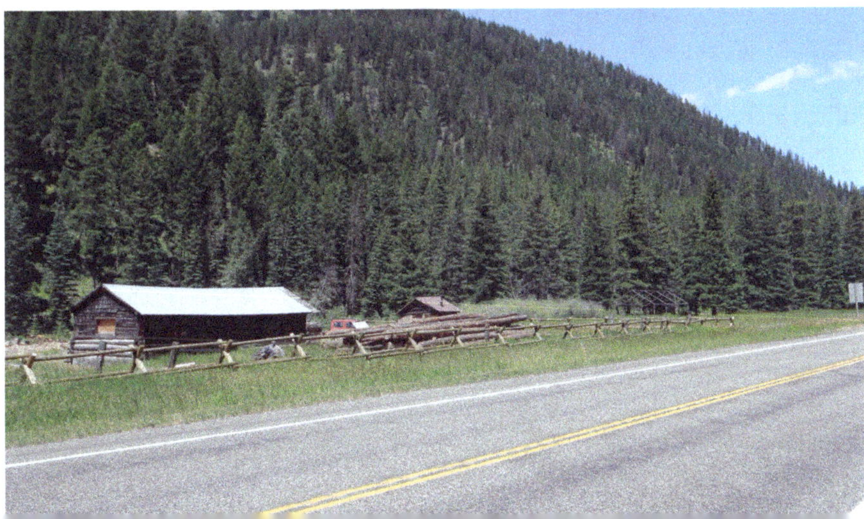

in-law, Edwin "Ed" J. Durnam, across the river from his buildings and north of what would become Durnam's lettuce fields (see below). Durnam was a professional golfer from Minnesota and in 1923 married Karst's stepdaughter, Isabella (the one on the stock bridge over House Rock in Figure 3.4). Some evidence of this course can be seen on early photos, which appear to show two holes with fairways. That area is now developed with homes in Park View West. To attract winter visitors, Karst developed Karst Hill for skiing across the road from the cabins. The first ski tow was built using 2,500 feet of cable from the asbestos mine, which made life easier for the skiers. Downhill and slalom races were held there. A 90-foot ski jump plus a practice ski jump were added. In 1938, the Montana Ski Jumping Championship, sponsored by the Bozeman Ski Club, was held at Karst Kamp, followed by events in 1939 and 1940, when the Northern Rockies Mountain Ski Association Jumping Tournament was held.

To supply power for his Kamp, in 1922 Karst built a small hydroelectric facility on Moose Creek a short distance north of the Kamp. At the open area, now Moose Creek Campground, there was a bridge to the west side of the river that allowed access to Karst's asbestos mine (see below). Moose Creek Campground is now popular for large RVs along with tents.

Karst's power plant, along with a small electric diesel generator installed in 1938 by Dr. McGill at 320 Ranch to the south, were the only sources of electricity in the canyon until 1948, when power lines were installed up the canyon as far as Elkhorn Ranch (MM#33.1) with funding from the Rural Electrification Administration (REA). Prior to electricity being run up the canyon, Elkhorn Ranch and other ranches used wood for heat and cooking and kerosene and white gas lanterns for light. At that time, guests at Elkhorn Ranch would go to Karst's facility to watch wildlife movies created by Ernest Miller, founder of Elkhorn (personal experience). One assumes the small generator at 320 Ranch was run irregularly and thus was not a source of electricity for such entertainment.

Karst Kamp continued to prosper under new ownership into the 1950s, until a main building burned to the ground in 1957. The building was rebuilt but burned down again a few years later. These buildings with bar and entertainment were one of the stops in the canyon into the 1950s for those looking for a "night out." Today, locals claim only two of the original twenty-six cabins remain in use (see the earlier photos).

Along with his well-developed Karst Kamp (Karst Cold Springs Resort), Karst discovered asbestos and developed a mine up the mountain west of the Gallatin River. Karst sold the mine in 1935 to the Karstolite

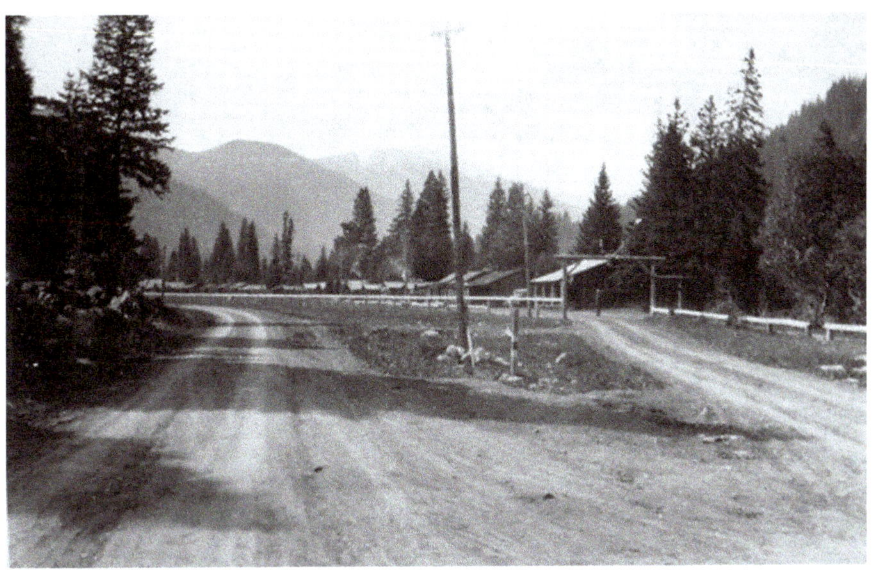

Figure 5.4. Karst Kamp cabin area (Karst Cold Springs Resort) (MM#55.4).
Above photo (circa 1927): Roadway to Karst's twenty-six cabins leads off to the right (south) from main Karst buildings. The main roadway goes to the left. *Gamel family.*
Below photo (2016): Most cabins are gone and the property now is owned by Montana Whitewater.

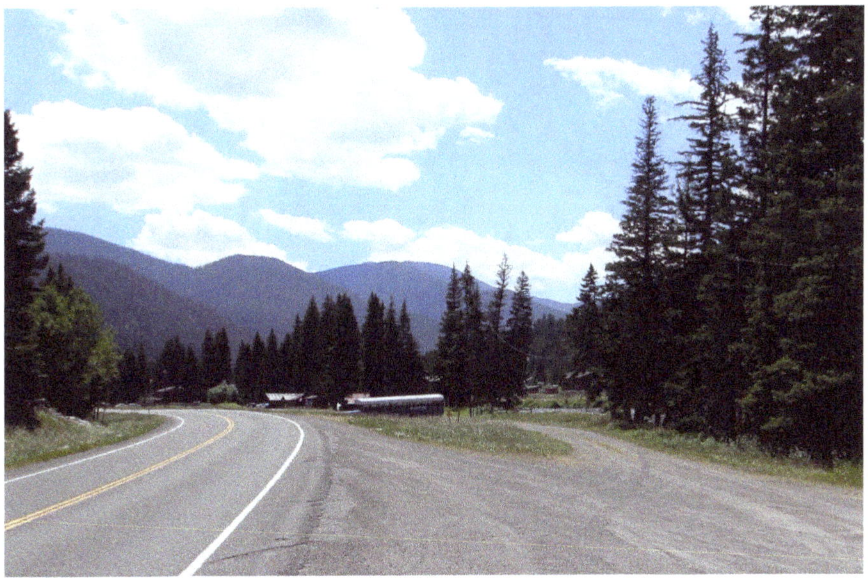

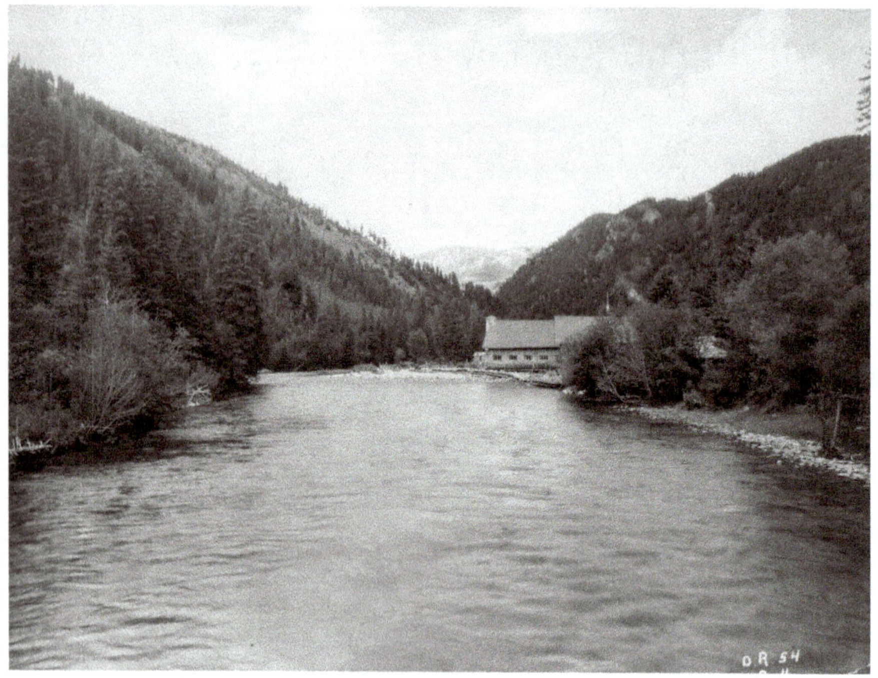

Figure 5.5. Looking north down the Gallatin River at Karst Cold Springs Resort in the Gallatin Canyon (MM#55.4).
Above photo (1954): The dance hall at Karst Cold Springs Resort built on the edge of the Gallatin River. From within the dance hall, one could look upstream with wonderful views. This photo was taken only a few years before Karst Kamp closed after the main building burned down. *MOR.*
Below photo (2016): Looking downstream toward the dance hall location, which was on the grassy point downstream near the right side of the river. The dance hall and most structures from Karst Cold Springs Resort no longer exist.

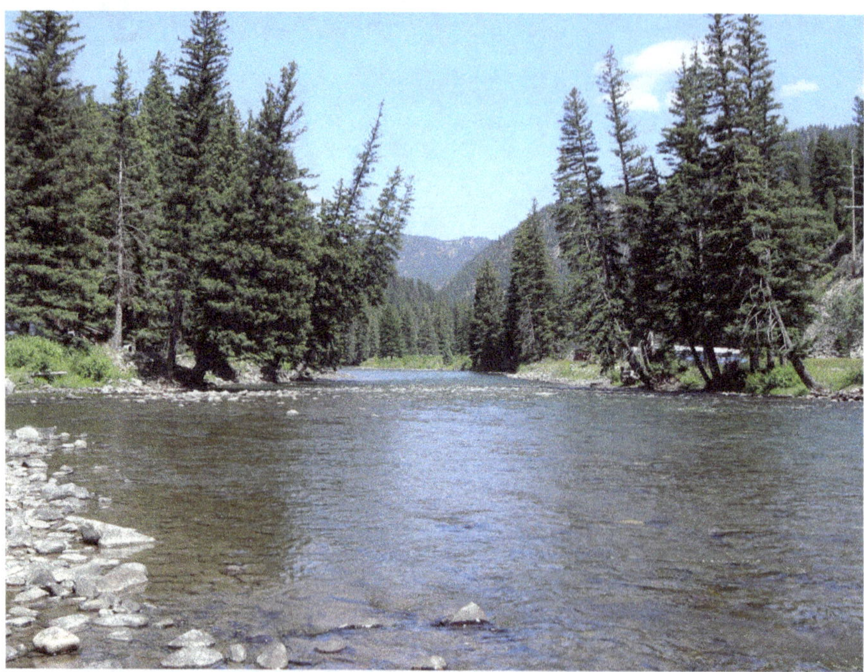

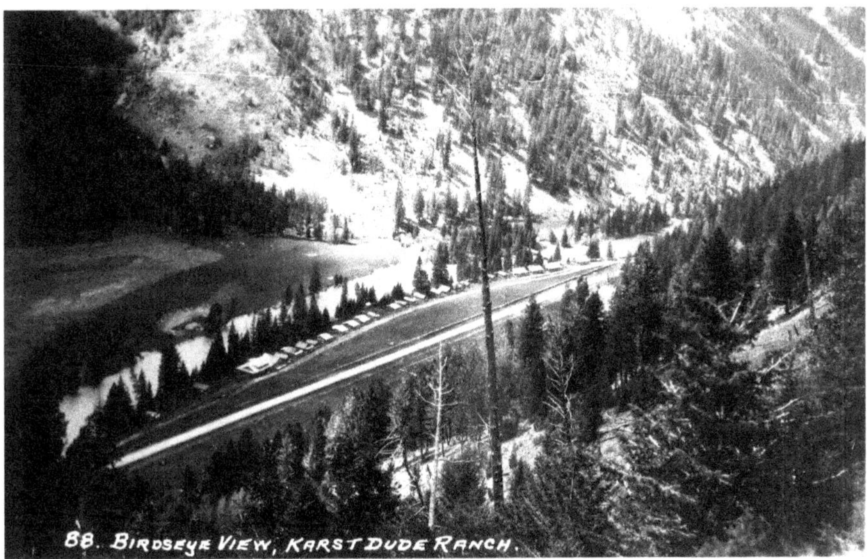

Figure 5.6. Karst Cold Springs Resort along the Gallatin River (MM#55.3) (1912). Many of the twenty-six cabins Karst had constructed in the early 1900s to serve travelers and guests passing up the canyon. Most of the cabins are now gone, and the area houses only a few people. *GHM.*
Repeat photo location was forested.

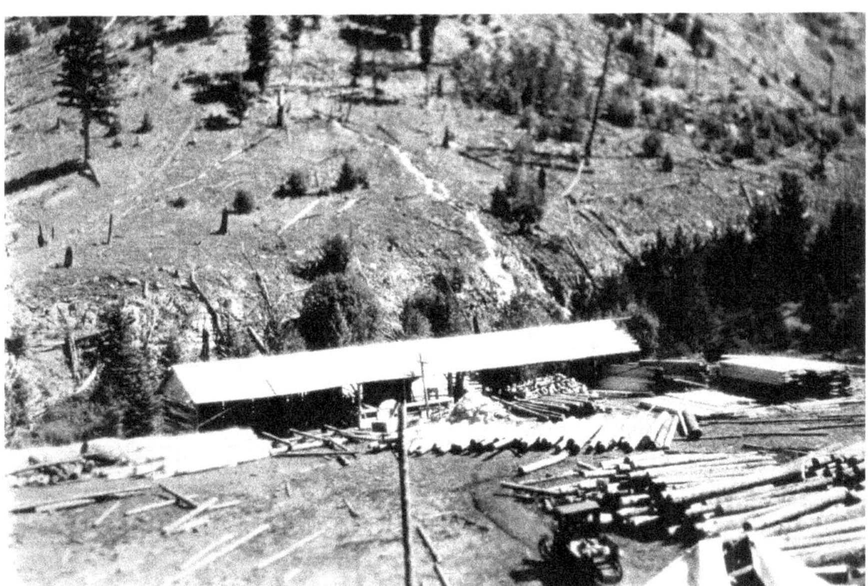

Figure 5.7. Karst sawmill up Moose Creek (circa MM#56) (circa early 1900s). It processed the many logs for all the cabins and structures Karst built at Karst Kamp in the early 1900s. *GHM.*

Company, which operated the deposit until 1938, when it was sold to the Montana Asbestos Company. In 1940, the property was closed down; however, in 1947, the Interstate Products Company reopened the mine and produced asbestos until it closed for good in 1975. A U.S. Forest Service trail passed right by the mine, creating an unsafe health condition. In 2007, the USFS rerouted the trail away from the mine, although the mine is still accessible.

Just south and upstream of Karst Kamp on the west side of the river, Ed Durnam developed extensive agricultural fields. These fields, purchased in 1936, were planted in lettuce and continued to produce for about thirty years, until Durnam changed to raising cattle. Ed Durnam died in 1970, and his family sold the lands in 1978 to the U.S. Forest Service, which purchased the land with Land and Water Conservation Funds. The land is accessible by Durnam's bridge (MM#53.9).

Several miles south of Durnam's bridge, there is another bridge crossing the Gallatin to the trailhead for Deer Creek trail. This bridge (MM#51.5), first built by C.F. High in the 1920s (Figure 5.8), was reconstructed by the Markleys in the 1950s and then improved again to its present condition. Locally, it is known as the Green Bridge (or Markley's Bridge) and is extensively used on hot days in summer for swimmers jumping into the river and picnicking nearby along the riverbank.

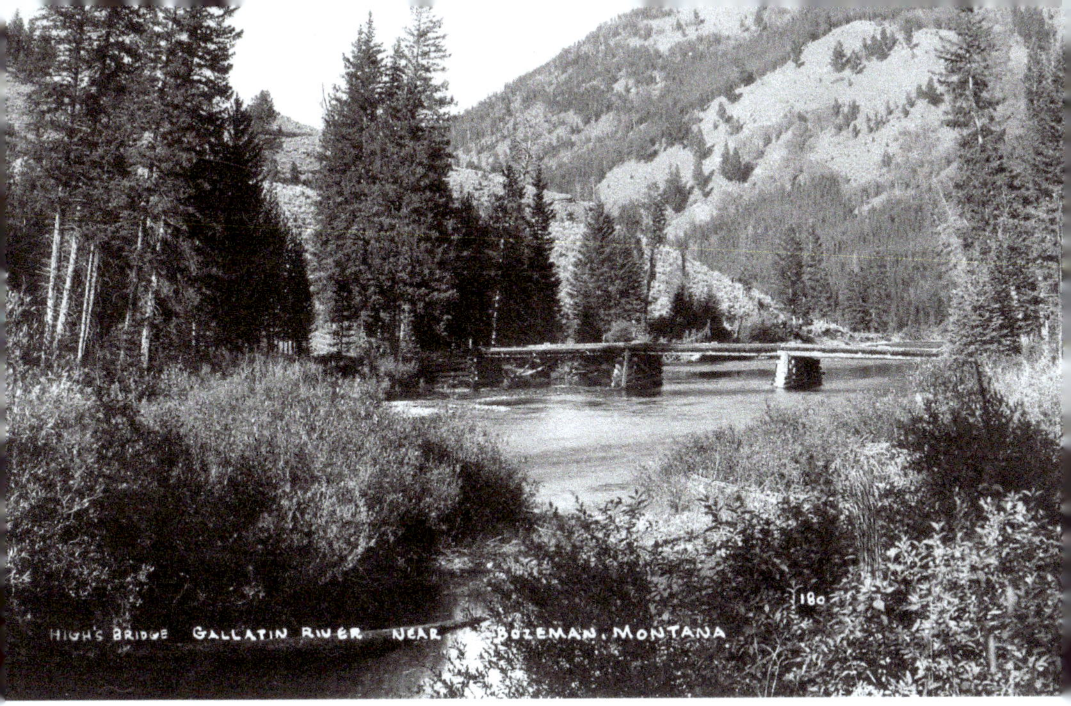

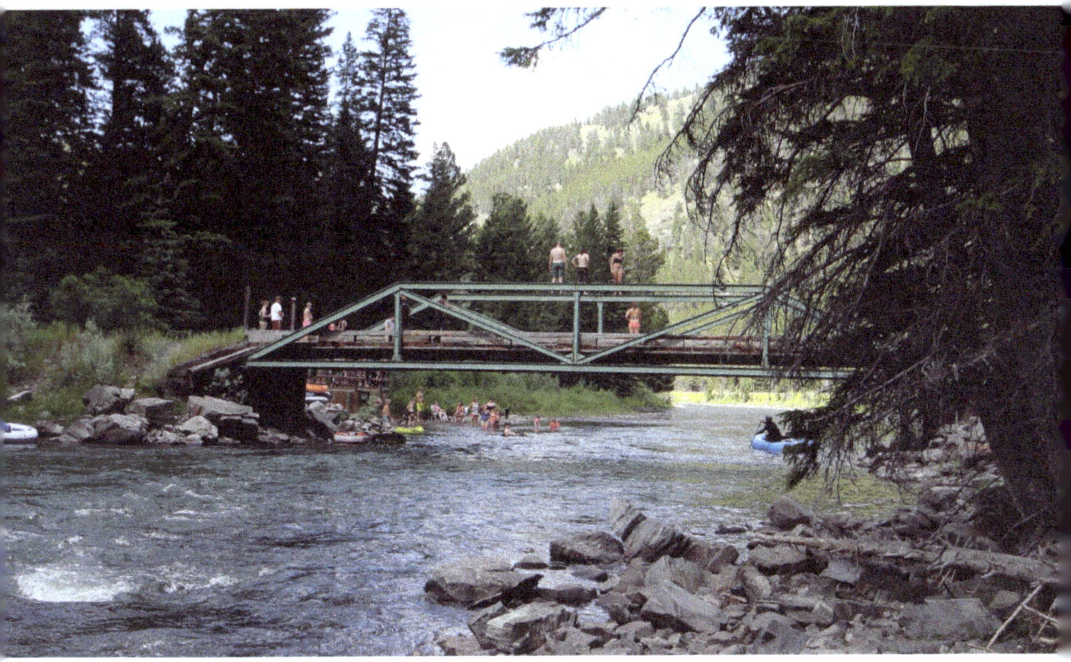

Figure 5.8. Bridge over Gallatin River at Deer Creek trailhead (MM# 51.5) looking north downstream.

Upper photo (circa 1920s): High's Bridge, built by C.F. High to access his property on the west side of the Gallatin. The bridge has log/rock cradles as abutments in the river, typical for abutments in those days. *GHM.*

Lower photo (2015): High bridge was replaced and then improved to the steel-framed bridge with wood-framed/rock abutments on each end. The bridge, now called Markley's or the green bridge, is very popular in summer for swimmers and picnicking.

Chapter 6

North of Big Sky to Buck Creek Road

(MM#49.8 to MM#44.6)

After leaving the Karst section of the canyon and passing the Green Bridge and some small developments, the traveler approaches the Big Sky area (Map 6.1). Before arriving at Big Sky, the road moves from east of the Gallatin River to west of the river, passing over Jack Smith Bridge (MM#49.8). This bridge has some history. The earliest bridge at this location was built about 1898, about the same time as the old bridge downstream of the curved bridge south of House Rock (MM#61.6) (see Figure 3.7). This was the period when a road was being built up the canyon, eventually getting to Taylor Fork to serve the Walter Cooper Company producing railroad ties. Jack Smith, a local pioneer, lived in a cabin near the bridge and perhaps helped build the original bridge. As stories also tell, he apparently charged a toll for use of the bridge. This is hard to believe if this was a county road, but so goes the story. The present bridge was built in 1952, when the West Gallatin Road was having major improvements.

The damsite near West Fork, proposed by the U.S. Army Corps in the early 1930s, was likely at a location where the canyon is narrow between Jack Smith Bridge and the entrance to Big Sky. This dam project was part of the New Deal, which was proposing and building dams across the country. This proposal eventually died, and the only proposal for a dam to surface later was for one near the entrance of the canyon (see chapter 2).

When coming from the north on Highway 191 and just before arriving at Lone Mountain Trail (MM#47.9), the spur road that heads west into the Big Sky area, one crosses a wide cement bridge over West Fork, built in 2009

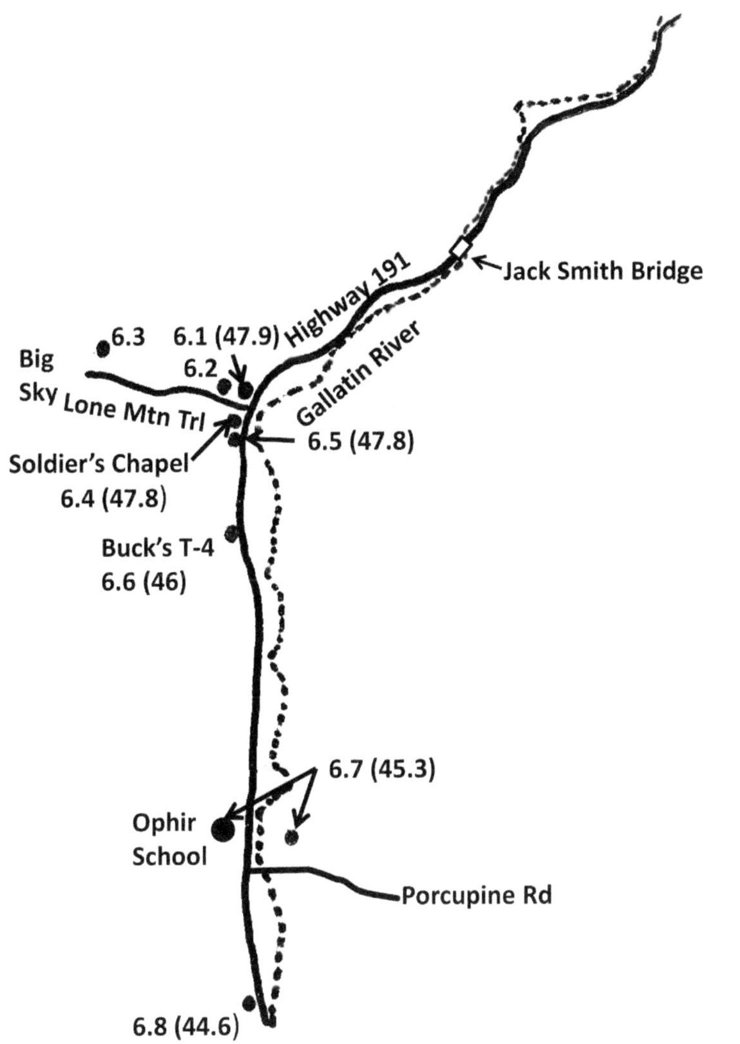

Map 6.1. North of Big Sky to Buck Creek Ridge Road (MM#51.5 to 44.6). Map of photo locations along Highway 191 and the Gallatin River (mile markers in parentheses).

replacing a narrower bridge. In the past, during the period when pioneers were looking for gold in the area and ranchers were bringing livestock here, the bridge over West Fork was a small wooden bridge and there were few, if any, buildings in the area (Figure 6.1). The area near the bridge is now occupied by shops and a bank to the north of the bridge, developed some time after Big Sky was established in 1972. In early days of Big Sky, there

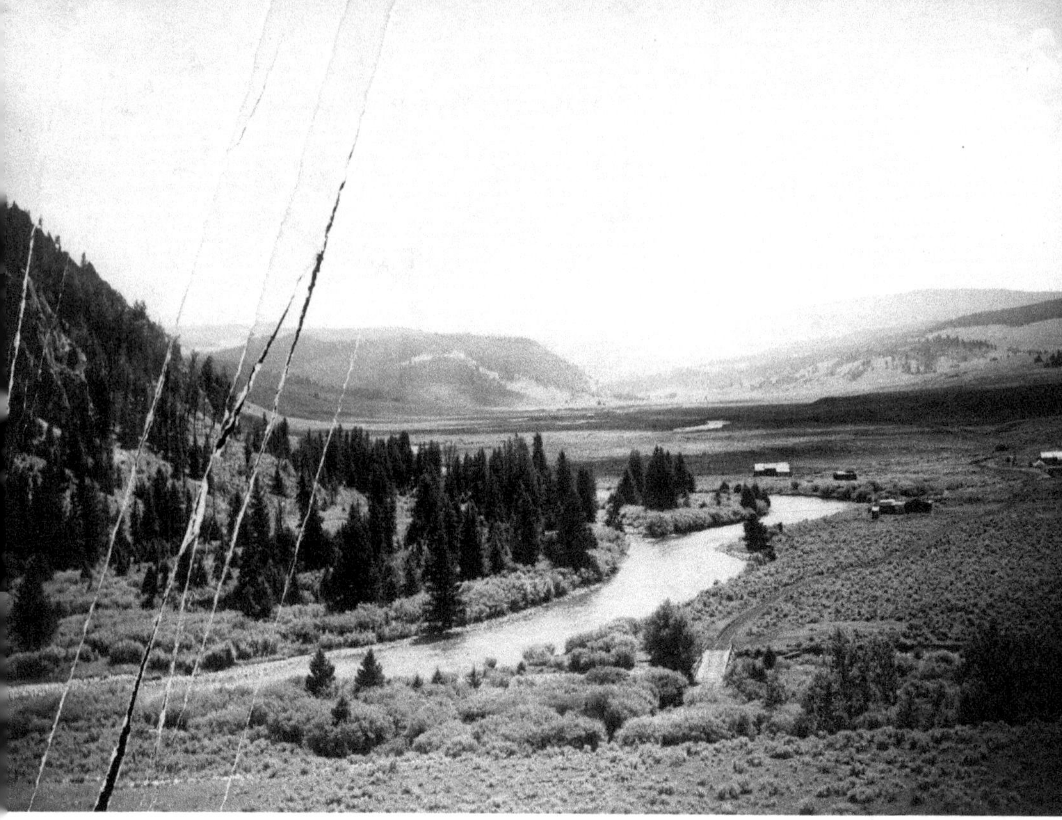

Figure 6.1. Confluence area of West Fork with the Gallatin River near present-day Big Sky (MM#47.9).
Left photo (pre-1920): Small wooden bridge over West Fork with extensive willow cover along the rivers. Limited home/cabin development in the distance, some cabins possibly belonging to Thomas Michener. *MOR.*
Right photo (2012): Large four-lane bridge over West Fork with photo showing roofs of businesses in foreground and expanded development in the distance. Streamside vegetation is mostly gone.

was a bank on the south side of West Fork just northwest of the junction of Lone Mountain Trail with Highway 191. This bank was founded by Jack Hume, who owned B-K Ranch, now Lone Mountain Ranch, as well as other properties in the Big Sky area.

Many explorers, ranchers and individuals or families looking for homesteads in the late 1800s and early 1900s while traveling up the Gallatin Canyon often traveled west toward Lone Mountain when reaching West Fork (Figure 6.2). In 1970, while vacationing at 320 Ranch farther south along Highway 191, with encouragement from Jim and Patty Goodrich, who owned the ranch, Chet Huntley, an NBC News anchorman, traveled west up West Fork and "found" the right site for a golf resort with Lone Mountain as the ski area. He convinced the governor of Montana to allow him to use the name Big Sky for the development. With help from Chrysler

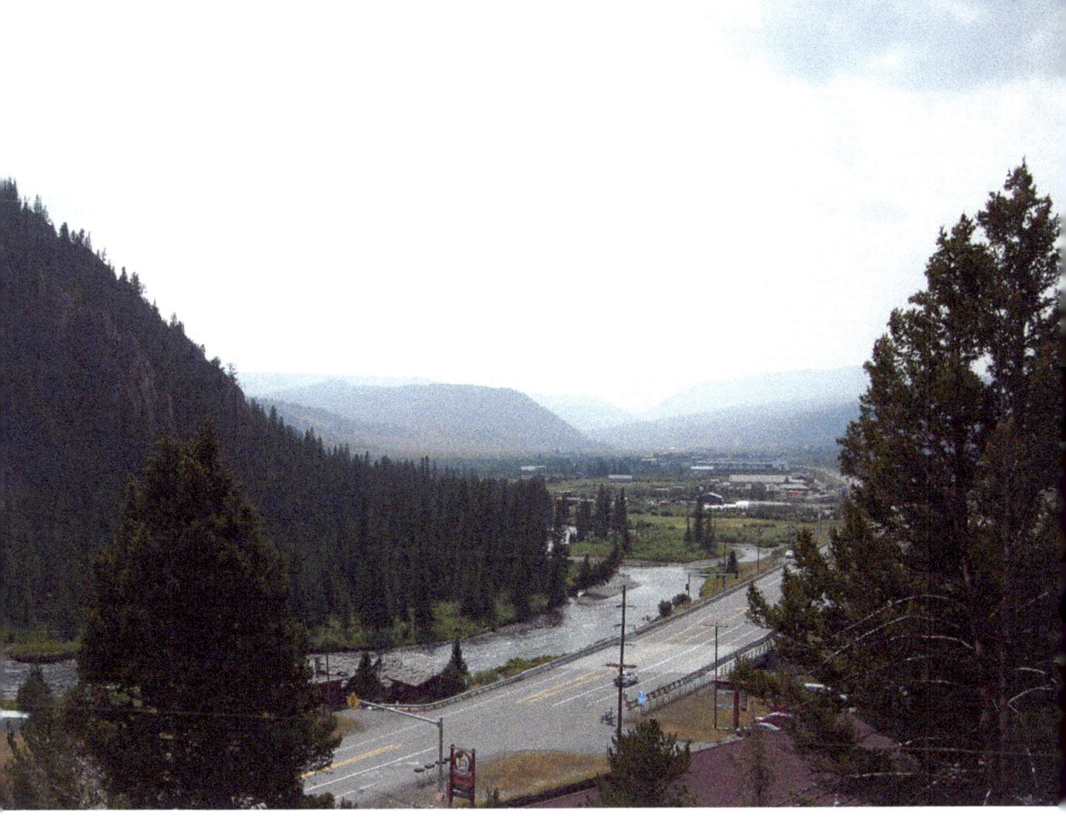

Realty and others, Huntley began development of Big Sky in 1972. In 1974, the first chairlifts opened.

A short way west from the Gallatin River up the West Fork valley, early travelers would come upon extensive rangeland, the Basin, today the location of the Lone Mountain Golf Course and City Center. Some would use this area for seasonal grazing, while others claimed homestead lands. One of the earliest ranchers to homestead here was Augustus Franklin Crail, who bought a 160-acre homestead in 1901 and expanded it to an extensive ranch spread over the following decades. Today, a few of the Crail homestead buildings remain, now used by the Crail Ranch Homestead Museum and maintained by the Historic Crail Ranch Conservators, while most of the rest of the Crail grazing lands are occupied by golf course, tennis courts, ponds, condominiums, City Center development and more (Figure 6.3). In the 1950s, Jack and Elaine Hume bought the Crail Ranch and continued to use it for rangeland. They also purchased the B-K Ranch, now Lone Mountain Ranch. The Humes eventually sold out and moved to Bozeman as Big Sky developed. In the southern part of the large rangeland parcel, Ken McBride ran livestock until selling off some parcels of his ranch and eventually selling the rest to Big Sky development in the 1970s.

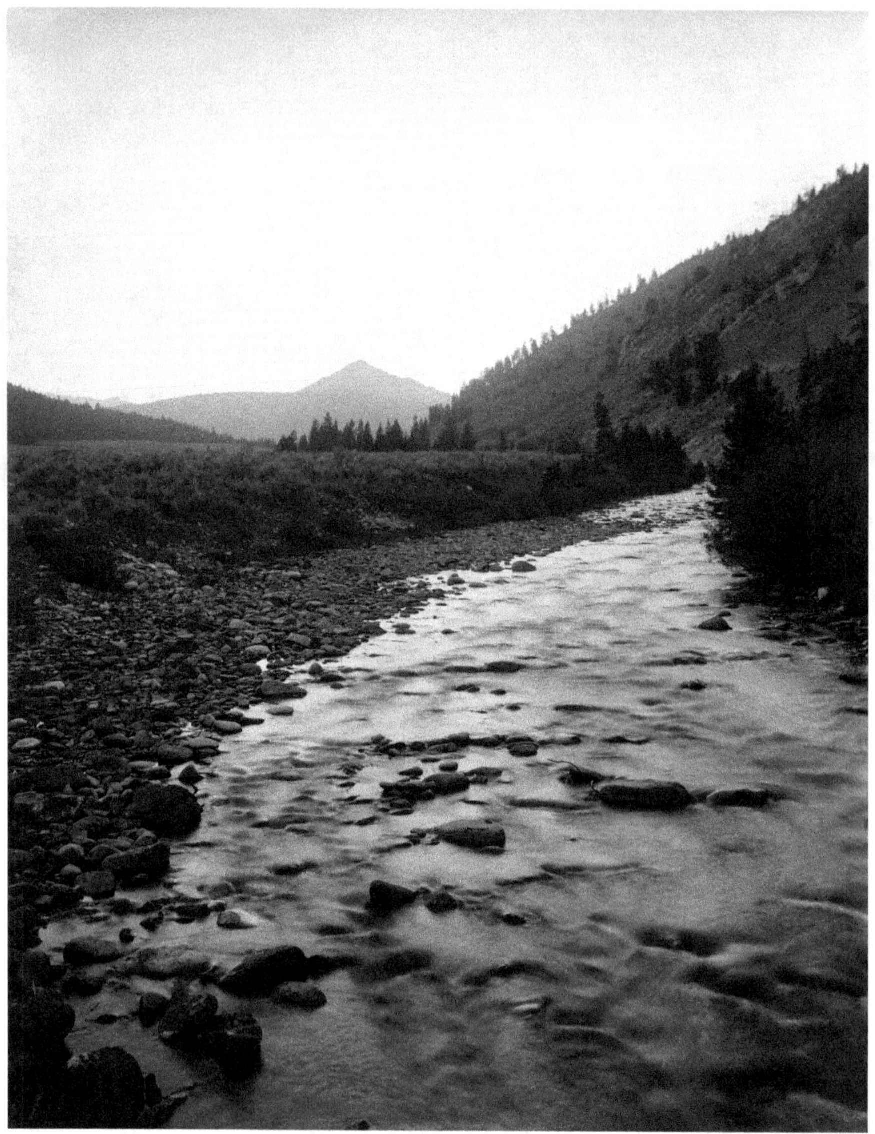

Figure 6.2. West Fork near its confluence with the Gallatin River looking west upstream toward Lone Mountain, only slightly visible in both photos.
Left photo (circa 1910): Scoured stream bank and no development. *MOR*.
Right photo (2012): A narrower river channel with riverbank stabilized by vegetation. Some buildings from Big Sky developments can be seen along the bank.

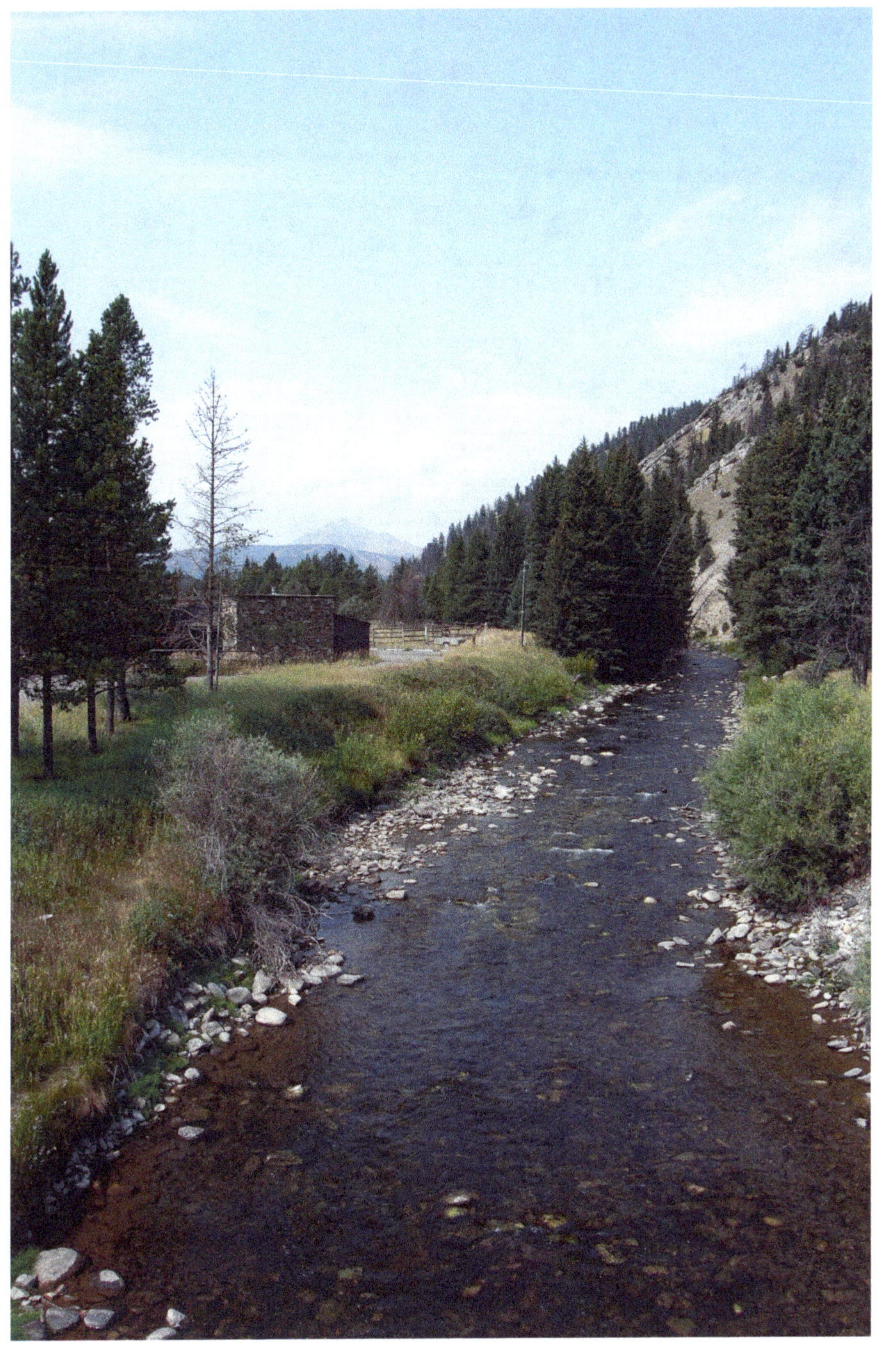

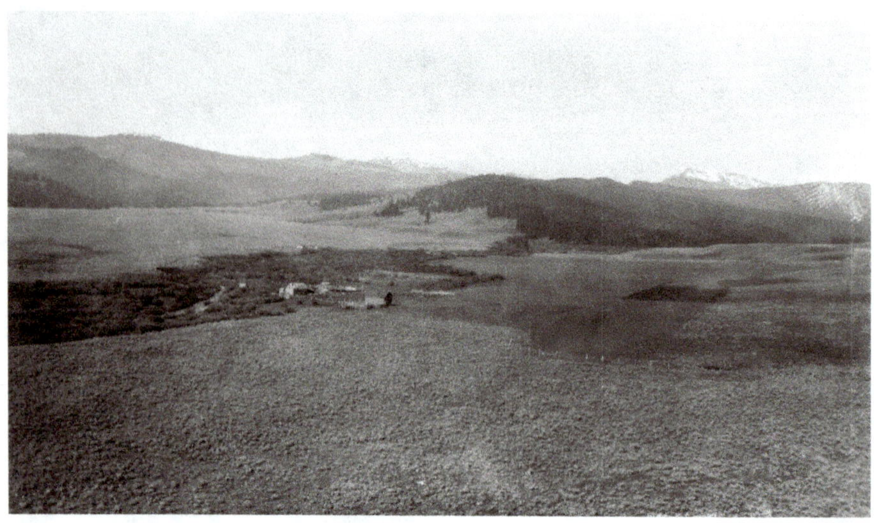

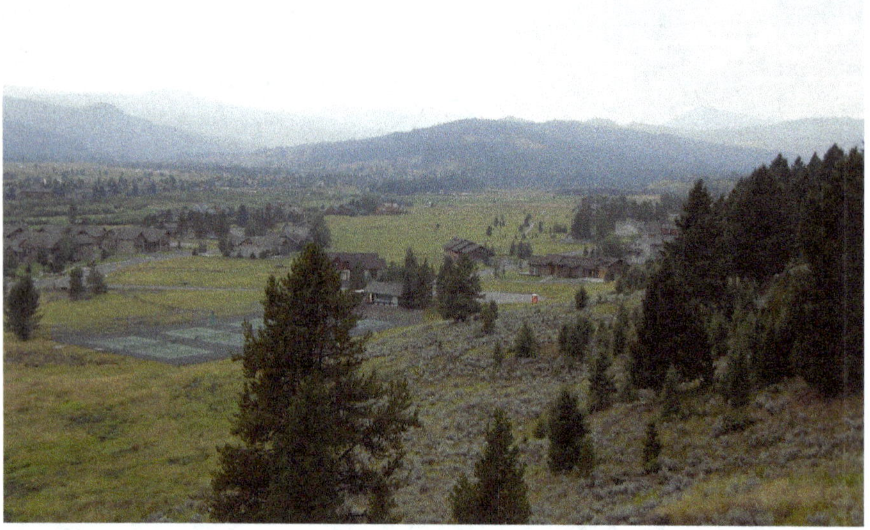

Figure 6.3. Basin area along West Fork about two miles west of the confluence of West Fork and the Gallatin River.
Upper photo (date unknown, est. circa 1920s): Crail Ranch along the West Fork in an extensive sagebrush flat. *HCRC.*
Lower photo (2013): Big Sky development showing condominiums, tennis courts and ballfield.

Beyond the Meadow Village and City Center, the West Fork Road (Lone Mountain Trail) winds up the valley toward the Mountain Village at the base of Lone Mountain. Development of this village and development of the chairlifts and access to alpine skiing were all part of the original Big Sky Resort development plan in 1972. The Mountain Village area is in Madison County and can be found chronicled in several historical documents of the area.

Immediately south of the spur road into Big Sky is Soldiers Chapel on the west side of the highway (Figure 6.4). This chapel was dedicated in 1955 in commemoration of Nelson Story IV and his regiment, who died in World War II. Story was a grandson of Nelson Story Sr., a Montana pioneer and early developer of Bozeman. Nelson Story Sr. brought cattle from Texas to the Montana Territory in 1866, the first major cattle drive from Texas to Montana. The book *Lonesome Dove* by Larry McMurtry is based, in part, on that event. Soldiers Chapel was constructed by local citizens out of local materials. The design of the chapel, created by Bozeman architect Fred Willson, with the picture window above the altar overlooking Lone Mountain follows a similar design of the Chapel of Transfiguration in Jackson Hole, where the window above the altar looks out on the Teton Range. Soldiers Chapel is a nondenominational memorial chapel and is often used for weddings and other special events.

Near Soldiers Chapel is the location of Thomas Michener's homestead. Michener was an early settler in this area, both raising livestock and exploring for minerals, especially gold. He established the Hercules Mining Company that had claims all the way from West Fork to the Yellowstone Park boundary about twenty miles south. Except for some small show of gold near West Fork and a couple of mines near the northwest corner of Yellowstone developed by other miners, little gold was found in the area, and the mining company folded. Michener rented his cabins to "dudes," working out weekly rates with Pete Karst and Sam Wilson (320 Ranch) (Figure 6.5). Dorothy and Joe Vick lived in this area in Michener's old homestead cabins from 1938 into the 1950s, operating it as a guest facility for part of that period. Dorothy was the daughter of Thomas Michener, and Joe, her husband, played a major role in the construction of Soldiers Chapel. After Joe's death, Dorothy sold the cabins, which were eventually destroyed or moved to make room for other development in the Big Sky area. Dorothy then built a new home on the rise south of the road into Soldiers Chapel. One of the old cabins was moved to the front of Ophir School as a historic exhibit.

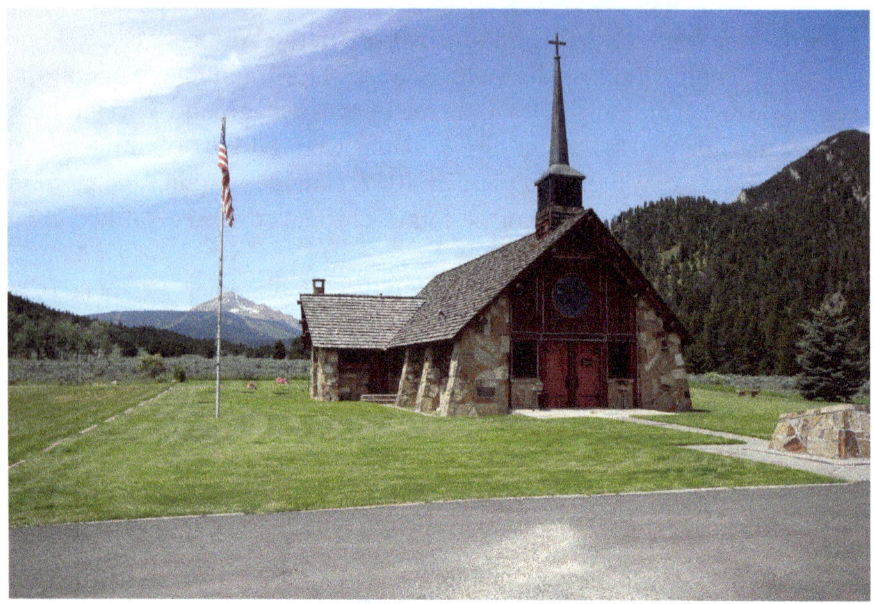

Figure 6.4. (2016). Soldiers Chapel, dedicated in 1955 in commemoration of Nelson Story IV and his regiment who died in World War II (MM#47.8).

Farther south along Highway 191, one passes a gravel pit that supplies many demands of expansion in Big Sky; a trailer park that has been in the area for many decades, predating Big Sky; and the Whitewater Inn, originally the Comfort Inn and the first standard motel in the area. At MM#46 is Buck's T-4, restaurant, bar and lodge (Figure 6.6). Buck's, as it is known by locals, dates back to 1946, when Buck and Helen Knight, its founders, acquired ten acres along the highway from Bert Stillman and built the first buildings for a hunting camp, which included cabins, a small bar and a restaurant. In 1950, the Knights expanded by combining two cabins into a lodge and expanded bar. With Buck tending bar and Helen cooking, Buck's T-4 became a favorite stop to drink and eat for locals, hunters and travelers headed for Yellowstone National Park.

With early development of Big Sky and potential greater demands on their business, Buck and Helen retired in 1972, sold the business to the Scholz family and moved to their new home on the ridge west above the location of Buck's T-4. Mike Scholz ran the place for thirty years. In 2006, the Scholz family sold the place. However, in 2009, Mike Scholz had an opportunity to buy Buck's T-4 back and joined Chuck Schommer

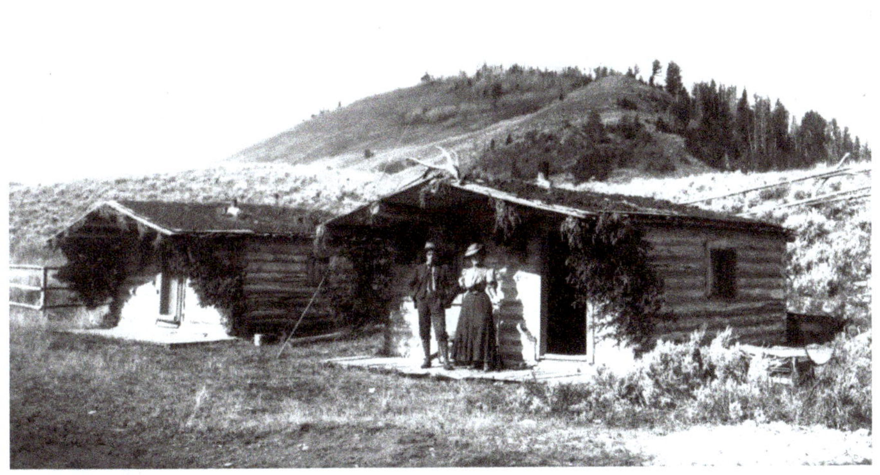

Figure 6.5. Location of the Thomas Michener cabin near the entrance to Big Sky (MM#47.8).
Above photo (circa 1910–15): The original Thomas Michener cabins, occasionally used for guests (Mr. and Mrs. Achilles Lamme from Bozeman are shown in photo), including Frank Butler of the Butler Paper Company and sons (see chapter 8 for history of Butler, Micheners and Nine Quarter Circle Ranch). Dorothy Vick (Michener's daughter) and her husband, Joe Vick, lived in these cabins from 1938 into the 1950s, using them for dude business and offering gold panning in a spring nearby. *GHM.*
Below photo (2016): Cabin site is now along a bike path and used by businesses near the Big Sky entrance. The house at right center was built by Dorothy Vick after Joe Vick died.

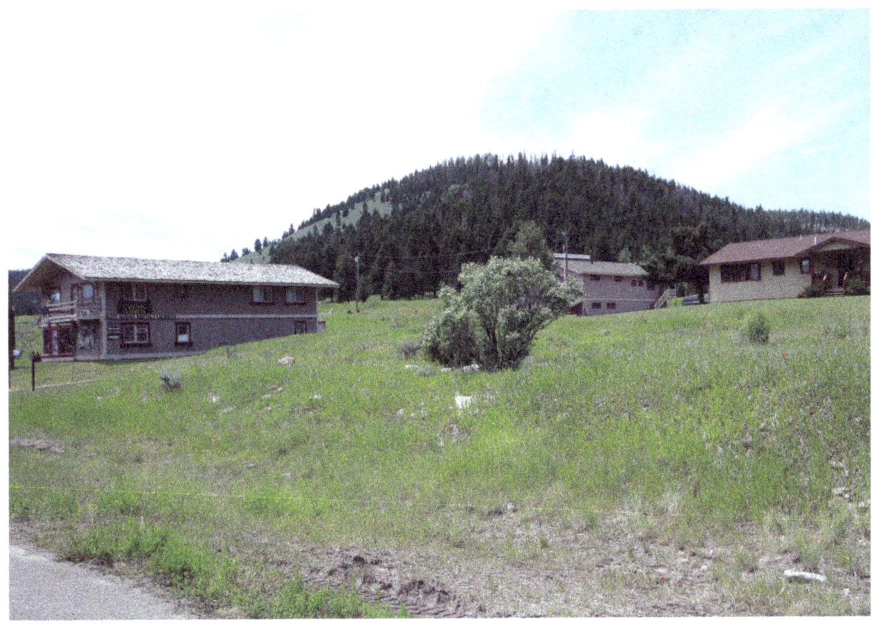

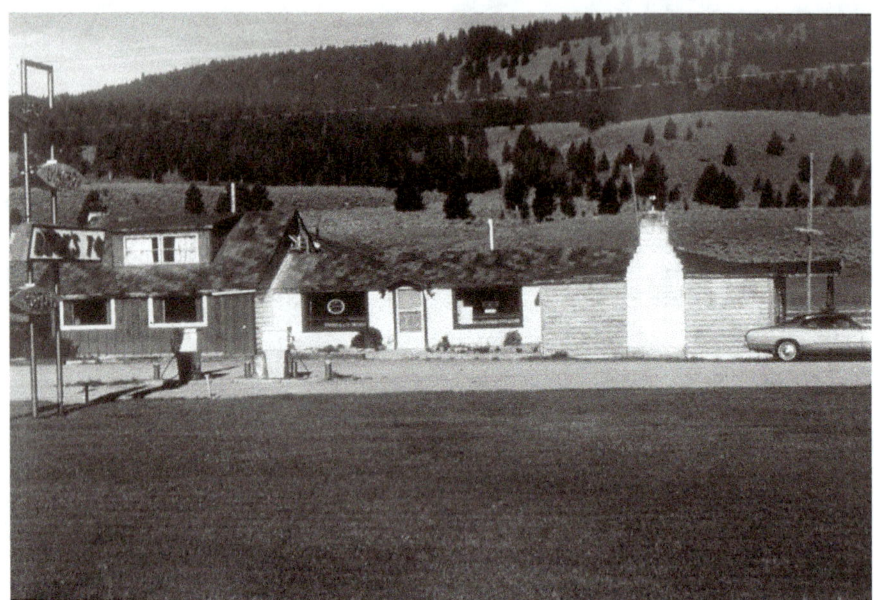

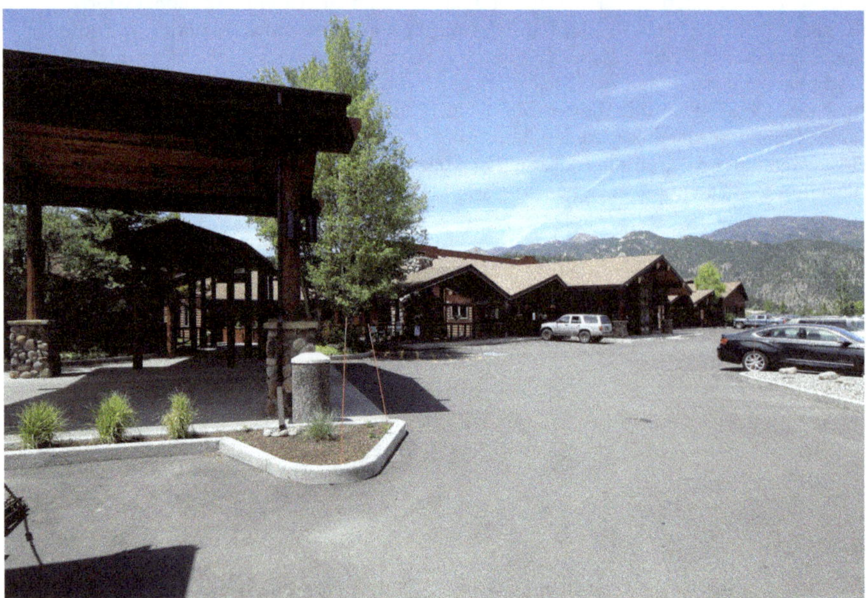

Figure 6.6. Buck's T-4 Lodge and Restaurant, Big Sky (MM#46.6).
Upper photo (circa 1972): Buck's T-4 after expansion, adding a dance hall. *Buck's T-4 Lodge.*
Lower photo (2016): Buck's T-4 with motel, restaurant and bar.

and David O'Connor, who had been operating the place. By that time, Buck's T-4 had greatly expanded, including a restaurant, lodging and all, to create what one sees today. In 2013, Mike Scholz sold out to his partners and retired from the business.

After passing new home developments, one approaches Ophir School (MM#45.1). Ophir School has two major buildings, high school and elementary school. Looking at these modern school buildings and knowing the potential expansion demands facing the school district as Big Sky grows, it is hard to imagine the history and development of this school over the decades.

The first Ophir School opened its doors in 1906 with five students. In 1908, Katherine Cope of Bozeman, a cousin of Thomas Michener, lived with the Micheners in the summer and taught school for the first six years; school was held only in summer. At that time, the homesteaders formed a school board, and in 1912, the State of Montana recognized Ophir as a school district (K–8). The first real schoolhouse was built in 1929 east of the Gallatin River and north of Porcupine Creek. It was called Porcupine School. Compared to today's school, a small one-room schoolhouse seems inadequate for the needs of the community (Figure 6.7). In 1964, the community decided to build a new school building at its present location. The Gallatin Women's Club made a major donation toward that building. The club had been willed some funds from Dr. McGill, who had owned the 320 Ranch. The group had to decide how to spend the funds. After some discussion, the group decided the best use of the funds was for education and aid in construction of the new school building.

Heading south from Ophir School, the traveler passes the Gallatin Riverhouse Grill and then San Marino, a complex of upscale small cabins situated along the river. The Grill was built in 1994 as the Half Moon Saloon. Under new ownership, it continues to serve barbecue dinners and other western fare. At this point along the road, the traveler leaves the Lower Basin or Porcupine Flat area. Looking back from Buck Creek Ridge Road on the south end of this open basin, one can see many changes that have taken place over the past one hundred years, including a very improved highway and some housing (Figure 6.8). At Buck Creek Ridge Road, the early road went over the side hill above the river. In order to level the road in the 1950s, the river was filled in, and the road was constructed where the river had been located.

What is apparent in the Porcupine Flat (Lower Basin) is the number of individual homes that have been constructed over the years, with many

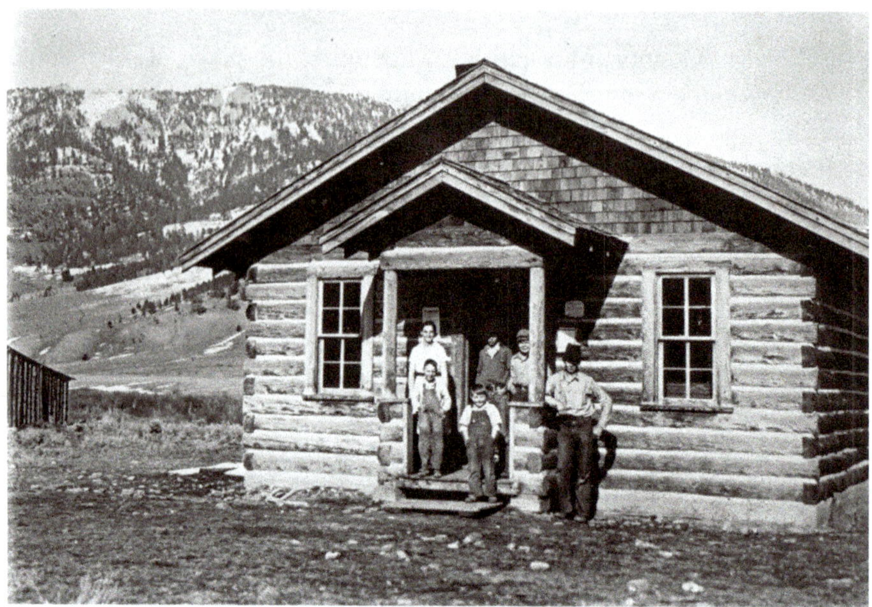

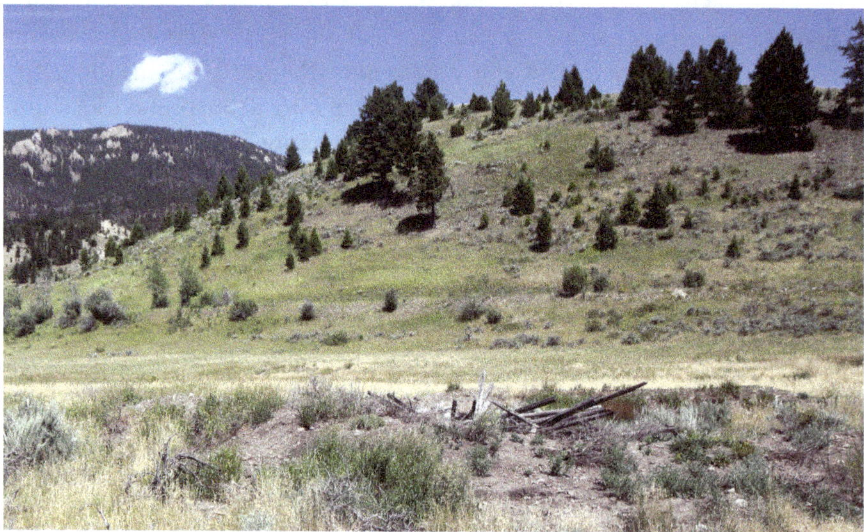

Figure 6.7. Ophir School (MM#45.3).
Upper photo (1936): Original schoolhouse built in 1929 on the east side of the Gallatin River known as Porcupine School. *GHM.*
Lower photo (2016): Possible present location (near a burn hole on FWP property).
Opposite page, upper photo (circa 1960s): Construction of the new Ophir School on the west side of Highway 191 near Beaver Creek. Some funding came from the Gallatin Women's Club. *MSU.*
Opposite page, lower photo (2016): Ophir School in 2016 with new elementary and middle school to the north (right in photo) and Lone Peak High School in foreground. Note the presence of the building that was being constructed in the 1960s.

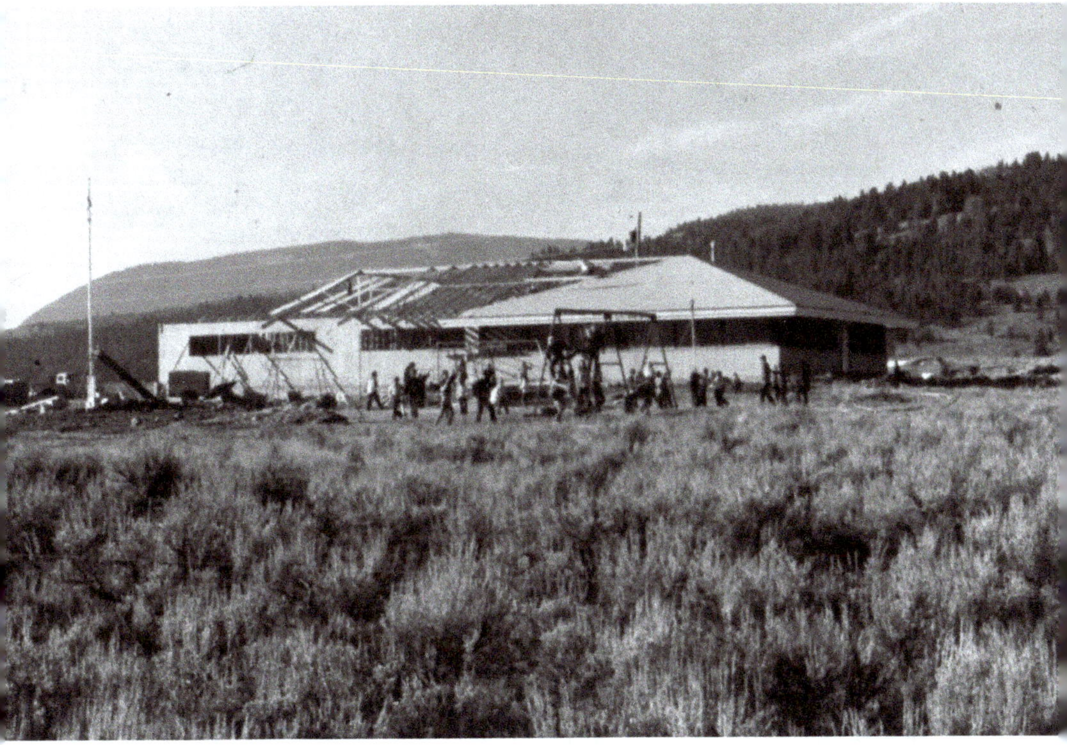

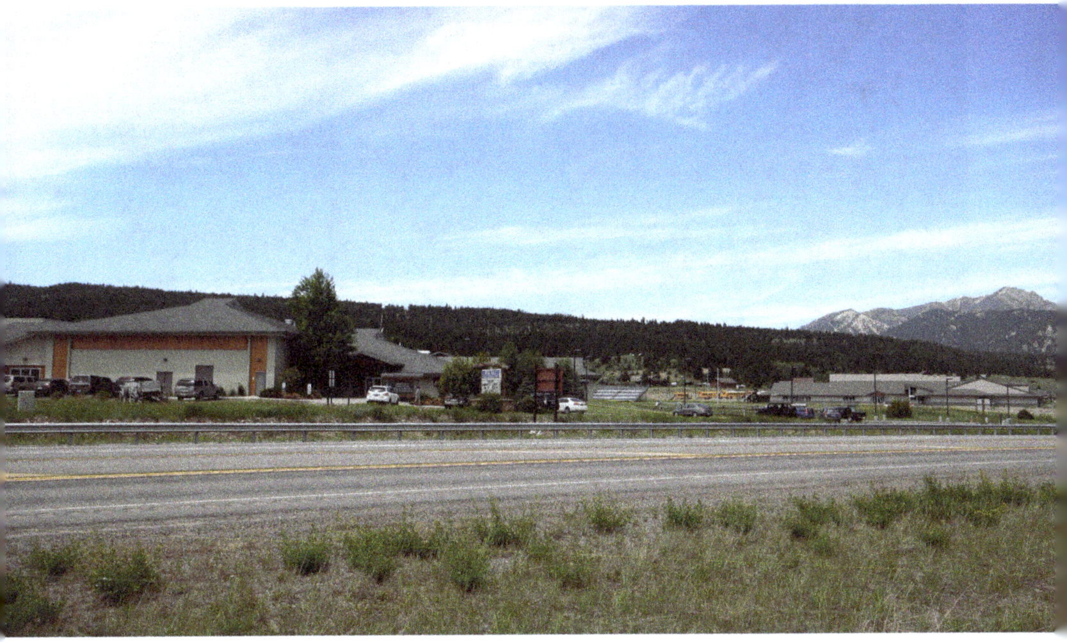

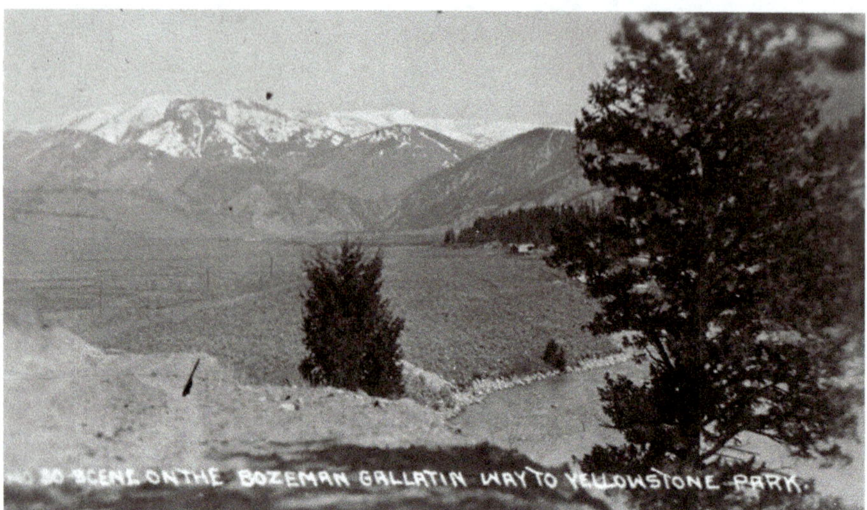

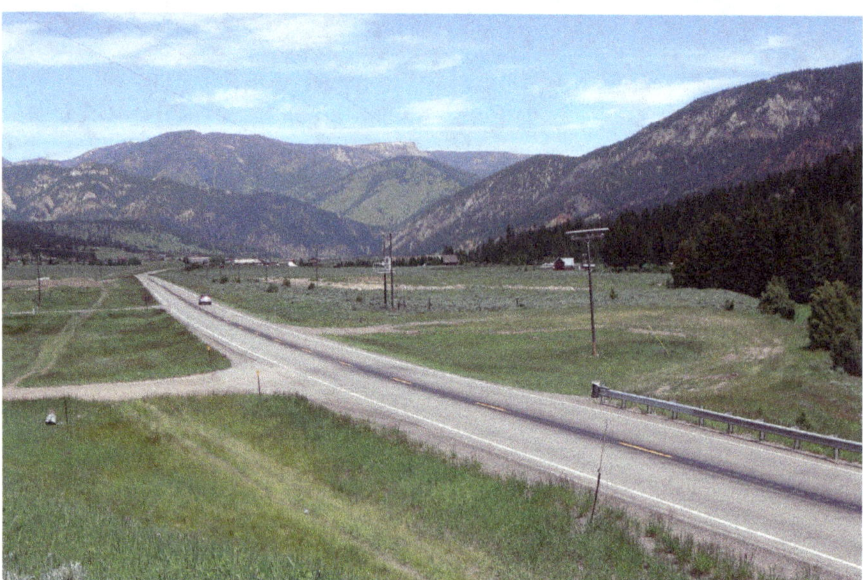

Figure 6.8. View north toward Spanish Peaks into the Lower Basin (Porcupine Flats) south of Big Sky (MM#44.3).
Upper photo (circa 1922): The old road, no more than a buggy road, comes up the hill in left foreground, avoiding the river. Old roadway is just visible crossing the sagebrush flat. *Gamel family*.
Lower photo (2016): The old roadway bed, grass covered, is still apparent in the lower left foreground. The new highway was built in this area by filling in the river. The roadway leading to the left in foreground is Buck Creek Ridge Road.

more plats available. In the old photo, one sees only one cabin, while the repeat photo shows several houses, Ophir School is slightly visible and the highway changes from a narrow road, heading over the hill by the river in the foreground and across the flat through the sagebrush, to a wide straight improved road with no hill.

Chapter 7

Buck Creek Road to North of 320 Ranch

(MM#44.6 to MM#35.5)

Heading south from where Buck Creek Road intersects Highway 191 (Map 7.1), the road passes a Montana Highway Department facility (MM# 44) that houses plows, sand and other equipment to keep this portion of Highway 191 open in winter. This facility has been at this location for many decades, predating the establishment of Big Sky.

Across from the Montana Highway Department facility and slightly south, there is an area on which large amounts of rocks were deposited. These rocks came from removal of the cliff near Red Cliff Campground (discussed later). The rocks were placed in a basin on the west side of the highway behind a berm paralleling the highway. The area behind the berm and within the depression was used in the 1940s to early 1960s as a refuse dump. Canyon residents would bring their "trash" some distance to deposit in this depression. Eventually, the waste was covered, and vegetation grew back on the surface. This area then became the depository for the rocks. Today, ranches and homes have their trash picked up at the ranch, along the curb or highway edge or they take it to a county collection point, for example, the one north of West Yellowstone.

A little farther south before arriving at Rainbow Ranch and the Corral Bar and Restaurant, a location once called Halfway Point—that is, halfway between Bozeman and West Yellowstone—the highway passes between the river on the left (east) and a low area on the right (west) (MM#43). Beyond the depressed area west of the highway, one can see the path of the old roadway. The low point between the present highway and the old highway

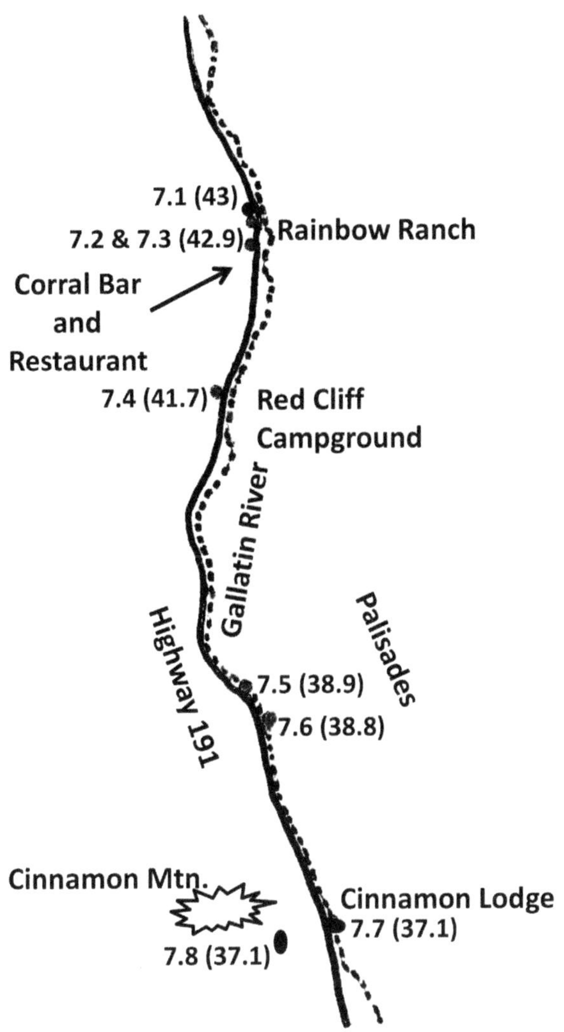

Map 7.1. Buck Creek Ridge Road to north of 320 Ranch (MM#44.6 to 36.5). Map of photo locations along Highway 191 and the Gallatin River (mile markers in parentheses).

route once was the river channel and is now often a wetland (Figure 7.1). However, when improving the highway at this location in the 1950s, the road was built on fill placed in the river and the river was moved to the east. Evidence of this can be seen as not only the abandoned roadway to the west but also as cut banks on the east side of the river.

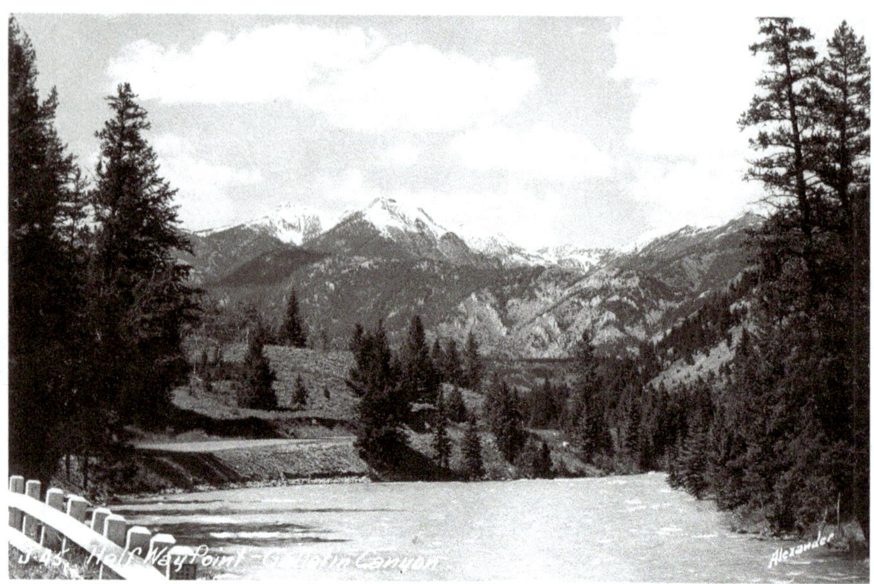

Figure 7.1. Halfway Point in the Gallatin Canyon: about halfway between Bozeman and West Yellowstone at MM#43.
Above photo (circa 1930s): Highway swings to the west around a bend in the Gallatin River. The white railings along the highway were placed along the road to West Yellowstone in the 1930s. *GHM.*
Below photo (2015): Highway curves to the east on fill placed in the Gallatin River. The river was moved to the east to make room for the highway improvement, and the old riverbed has become a wetland.

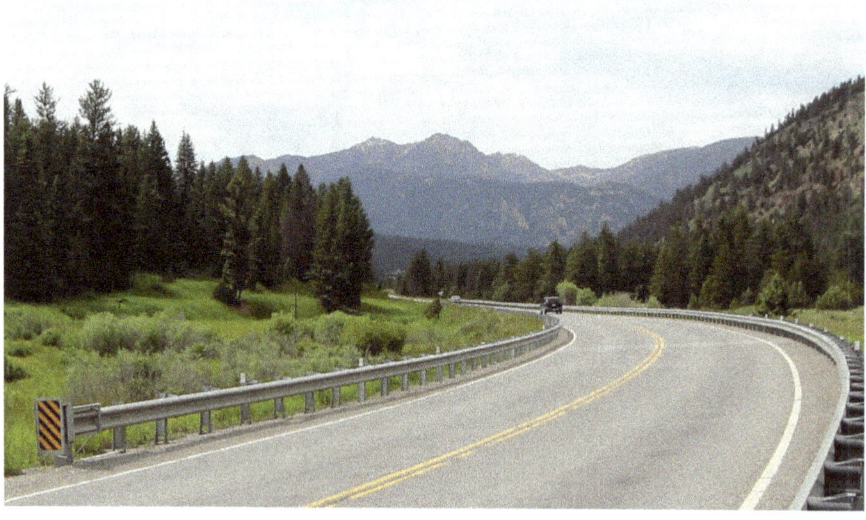

Just south of this section of highway are Rainbow Ranch and the Corral Bar and Restaurant (MM#42.9). Both of these locations have history going back many decades. Rainbow Ranch was first built in 1919 and originally named Dew Drop Inn by the Lemons when they homesteaded it as a cattle ranch (Figure 7.2). The name was then changed to the Halfway Inn, possibly after it was sold to the Cotrells. The Lemons rented rooms and served meals for travelers. It was a center of community activity into the 1940s. When the property was sold in 1946 to Fran and Walter Cotrell, they improved its services to include a gas pump, store, auto shop, smokehouse, blacksmith and sawmill (Figure 7.3). The Cotrells then sold to the present-day owners. Today, the Rainbow Ranch no longer has many of the services from the 1940s but is an upscale resort with a restaurant, rooms and facilities for special events, having benefited greatly from the development at Big Sky. The main lodge of Rainbow Ranch burned to the ground in 2008 but was replaced with the elegant rustic ranch building one sees today.

On the west side of the highway at the Halfway Point is the Corral Bar and Restaurant. The Corral, as it is known, was built in the 1940s as a bar. The original bar, if one goes inside, was on the south end of the big room where there is now seating for eating at a counter near a kitchen that was added in the 1980s. The rest of the space was originally used for dancing and entertaining. In the 1950s and '60s, the Corral and Buck's were the only two watering holes in the area now served by a multitude of bars, restaurants and resorts. There are many local stories from the early days of the Corral. In the late '40s or early '50s, a local rancher had turned off an irrigation ditch of another rancher, infuriating that rancher, who tracked the "offender" to the Corral. There, he shot at the offender, fortunately missing, but if one knows where to look, there still is a bullet hole near the fireplace. Under the present ownership, many local ranches were asked to burn their brands into the fireplace mantel. This wide array of brands shows how important the Corral was as a watering hole for the locals and present residents who have registered brands. In the 1980s, the Corral added a motel, and the present owners purchased the place in 1988.

A little more than a mile south of the Halfway Point (location of Rainbow Ranch and the Corral) is Red Cliff Campground (MM#41.5). This campground, open only in the summer, lies just below some reddish-stained limestone cliffs, thus the name. The red color comes from erosion of a reddish geological formation overlying the limestone. West of the highway just north of the turnoff into the campground is a large cliff

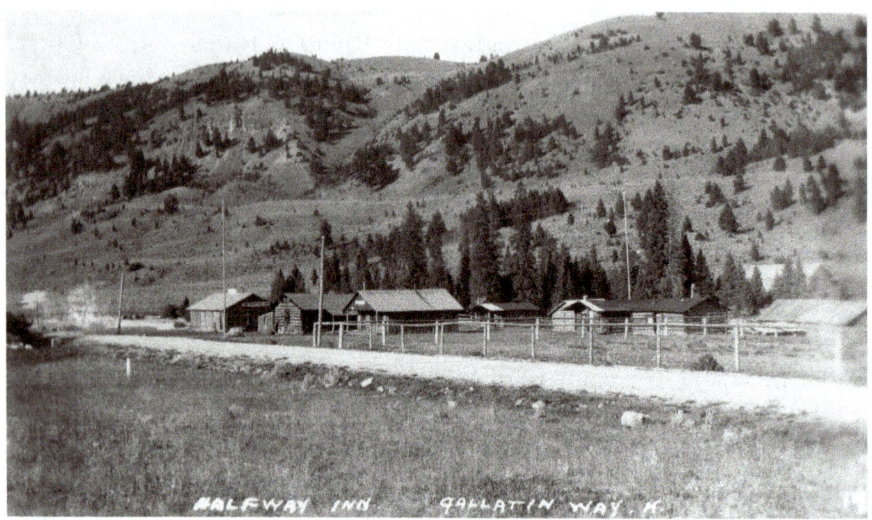

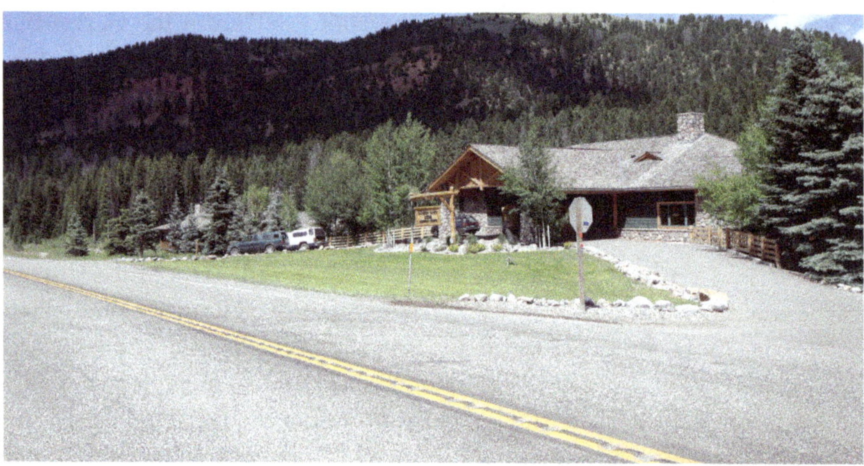

Figure 7.2. Rainbow Ranch at Halfway Point in the Gallatin Canyon (MM#42.9).
Upper photo (circa 1930–40): Halfway Inn owned by the Lemons, who had some facilities for food and beds for travelers. The Lemons were the homesteaders and founders of this property. *MOR.*
Lower photo (2016): Rainbow Ranch, which replaced the Halfway Inn, at its most modern state following a destructive fire in 2008.

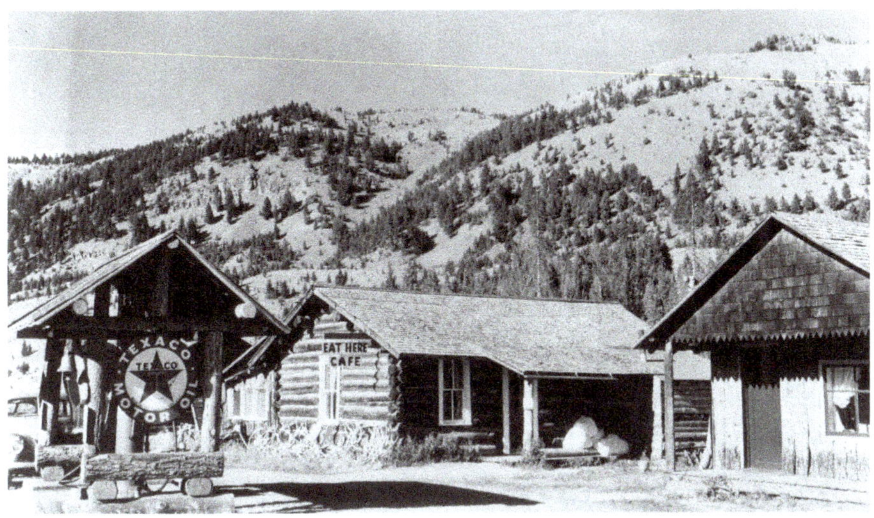

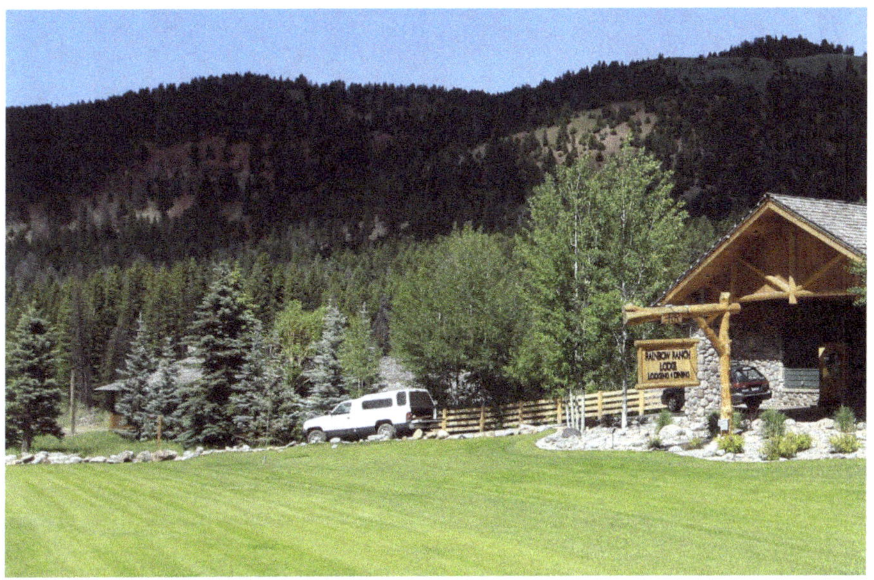

Figure 7.3. Rainbow Ranch at Halfway Point in the canyon (MM#42.9).
Upper photo (circa 1946): Rainbow Ranch owned by the Cotrells, who added many more services to the property, including a gas pump. *GHM.*
Lower photo (2016): Present-day Rainbow Ranch.

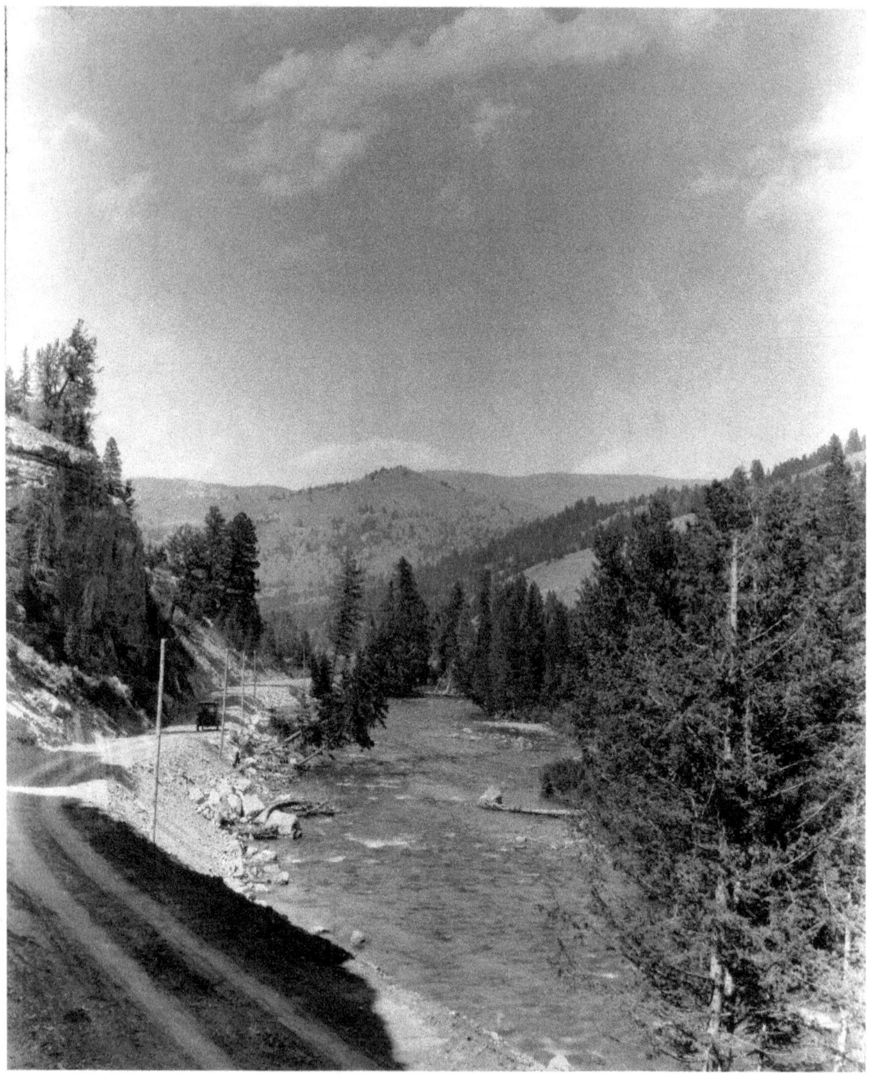

Figure 7.4. Curve in Gallatin Road just north of Red Cliff campground looking north (downstream) (MM#41.7).
Above photo (circa early 1920s): Dirt road with no railings shows this stretch of road is still a rough roadway. *GHM.*
Opposite page, upper photo (circa early 1930s): Improved gravel surfaced road with early railings. *HCRC.*
Opposite page, middle photo (circa late 1930s): Highway has been paved and lined but remains tight to the rock cliffs. *GHM.*
Opposite page, lower photo (2015): In the 1950s, the highway was widened into the river channel, moving the river over. Recently, it has been improved with turning lanes for Red Cliff Campground, and the right of way has been widened with the removal of much of the rock cliffs to the west (*left*) of roadway.

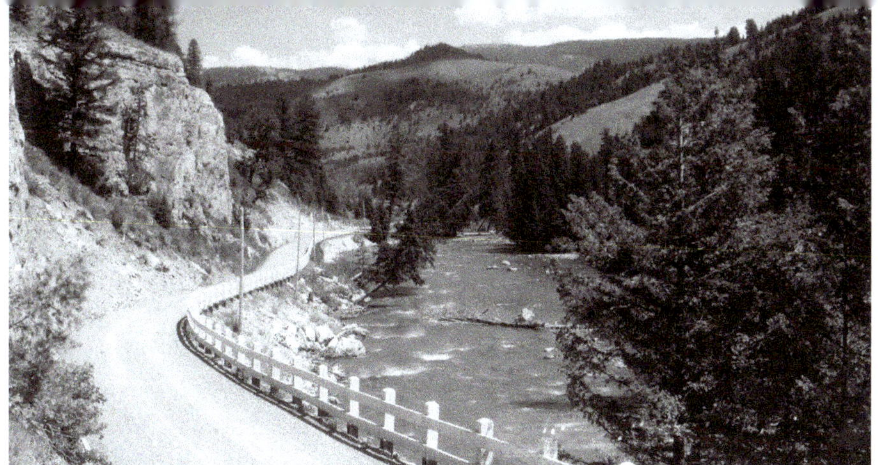

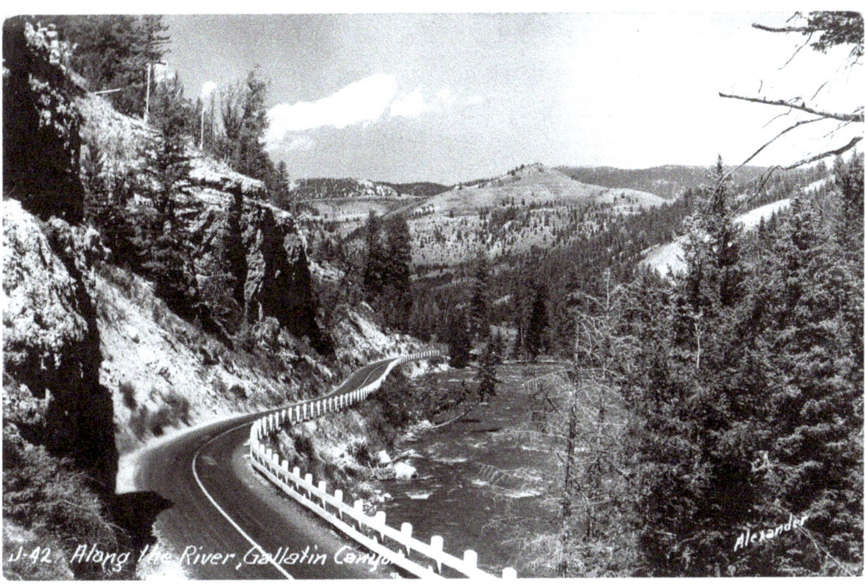

J-42 Along the River, Gallatin Canyo

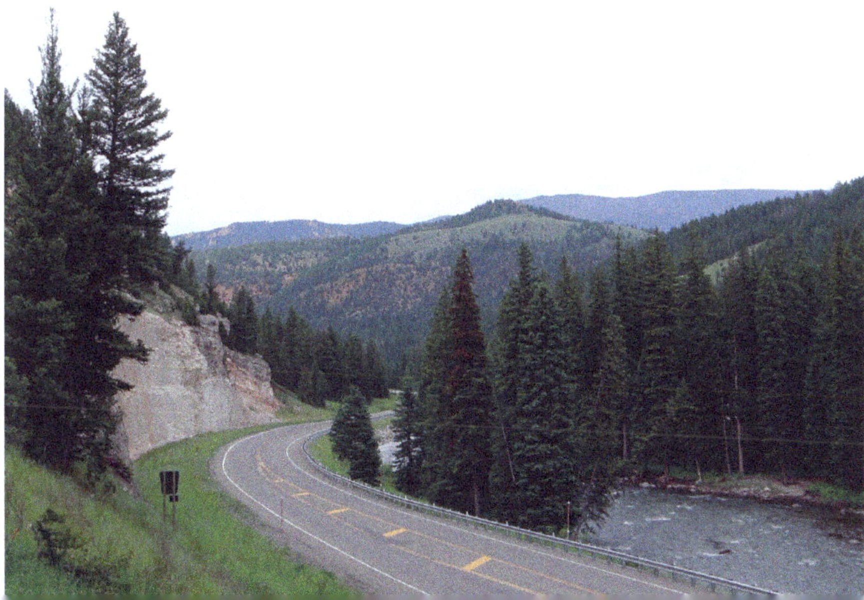

that was blasted and moved back, allowing construction of a turning lane into the campground. The rocks from this project were deposited in the depression north of Halfway Point mentioned earlier. The removal of part of the cliff has greatly changed the appearance of this curve in the highway (Figure 7.4). The present exposed surface of the cliff is a rich source of marine fossil imprints.

South of Red Cliff campground on the east side of the highway across from Buck Creek (MM#41) is a large open pasture. This pasture area was homesteaded in the late 1800s by Burt Corwin. Corwin sold the property to Joe Philips, who sold it for $100 in 1916 to Earl Benham. Benham's father had homesteaded at Sheep Rock near the entrance to the canyon in 1886. In 1941, Benham sold the property to Dr. Caroline McGill, owner of 320 Ranch. At her death, the property went to the Goodriches, who had become owners of 320 Ranch. The Goodriches sold the property in the 1970s. The present owners put a conservation easement on the property. Thus, this large pasture will remain undeveloped into perpetuity, and the canyon at this point will remain in its more or less historic state.

As one travels south along Highway 191from the Red Cliff area, one will notice the cliffs to the east, where there are extensive ornate outcrops of limestone. These outcrops, variously called Cathedral Rocks or Palisades, were a common attraction for early travelers up the canyon. Today, with an improved highway, faster speeds and interest in "getting where we are going," few travelers see or appreciate these geological gems. They were not overlooked by earlier travelers even as far back as 1872, when Jackson, the Hayden expedition photographer traveling south through the canyon, photographed them (Figure 7.5). In 1923, Alden, a photographer for the U.S. Forest Service, also photographed this outcrop (Figure 7.6). Hayden, a geologist and leader of the 1872 expedition, described the formations in this way:

> *For about fifteen miles the river has carved out a canyon with the nearly horizontal strata of limestones rising with vertical walls on either side 800 to 1,200 feet. The inclination of the strata appears slight, not more than 1° to 3°. The limestones are mostly in rather thin layers, but some of them form massive beds. The entire group presents the usual variety of texture common to limestones of this age. The fossils are quite abundant, and all, so far as could be determined, of well-known Carboniferous types. This part of the canyon is most picturesque; the high limestone-walls on either side are weathered into towers and Gothic pinnacles and in some instances wonderfully grotesque forms.*

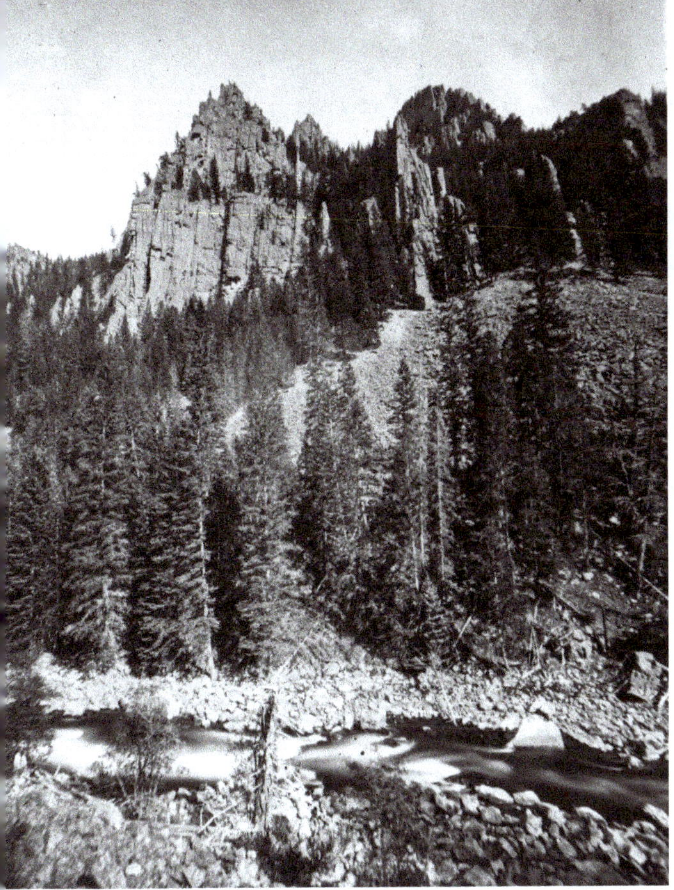

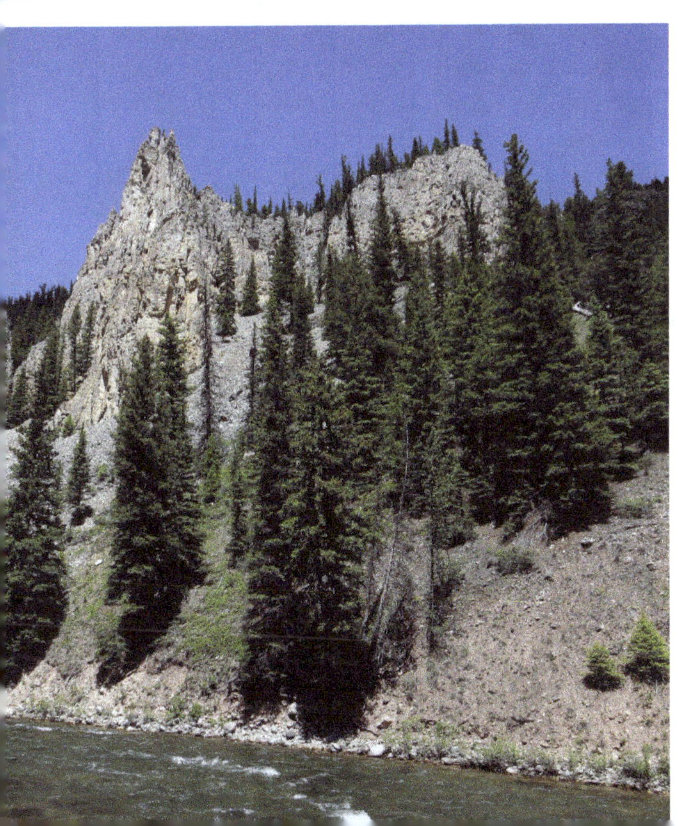

Figure 7.5. Palisades of the West Gallatin River Canyon (MM#38+/-).
Upper photo (1872): Palisades photo, part of a stereo set. Photograph by W.H. Jackson during the 1872 Hayden Expedition. *USGS.*
Lower photo (2016): Appearance of the Palisades in the twenty-first century.

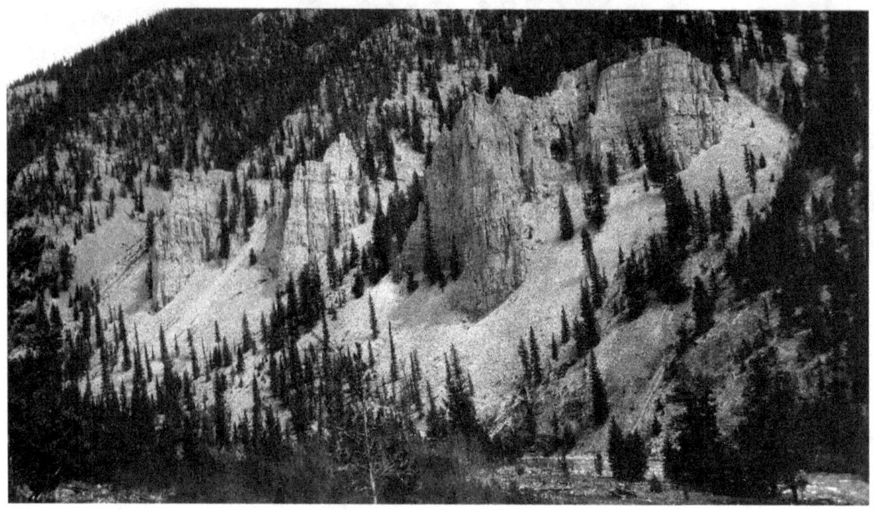

Figure 7.6. Palisades in the Gallatin Canyon (MM#38.8).
Left photo (1923): Palisades with little forest on the slopes. *USGS.*
Right photo (2016): Palisades with more forest. Highway 191 embankment can be seen to the left in photo.

Farther along to the south, one comes upon Cinnamon Lodge on the east side of the road at MM#37.1 and the dirt road to the USFS Cinnamon Ranger Station on the west. The Cinnamon Lodge was founded by Alma and Art Vandecar in 1947 and called Almart Lodge (Figure 7.7). They maintained some lodging and services, including a gas pump. In 1993, Jim and Jo Snyder bought the lodge and renovated it. On February 25, 2002, the Cinnamon Lodge burned down and was rebuilt to the present structure. Today, Cinnamon Lodge has a large restaurant and attached bar. It also has cabins for rent and stays busy during the tourist season. Apparently, some cabins are occupied year-round by employees from Big Sky, where there is limited affordable housing.

The history of the Cinnamon Ranger Station goes back to the very beginning of the twentieth century. It is a short drive up the dirt road and is near the trailhead for the trail going up Cinnamon Mountain adjacent to the station. Cinnamon Mountain is visible in photos shown later taken from the 320 Ranch bridge. Many of the Cinnamon Station buildings were built in the early twentieth century. Rhesis Franshan, the first forest ranger in the canyon at Squaw Creek in 1906, built a cabin at Cinnamon in 1907 and then made it his headquarters in 1908. There also were some cabins built by homesteaders, taken over by the Forest Service and occupied by rangers who

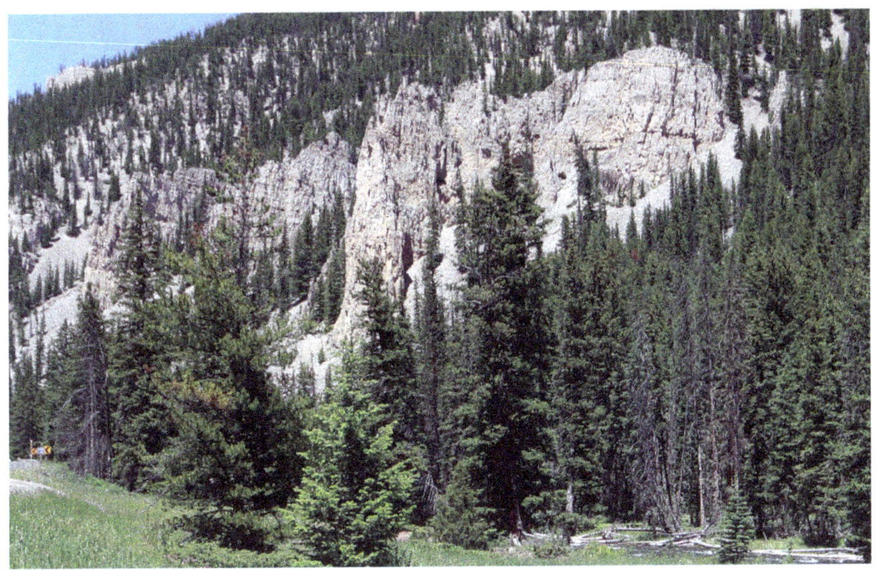

were assigned to elk and range surveying. The 1907 cabin was quite rustic but improved in later years. The main building present today was built in 1922 (Figure 7.8). A quote from a ranger assigned to the station in 1917, who brought his wife along, tells the story of the place before the newer building was constructed:

> *The Station residence was a very old cabin, 16 by 28 feet, divided into three rooms. The south end was living room, dining room and kitchen, the north end divided into two sleeping rooms. Partitions were one inch matched flooring, no sound proofing. There was a good floor, not very old, the original roof, almost flat, had been poles with moss filler in the cracks between poles covered with 6 or 8 inches of dirt. The cabin had been built by a would-be homesteader and had been taken over by the Forest Service for a Ranger Station when the homesteader gave up and moved out. A year or so before my time, a board roof had been installed over the dirt roof to make it more waterproof.... The water supply was a water trough at a big spring about 50 feet from the back door. The rest room facility was a log affair about 50 yards from the back door.*

There is a question whether this report was about an old homestead cabin or the one built for the Forest Service by Franshan in 1907. Still, it describes a very rustic situation.

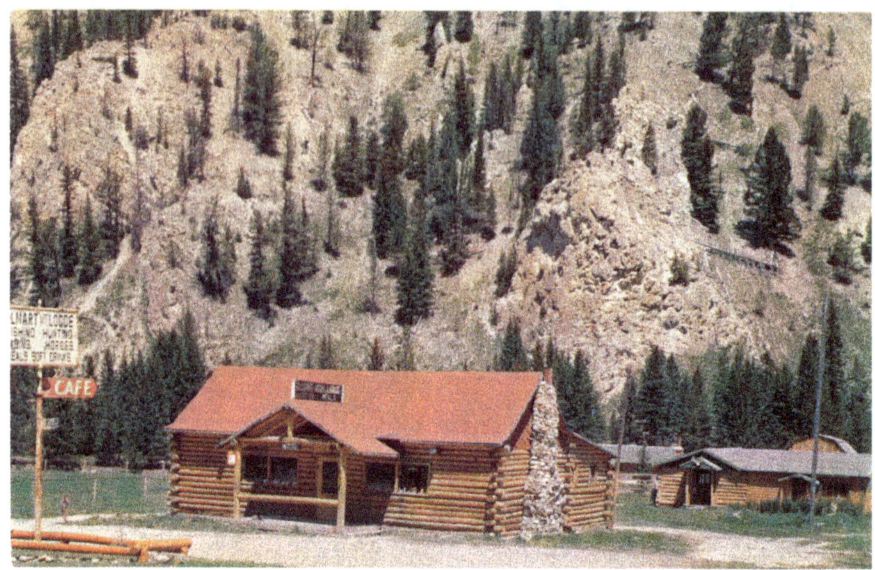

Figure 7.7. Almart Lodge (Cinnamon Lodge) location along the Gallatin Road (MM#37.1). *Above photo* (late 1940s): Almart Lodge shortly after opening in 1947 (tinted photo). *GHM*. *Below photo* (2016): Cinnamon Lodge, which replaced the original Almart Lodge. The original Cinnamon Lodge burned to the ground in February 2002 and was rebuilt with this building.

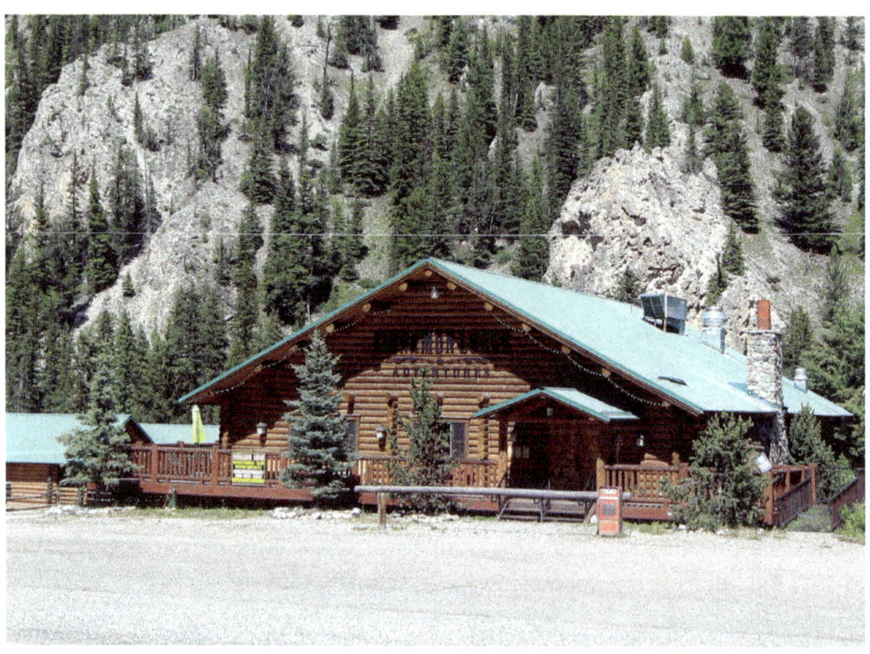

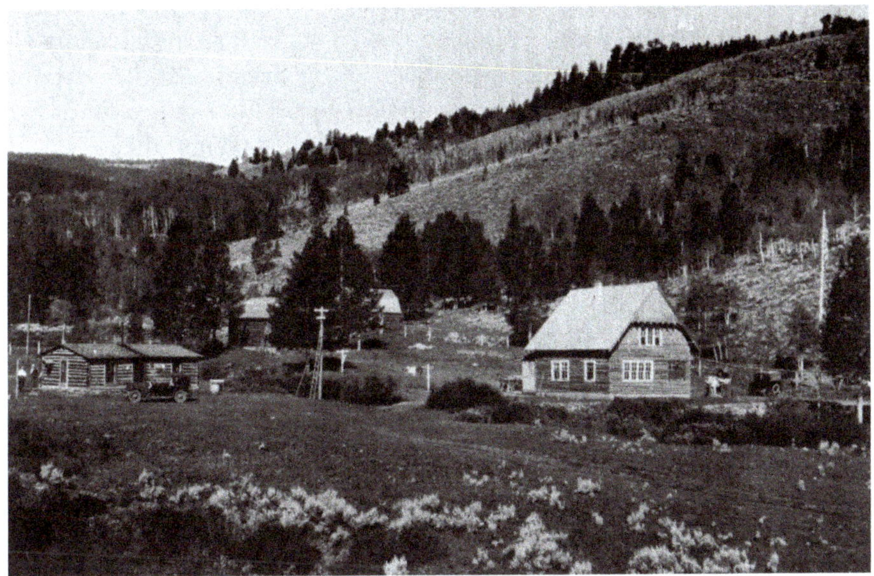

Figure 7.8. Cinnamon Ranger Station in the Gallatin National Forest (MM#37.1).
Above photo (1922): Early photo of the ranger station taken shortly after the building was constructed. The station was established a couple of decades earlier. The old station cabin described in the text is on the left. *Forest History Society*.
Below photo (2016): Present ranger station; the building is going to be restored, and the station has a relatively new barn behind the trees to the left of the building. The station is used irregularly by USFS staff.

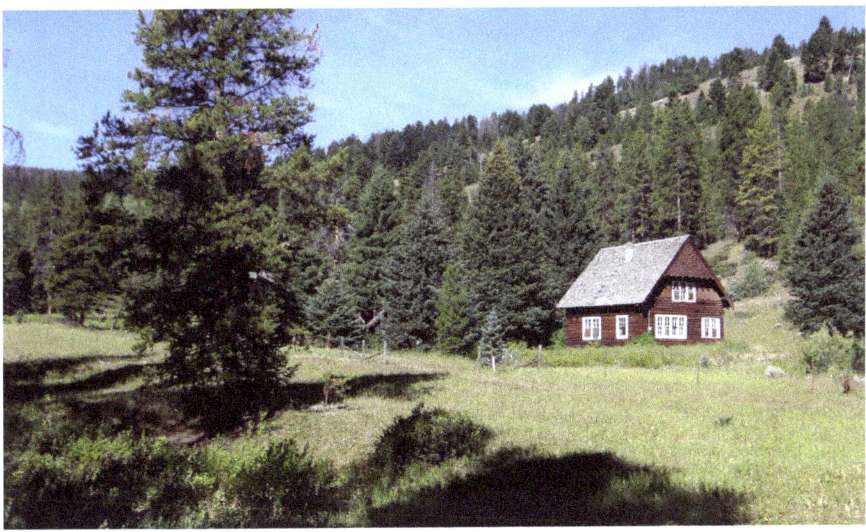

This section of the Gallatin Canyon was an active area in the killing of two bank robbers in July 1932. Two robbers of the Security Bank and Trust in Bozeman got away and escaped up the canyon. They stopped for gas at Karst Kamp, and Pete Karst reported their passing. When they reached the section of canyon near Cinnamon, they first went into the forest but then entered the Henke cabin in the area near today's Cinnamon Lodge and held the Henkes and friends hostage, asking Henke to buy food at 320 Ranch just down the road to the south. The sheriff, knowing the robbers were in the area, had set up headquarters at 320 Ranch, but Henke, fearing for the hostages at his cabin, did not tell the sheriff and returned with the food and put it under a tree near the cabin for the robbers to retrieve. The Henke group then made a dash for their car and escaped down the canyon. Some of the locals who were acting as vigilantes took over the Henke cabin and waited for the robbers, who had retreated into the forest, to retrieve the food. The youngest robber approached the cabin and was shot by those inside, who had concealed themselves behind closed blinds. The sheriff and two other experienced men—one of these being Lester Pierstorff, who had owned a homestead on land that is now part of the Black Butte Ranch—tracked down the older bank robber, confronting him in the nearby forest. The robber shot and wounded the sheriff but was gunned down by the other two men, thus ending the robbery episode in the canyon.

Chapter 8

320 Ranch to Yellowstone National Park's Northwestern Boundary

(MM#35.2 to MM#31.2)

After leaving the area near Cinnamon Lodge and Cinnamon Ranger Station and heading south, one enters a part of the canyon and West Gallatin drainage that is occupied by several guest/dude ranches (Map 8.1). This, in itself, tells the visitor that this part of the canyon near Yellowstone National Park is a special place for recreation, wildlife viewing and relaxation. This has not always been the case, as our story will tell.

The first ranch to come up while driving south after leaving Cinnamon Lodge is the 320 Ranch on the east side of the river at MM#35. The history of this ranch goes back to 1898, when Sam Wilson homesteaded 160 acres on Buffalo Horn Creek, which flows out of the mountains on the east side of the valley. Sam Wilson had been grazing cattle up Taylor Fork in 1895 and knew the area well. In 1900, Sam's father, Clinton, homesteaded an adjoining 160 acres, and they combined their two properties, naming the ranch the Buffalo Horn Resort. With 320 acres, this eventually became the 320 Ranch (Figure 8.1). Sam Wilson started taking in guests, an opportunity taken by other canyon ranchers or landowners. In discussions with Pete Karst at Karst Cold Springs Resort and Tom Michener at West Fork, the group established a common charge of twelve dollars per week for cabin and board and six dollars per week for a saddle horse. This might be considered the beginning of the dude business in the canyon.

In 1906–7, the Eldridge Post Office was moved from the Walter Cooper Company headquarters up Taylor Fork (the company produced railroad

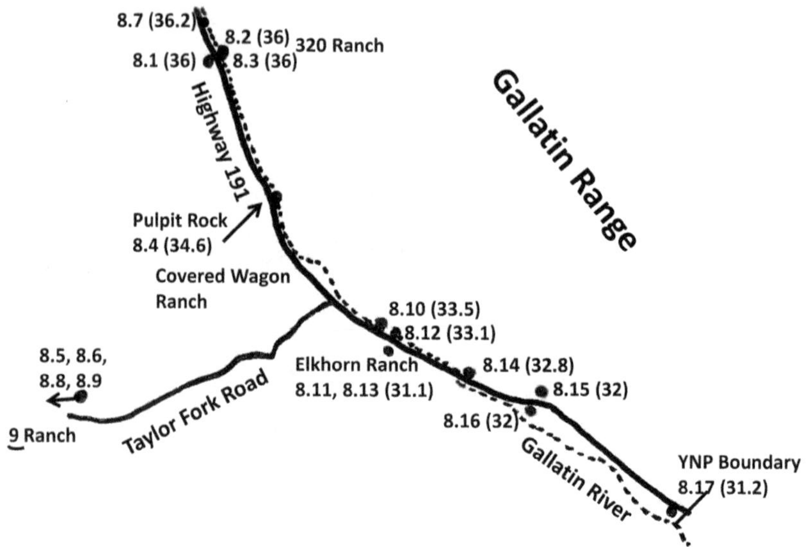

Map 8.1. North of 320 Ranch to the Yellowstone National Park boundary (MM#36.5 to 31.2). Map of photo locations along Highway 191 and the Gallatin River (mile markers in parentheses).

ties) to the 320 Ranch when the tie company went out of business. The name Eldridge for the post office was selected by Walter Cooper, owner of the tie company, after Hugh Eldridge, who was the postmaster general in Washington State. George Dean was the postmaster until the Eldridge Post Office was transferred to 320 Ranch. Cooper also named a small tributary of Taylor Fork near his headquarters Eldridge Creek. The story of the tie company is discussed later when describing locations up Taylor Fork, but ties from that outfit floated downriver every spring past the 320 Ranch Bridge (Figure 8.2). Josephine Wilson, wife of the founder of 320 Ranch, was Eldridge postmistress until approximately 1938–40, when the post office closed. By then, 320 Ranch had changed hands. The post office was a gathering place for many of the pioneers and locals in this area. They would come to collect their mail, visit with acquaintances and stay on for a few days, especially in winter when travel was difficult.

In 1936, Dr. Caroline McGill, Montana's first woman doctor, purchased Wilson's resort ranch. McGill had visited the canyon several times prior to purchasing the 320 Ranch, staying one night at the ranch of Dr. Safley near Snow Flake Springs (MM#33.2), about a mile north of today's Yellowstone

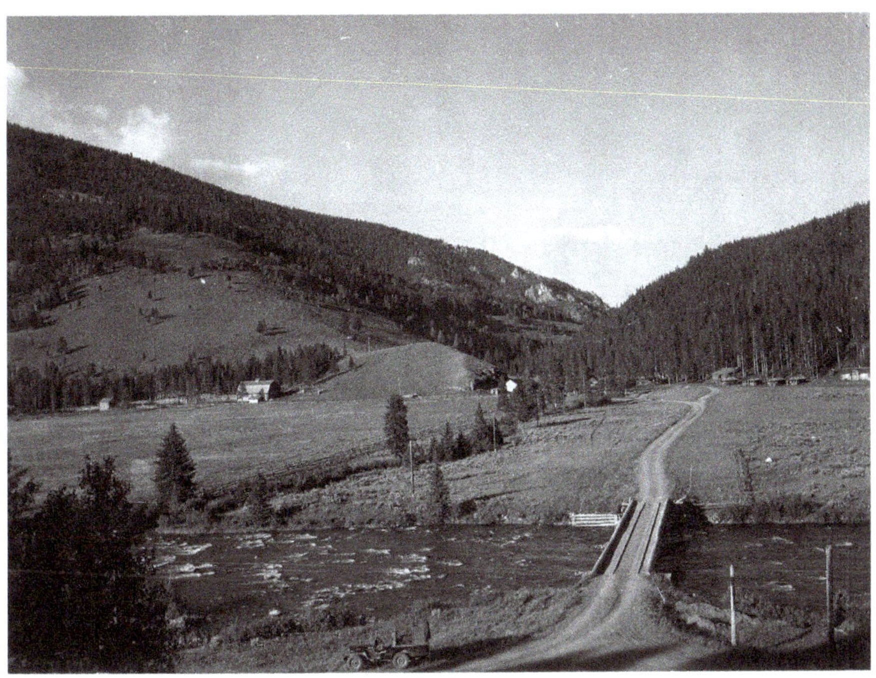

Figure 8.1. 320 Ranch (MM#36).
Above photo (circa 1950s): The 320 Ranch entrance with the old wooden bridge. Barn and limited number of cabins are apparent in the photo. *GHM*.
Below photo (2013): 320 Ranch entrance with new steel bridge. Many more cabins and structures now exist on the property.

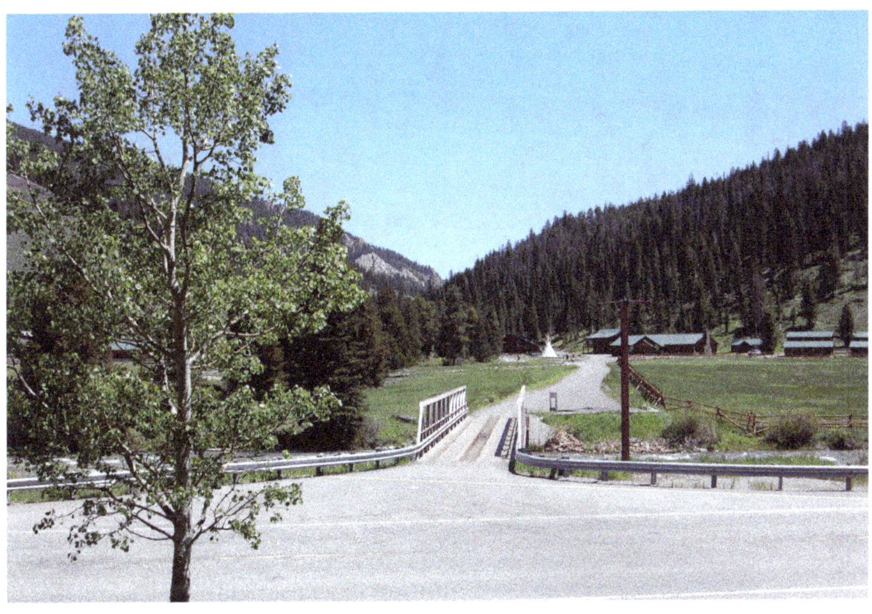

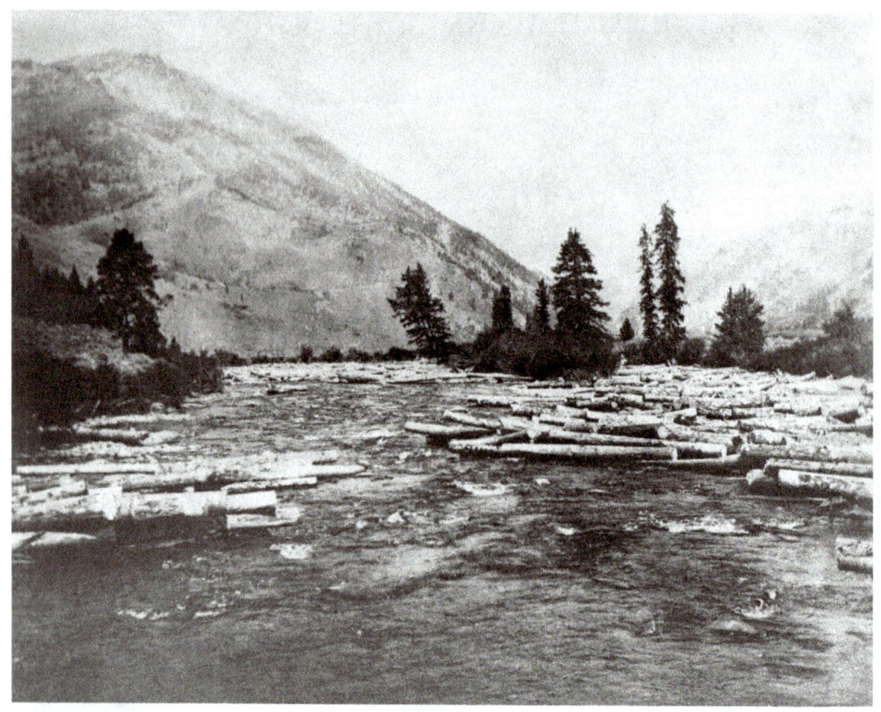

Figure 8.2. Cinnamon Mountain and the Gallatin River photographed from 320 Ranch bridge (MM#36).
Above photo (1906): Last run of logs on the Gallatin River from the Cooper Tie Camp up Taylor Fork. *GHM.*
Below photo (2013): Note how the river channel is not as wide as in 1906, perhaps a result of no tie drives for over a century.

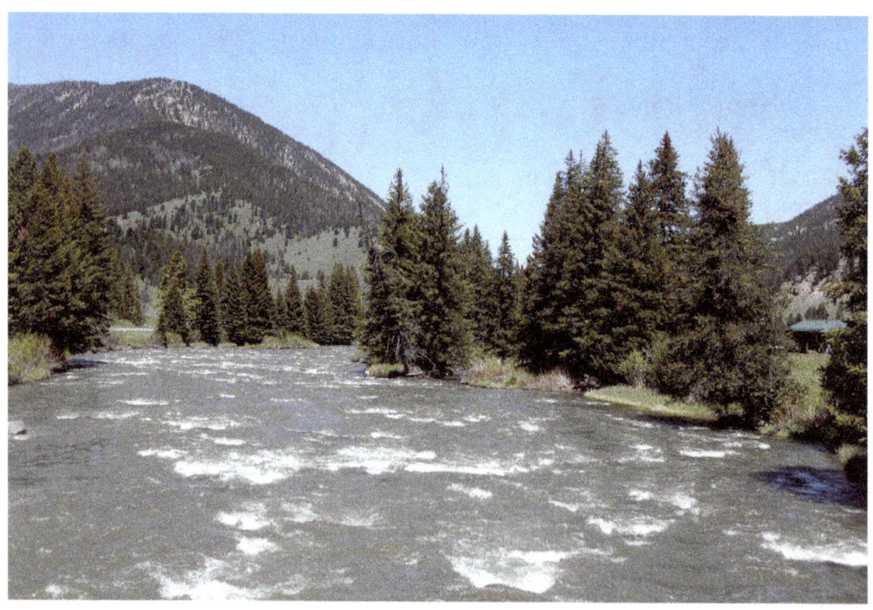

National Park northwestern entrance. Dr. McGill bought the 320 Ranch as a retreat for patients and friends.

Dr. McGill passed away in 1959 at 320 Ranch. In her will, she gave an option to purchase the ranch and lands she held up Taylor Fork to Jim and Patty Goodrich (Figure 8.3), who had been managing the ranch for many years. They purchased the properties and ran the ranch until 1987, when they sold it to David Brask, the current owner. Brask has turned the ranch into a resort/restaurant location.

Some interesting stories about 320 Ranch, in addition to its being involved in the 1932 bank robber events, include one about Dr. McGill buying an old Cadillac engine and installing it as a generator at the ranch in 1938, ten years before electricity was extended this far up the canyon. The other early source of electricity in the canyon was at Karst Resort, where Pete Karst had built a small hydroelectric plant on Moose Creek in 1922.

Leaving 320 Ranch and heading south, one comes to another guest ranch, Covered Wagon Ranch (MM#34.1). In the 1930s, a dam was proposed where the canyon narrows just north of Covered Wagon Ranch. That proposal eventually died for lack of funding. Also along the route between the two ranches is a tall rock formation jutting above the forest on the west side of the road. This formation with a flat top is called Pulpit Rock based on its shape (Figure 8.4). It can be seen clearly from a turnoff on the east side of the highway immediately opposite it (MM#34.6). This rock structure has been a challenge to many rock climbers.

Covered Wagon Ranch, like so many guest ranches in this part of the canyon, has a history of its own. Most of the Covered Wagon Ranch property is on U.S. Forest Service land. The ranch has had a lease on the property since 1925, when it was started by Vic and Eda Benson. Many of the early cabins are still being used by the ranch and occupied by guests. After Vic Sr. and Eda passed away, Vic Jr. "Benny" Benson managed the ranch and maintained the spirit of the old guest ranch until he sold in 1992 to Will King, who sold to Debi Narrcato and Jerry Taylor in 2005. The Covered Wagon Ranch is now owned by Kurt and Melissa Puckett, who, after working there, purchased it in 2013. Benny lived on the ranch until his passing in 1998. Since then, there have been several owners, and yet, Covered Wagon Ranch seems little changed to those who knew the ranch in the early days of Vic Sr. and Eda Benson.

Just south of the Covered Wagon Ranch gate, one crosses the bridge over Taylor Fork, arriving at Taylor Fork Road (MM#33.7). Taylor Fork often runs milky, which is caused by bentonite (very fine clay) eroded

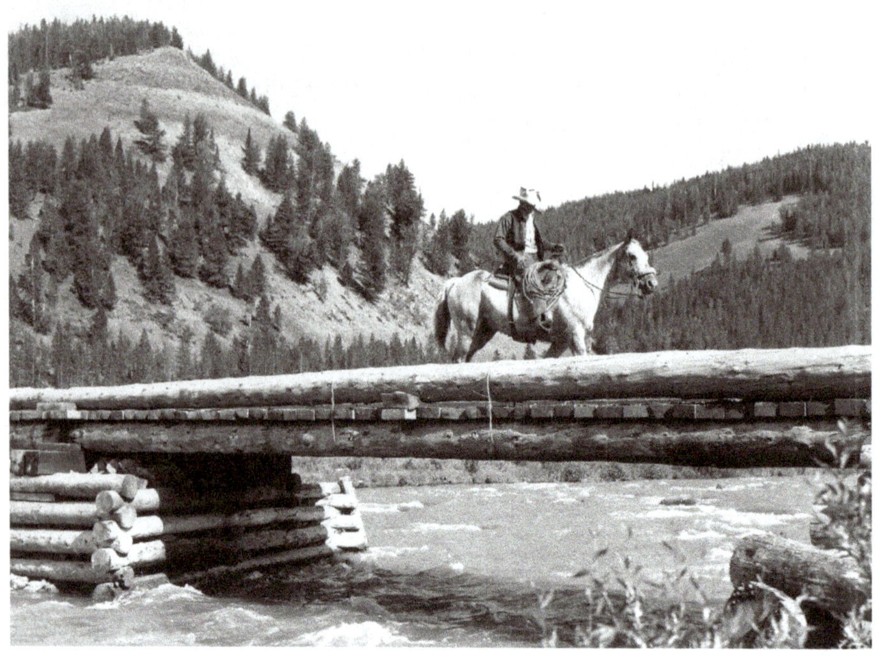

Figure 8.3. Bridge at 320 Ranch (MM#36).
Above photo (1952): Log bridge at 320 Ranch with Jim Goodrich, owner of the ranch at the time of the photo. Note the rock-filled log cradles (ends and center) used for early bridges. Date of bridge construction is unknown but probably in the 1930s. *GHM.*
Below photo (2016): Present 320 Bridge is a steel truss structure extending across the river with no center support. Note 320 Ranch guest ride crossing bridge.

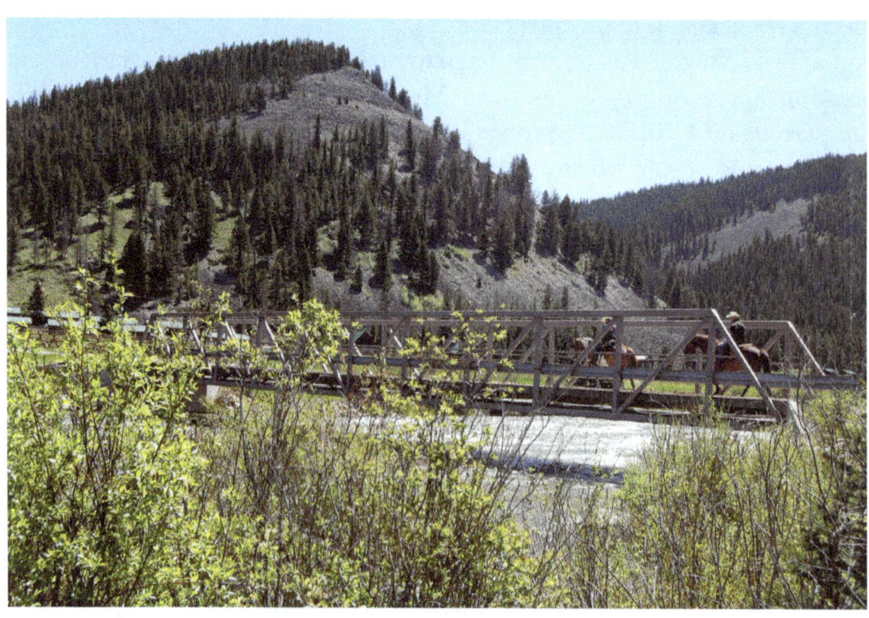

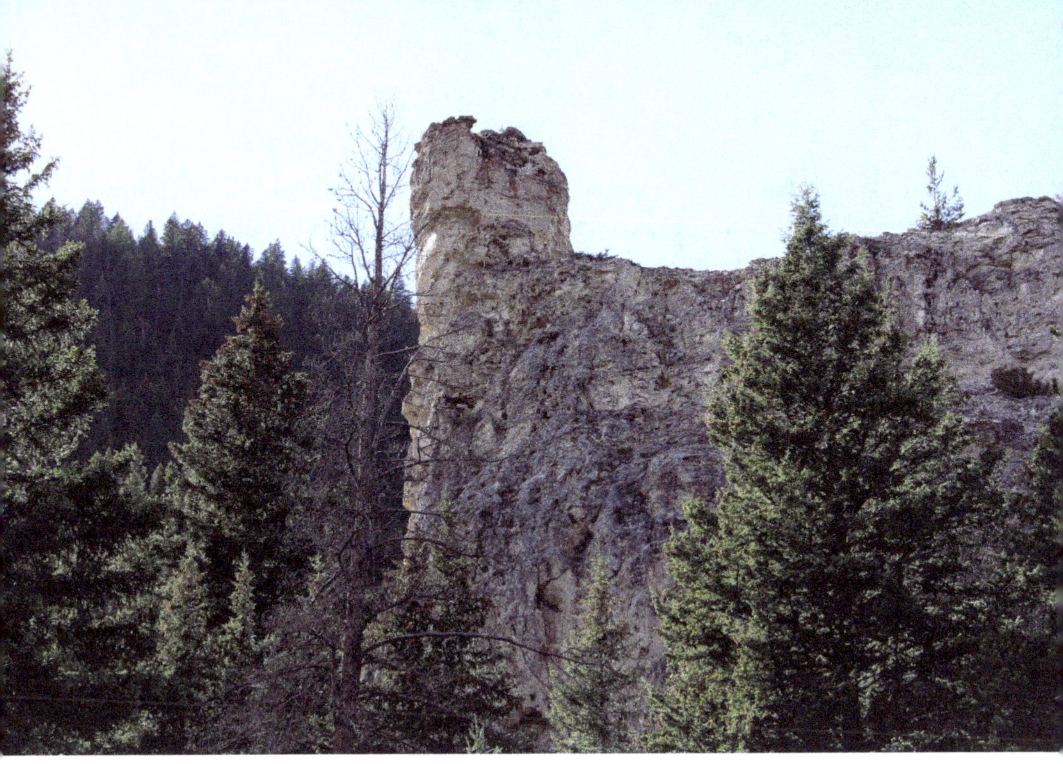

Figure 8.4 (2016). Pulpit Rock (MM# 34.6) along the Gallatin Way just north of Covered Wagon Ranch and about a half mile south of 320 Ranch. A pull-out is east across the highway from the rock.

from outcrops upstream. Rainfall entrains the bentonite, which stays in suspension for a long time. Because bentonite tends to seal soils in irrigated fields, farmers in the Gallatin Valley once proposed sealing the outcrops with asphalt. Fortunately, nature was left alone. The present Taylor Fork Bridge, built in the 1950s, replaced one just downstream. The location of the road leading away from the old bridge is still visible in the sagebrush to the east. If one turns up Taylor Fork Road, one passes a jack fence belonging to Covered Wagon Ranch, which maintains horse pasture along this first mile or so of the road.

Taylor Fork was the southern destination of the first early road up the canyon, constructed to this point about 1898 (this date varies depending on the source). As pointed out in earlier sections, the reason for extending the road this far at that time—other than people of Bozeman clamoring for a road all the way to the west gate of Yellowstone National Park thirty-four miles farther south—was to serve the Walter Cooper Company that produced railroad ties about seven miles up Taylor Fork. The condition of any road up Taylor Fork to the tie company was questionable, but other forms of access to the company buildings and logging areas still existed.

The Walter Cooper Company, which started in 1902, had three camps up Taylor Fork. Camp #1, company headquarters, was about nine miles up Taylor Fork on Eldridge Creek (Figure 8.5). This is where the original Eldridge Post Office was located. J.L. Taylor was the bookkeeper for all three camps and was postmaster. He also was in charge of the commissary for the camps. Taylor Fork was named after him, being changed from Dodge Creek, named after Ira Dodge, an early pioneer and trapper. Camp #2 was located about four miles west and upstream of Eldridge (Camp #1) on Taylor Fork, and Camp #3 was about three miles southwest. In the 1950s, when traveling through the forest where these camps once were located, one could still see remnants of some of the loggers' cabins (likely Camp #2). Also, the forest had many tree stumps more or less of the same diameter. This was selective cutting for trees of the right size for railroad ties, leaving trees of other sizes—larger and smaller—unharvested. In addition to the main camps, there also were subcontractors' camps, some on Buck Creek and one located on Wapiti Creek. Headquarters on Eldridge Creek had about two hundred men, other main camps had about fifty men and the subcontractor camps had about thirty-five to forty men. Consequently, with this manpower, one can imagine how many ties would be cut out of these forests each year.

The newly cut railroad ties were usually stacked near the rivers (Figure 8.6). On Taylor Fork and adjacent rivers, retaining dams were constructed, with ties floated onto the lakes in spring. During spring high water, the dams would be broken and the ties floated down Taylor Fork to the Gallatin River and then down the Gallatin River (Figures 8.2 and 8.7) to Cooper's lumber mill at Central Park in Belgrade.

It is astonishing to read how the ties were handled on the float downstream. The following is a quotation from a person who appears to be the daughter of Walter Cooper (his only surviving child), as she refers to him as "my father" in her memories of the tie company (held in the McGill papers at the Museum of the Rockies):

> *Expert river men were hired for that purpose. Most of these came from Canada or Oregon. The way they were able to handle the ties in that swift water was amazing and nothing short of miraculous. My father had two long river boats built which followed the ties and with long steal hooks the men in the boats untangled the tie jams that formed* [see Figure 8.7]. *These men were so expert that they always stood up in the boats sending the ties ahead of them. The worst jam that I saw was at Cave Creek* [near House Rock or the Mad Mile] *in those rapids where the river*

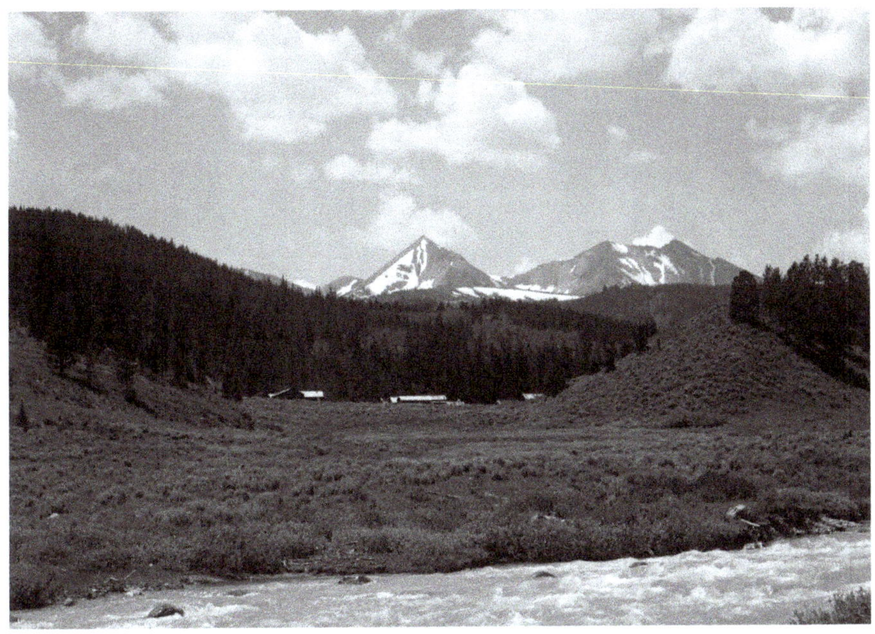

Figure 8.5. Walter Cooper Tie Company headquarters location on Eldridge Creek up Taylor Fork.
Above photo (1906): Headquarters of Walter Cooper Company. Original photo cropped to enlarge buildings. *Merrill Burlingame.*
Below photo (2013): Buildings have been removed, and the forest continues to expand.

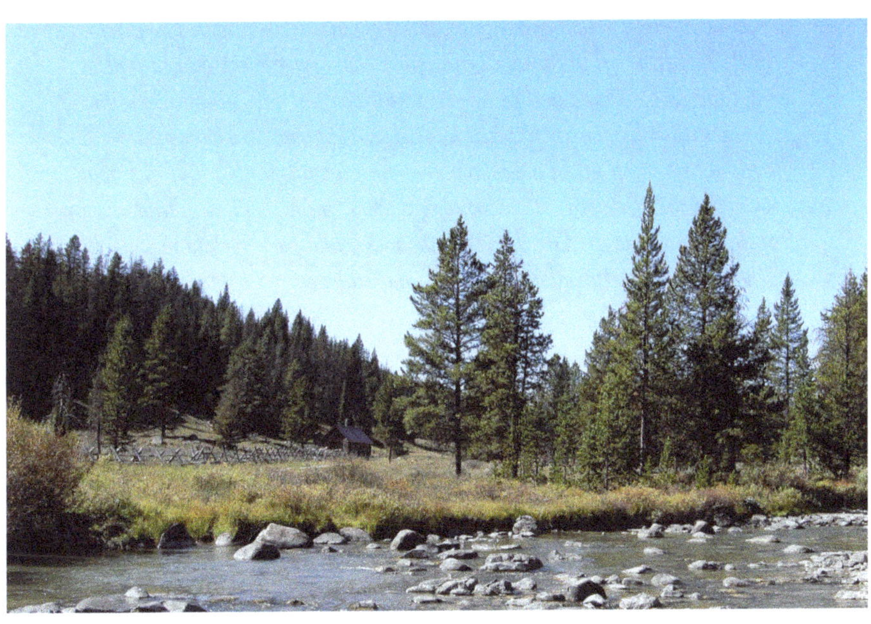

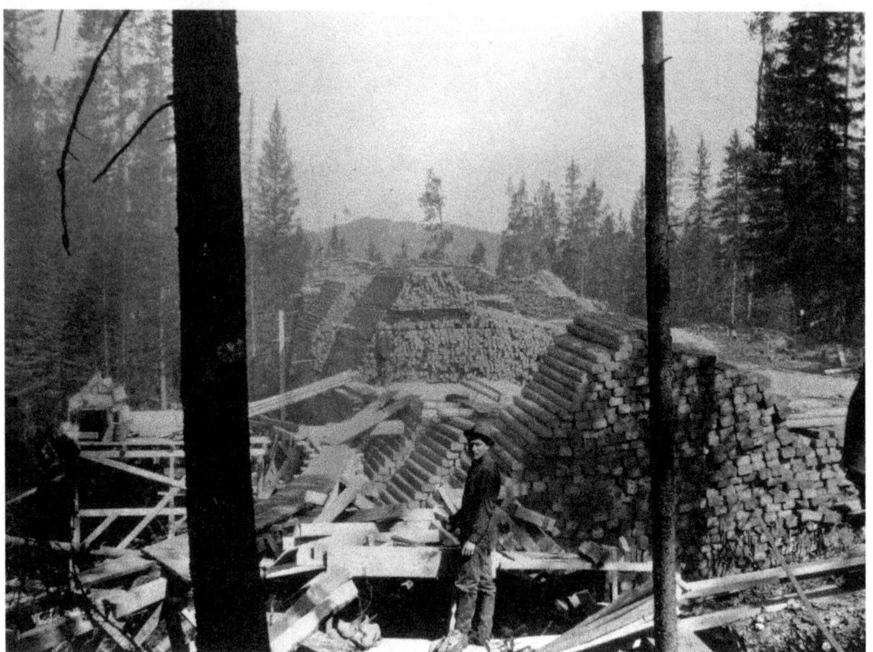

Figure 8.6 (1904–7). Walter Cooper Tie Company lumber camp. Piles of cut ties ready to be pushed into the river for a trip down Taylor Fork and the Gallatin River to Central Park near Belgrade, Montana. *GHM.*

> *is extremely swift and narrow and the rocks are very large. There were literally hundreds of ties wedged in around those huge rocks on end and in every conceivable shape and position. That was the only place where they had to wait till the waters lowered to disentangle them.... The men shot all the rapids standing up in the boats....A man would jump out of the boat onto a bunch of lodged ties, disentangle them, push them on ahead, then leap from one tie to another then onto the rocks, and from rock to rock till he reached shore then run along the bank and catch up with the boat farther down the river.*

By the 1890s, stockmen were entering the upper Gallatin and grazing herds in the Taylor Fork drainage. Sam Wilson, founder of 320 Ranch, grazed herds in the Taylor Fork vicinity prior to 1895. In 1898, one-time state land agent Hans Behring and his associate Marshall Cunningham, along with nine other associates, created the Taylor Fork Cattle Company (later the South Montana Live Stock Company). They ran sizable herds on the upper Gallatin to the late 1920s (Figure 8.8).

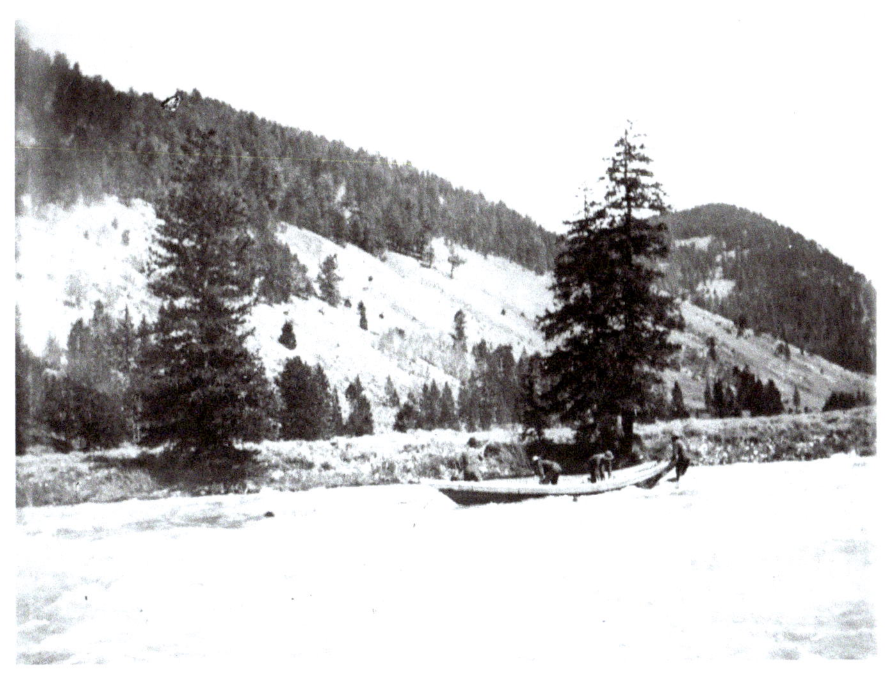

Figure 8.7. Gallatin River downstream from Taylor Fork and the 320 Bridge (MM#36.2).
Above photo (circa 1906): Long boats accompanied log/ties from the Cooper Tie Camps up Taylor Fork as they were being floated down the Gallatin River to a lumber mill at Central Park near Belgrade, Montana. *GHM.*
Below photo (2013): High flow river at location where the long boat had passed 107 years earlier.

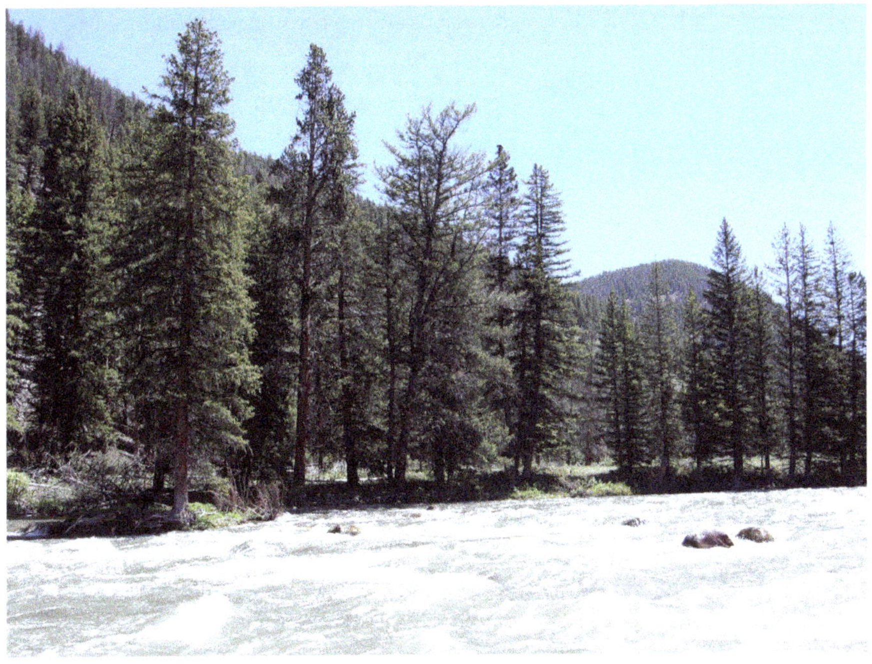

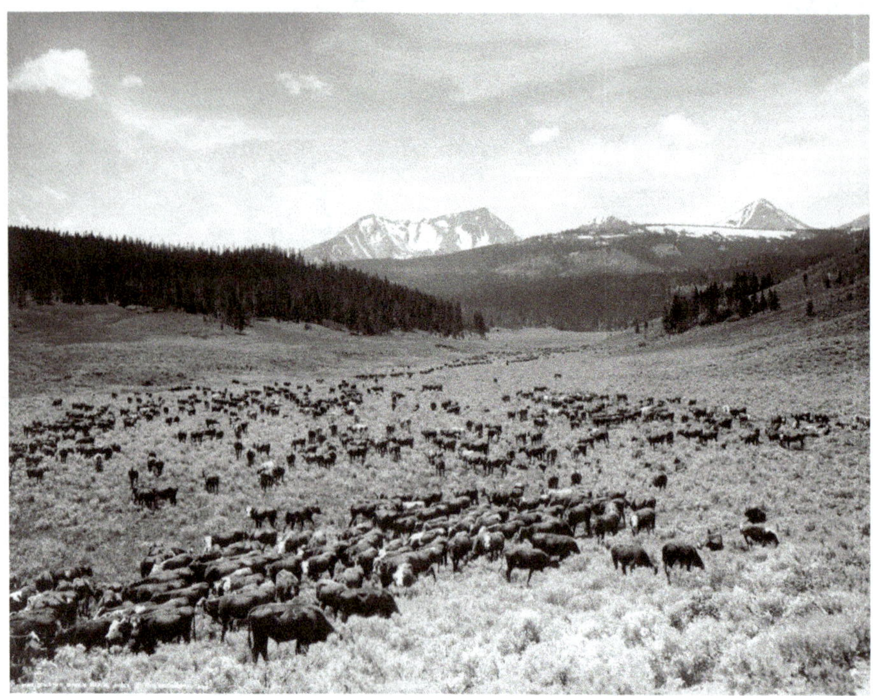

Figure 8.8. Rangeland in the upper Taylor Fork/Cache Creek basin.
Above photo (1911): Cattle belonging to the Taylor Fork Cattle Company associated with the Nine Quarter Circle Ranch graze the upper basins of Taylor Fork. *MOR.*
Below photo (2016): Present condition of the Taylor Fork/Cache Creek rangeland, which no longer supports cattle. Cattle were on these lands into the late twentieth century.

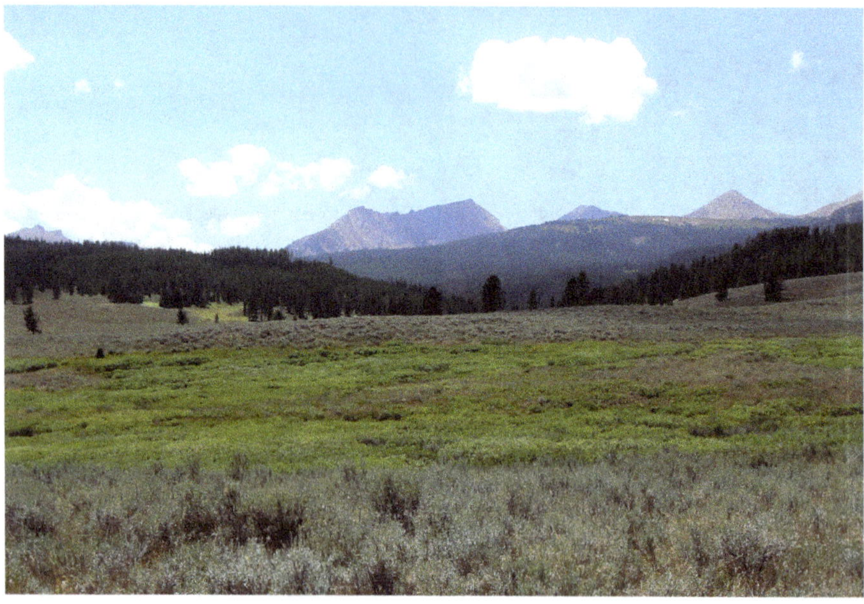

Taylor Fork is the location of one of several guest ranches started and/or encouraged by members of the Butler family of the Butler Paper Company in Chicago. Two of these ranches became the Rising Sun Ranches. Cunningham and Behring had created the Nine Quarter Circle cattle ranch, which is about five miles up the Taylor Fork road from Highway 191. Frank O. Butler, a regular guest of the Michener Ranch near West Fork since 1906, convinced Cunningham to let his family summer at the Nine Quarter Circle, where his sons, Paul and Julius, "could join in the operation of running a cattle outfit." This initiated the expansion of Cunningham and Behring's Nine Quarter Circle Ranch into dude ranching. Cunningham and Behring constructed their first guest cabins in the spring of 1910 for the exclusive use of the Butler family. This became the parent ranch of the Rising Sun Ranches, composed of Nine Quarter Circle Ranch and Seven Eleven Ranch on Sage Creek just over the ridge from Taylor Fork. Nine Quarter Circle Ranch was originally a horse and cattle ranch, and Seven Eleven Ranch, built in the early 1920s, was a "modern" ranch where polo ponies were raised and trained. During the 1930s, Nine Quarter Circle Ranch had one of the largest private herds of bison, according to a Milwaukee Railroad brochure on guest ranches in Montana. Owners of the Rising Sun Ranches were the two brothers, Julius and Paul Butler, and Marshall Cunningham. Paul Butler is also known for buying ranchland in the West Fork basin in 1927, homesteaded in 1917 by Clarence Lytle. From that, in 1930, he started the B-K Ranch as a guest ranch along the North Fork of West Fork near Lone Mountain, now called Lone Mountain Ranch in the Big Sky area. Nine Quarter Circle Ranch, now owned by Kim Kelsey and family—the son of Howard Kelsey who purchased it from the Rising Sun Ranches in 1945—continues as one of the historic guest ranches in the Gallatin Canyon (Figure 8.9).

The Seven Eleven Ranch location up Sage Creek was homesteaded by Mary Sales in the late 1890s and, when she got sick and left, was taken over and perhaps proved up by Victor "Vic" Adams sometime before the early 1900s. This property was purchased in the 1940s by Elkhorn Ranch from Rising Sun Ranches, which acquired it in 1923 from a man named Bittner who had purchased it earlier from Adams. Adams lived on in Bozeman until 1957. Elkhorn used it as a boys' camp, then to house employees and then leased it to Marc and Doris Patten from Michigan in 1951. The Pattens greatly improved the condition of the buildings, which Elkhorn Ranch removed in the 1960s or '70s. Many of the buildings were moved to the main Elkhorn Ranch property, and the three-sided logs from the main buildings at Seven

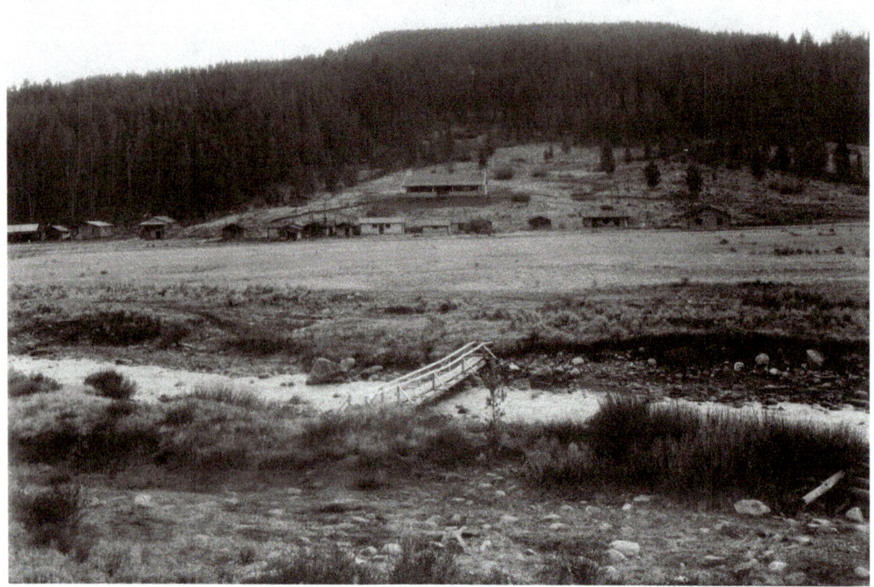

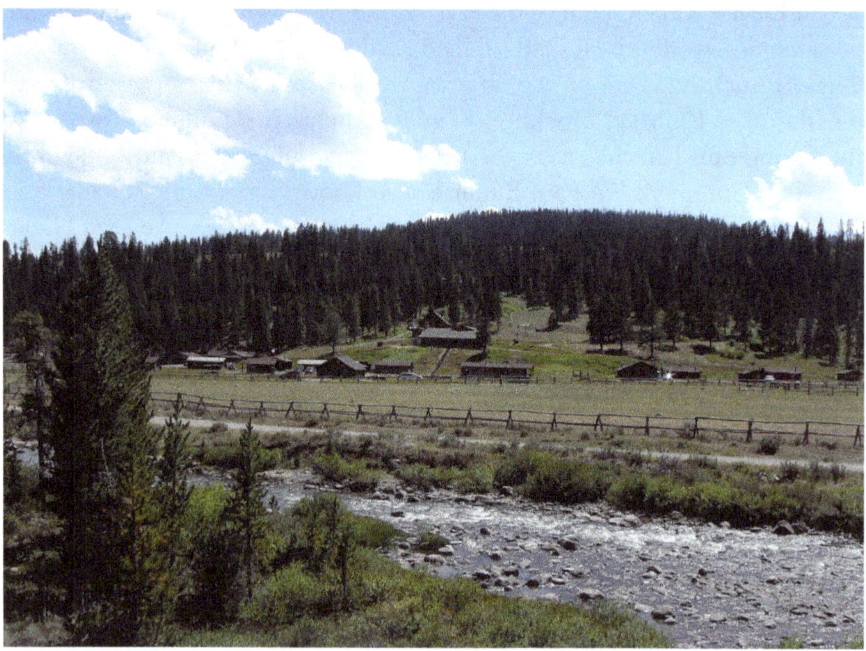

Figure 8.9. Nine Quarter Circle Ranch in the Taylor Fork valley.
Upper photo (early 1900s): The ranch in its early days. The footbridge across the river would not hold up with high spring flows. *MOR*.
Lower photo (August 2016): The ranch has added several buildings but still looks very much like the early days.

Eleven were sold to another Canyon family who used them to construct a log house in the Big Sky area. That house was eventually dismantled to make room for the large storage facility to the north of the Whitewater Motel. The Seven Eleven location is now used by Elkhorn for evening barbecues, from which guests ride back to the main ranch. The Pattens stopped leasing Seven Eleven Ranch in 1956 after they purchased land on Monument Creek in 1955 from Mayo Story Dean (granddaughter of Nelson Story). Monument Creek is a small tributary to the Gallatin River about three miles south of the northwestern entrance to Yellowstone National Park. Here, the Pattens developed the Black Butte Ranch. More history of the Black Butte Ranch area is covered in the next chapter.

East of Highway 191, across from Taylor Fork road, the limestone cliffs are quite dramatic. These are similar to the Palisades along the canyon walls farther to the north. One limestone cliff caught the eye of William Henry Jackson as he passed through this area with the 1872 Hayden Expedition on its way back to Yellowstone. Except for more trees, the cliff, river and area around it appear little changed from 1872 (Figure 8.10). One can only imagine riding past this cliff along the Gallatin River in 1872 and then think how we fly by this magnificent formation in our cars today.

In 1922, Ernest and Grace Miller founded the Elkhorn Ranch on Sage Creek (MM#33.1) (Figure 8.11). For $500, they purchased a small portion of property patented (homesteaded) by Charles A. "Axe" Johnson in 1912 and lost to H. Green, a Bozeman banker, who acquired it for back taxes. When the Millers bought the property, it had a cabin with two bedrooms and a kitchen. The banker and his family had fixed it up, but a bear broke in and destroyed much of the interior; that was enough for the banker's family. The year Elkhorn Ranch started, there were four guests whom Grace was accompanying from the East originally destined for Karst Kamp, where Ernest was working. Ernest had a falling out with Pete Karst over his commissions and a job for Grace, so they took the guests to their property on Sage Creek. The guests stayed in the cabin, and Ernest and Grace slept under a tree. Additional cabins were built over the next several years, so by the 1940s the ranch had many of the guest cabins one sees today, plus a kitchen, dining hall, barn and corrals, many of these built by Cruse Black, Ernest and Ernest's son Robert.

Cruse Black joined Elkhorn Ranch as guide, caretaker and jack-of-all-trades shortly after it started and worked for the Millers until he died in 1972. He was instrumental in much of the building expansion of the ranch. He wintered at the ranch as caretaker until his later years, when he joined

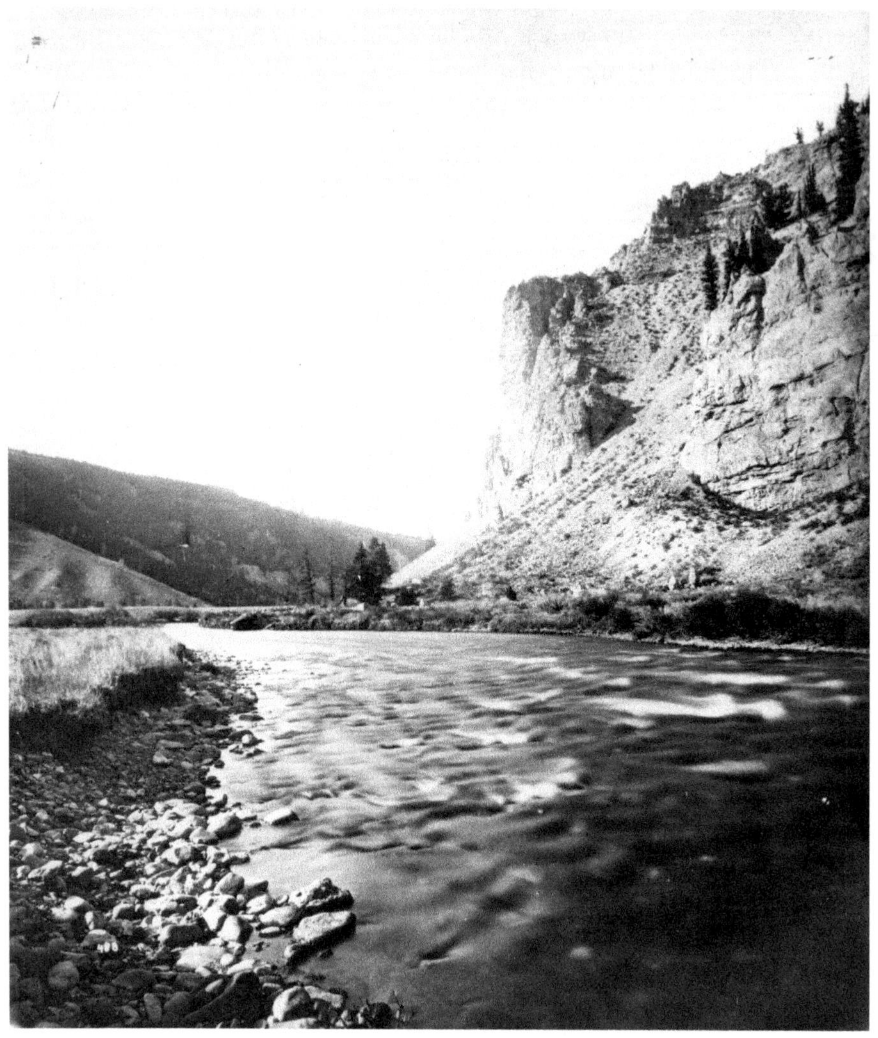

Figure 8.10. Bluffs along the upper West Gallatin (MM#33.5).
Left photo (1872): One of earliest photos in the Upper Gallatin. Photograph by W.H. Jackson during the 1872 Hayden Expedition. *USGS.*
Right photo (2013): Little has changed along this reach of river except for more trees along the river and some differences in the stream bank.

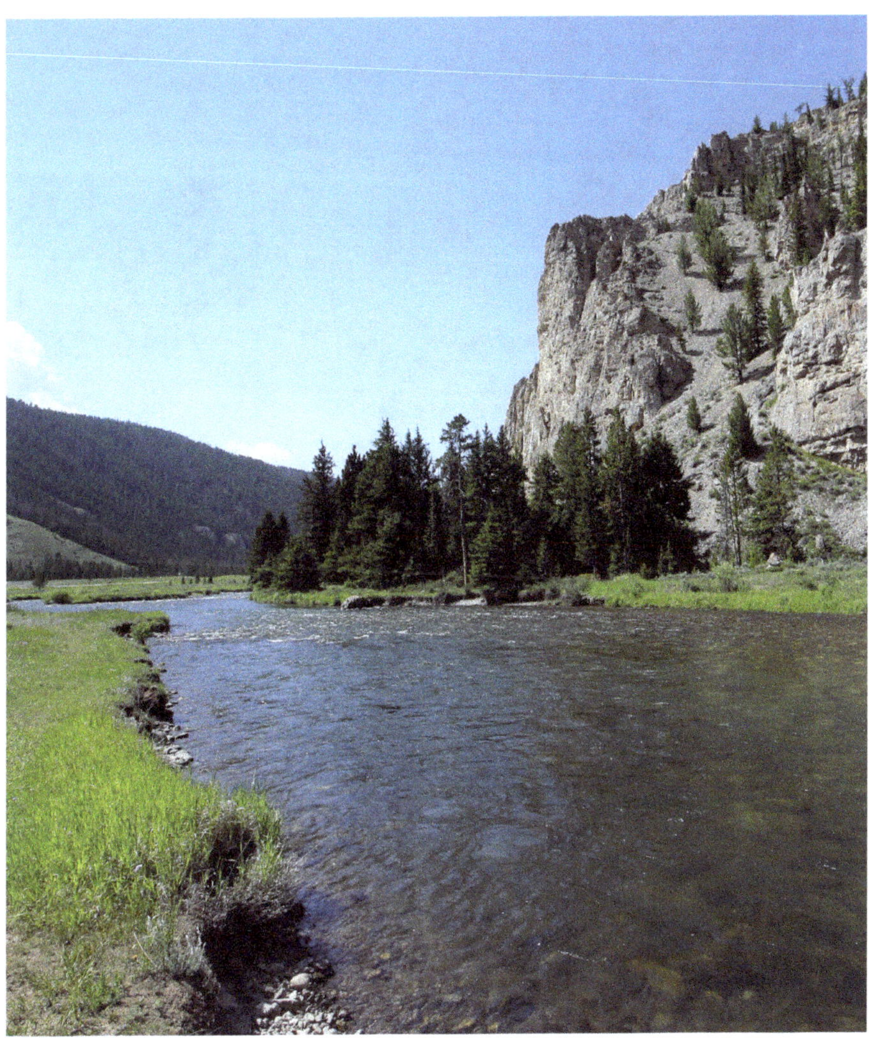

the family at the Arizona Elkhorn Ranch outside Tucson. I worked with Cruse in the early 1950s, and although he was at least fifty years older than me, he would work circles around me. I recall being at the Corral Bar, his favorite watering hole, once when Cruse was there. He was playing pinball, and a fellow came up to him to "coach" him on how to move the machine in your favor. After constant prodding by the man, Cruse had had enough, turned to the man, hit him square on the jaw and floored him—and then went back to his pinball game. That was Cruse—tough as nails but kind and helpful as anyone I've known.

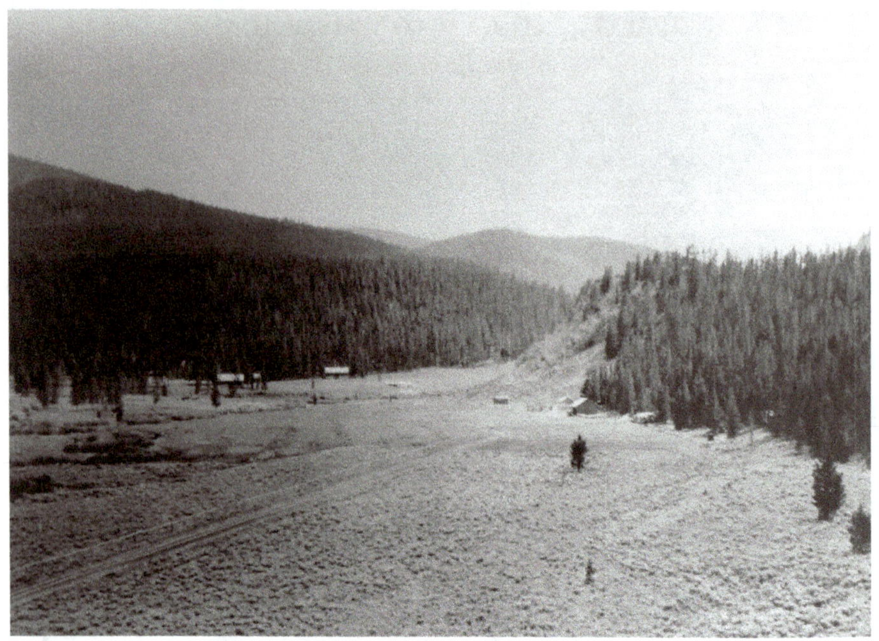

Figure 8.11. Elkhorn Ranch on Sage Creek, a tributary of the Gallatin River (MM#33.1).
Above photo (circa 1948): By this date, many of Elkhorn Ranch's cabins were constructed. In view are the barn and corrals on the right against the forest and a few of the guest cabins in the distance center. *MOR*.
Below photo (June 2016): By this date, all new cabins had been added, some having been moved from Seven Eleven Ranch up Sage Creek to the main ranch. In general, except for more cabins and barn buildings, including improvements of older cabins and the road into the ranch, much appears unchanged. (Repeat photo is wider to show more cabins.)

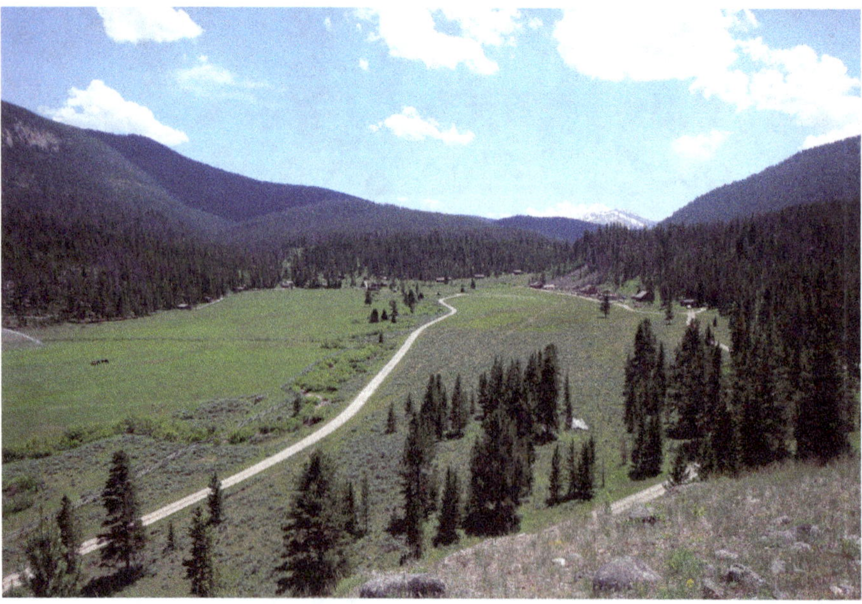

In the early years of Elkhorn Ranch, the Millers purchased two adjacent properties. One, purchased about 1925, was just south of the ranch near Snowflake Springs. This was called the Cow Camp because they kept a dairy herd there in early years. This property once belonged to Dr. Safley. It was homesteaded by Charles Marble in the 1890s and was proved up by Safley in 1911. The spring was then called Safley Spring. At the time Elkhorn bought this property, the Ruegemar family was living on it. At some earlier time, the Ruegemars probably were on some of the property the Millers had purchased as they expanded the original ranch property as Ruegemar apparently built the bridge over Sage Creek on the ranch, as it is now historically named after him. The other property was Seven Eleven Ranch up Sage Creek, discussed earlier as part of the Rising Sun Ranches. In 1988, the Miller family sold the Elkhorn Ranch to Dwight and Marian "Minxie" Minton, who, having been guests for many years, recognized its historic character and brought it back to its original condition with some necessary modern improvements (e.g., a modern kitchen). Much of the Elkhorn Ranch is now in the National Register of Historic Places. The Millers and Elkhorn Ranch played an important role in the 1926 founding of the Dude Ranch Association. At an informal meeting of dude ranchers hosted by the Northern Pacific Railroad in Bozeman, the group decided to form the Dude Ranch Association, selecting Ernest Miller of Elkhorn Ranch as secretary-treasurer.

Several photographs have been taken over time with Black Butte in the distance (Figures 8.12, 8.13 and 8.15 in sequence). Like Castle Rock (now Storm Castle) on the north end of the Canyon, Black Butte was a point of interest. Two of the photos, in 1907 (Figure 8.15) and in the early 1920s (Figure 8.13), show little evidence of a road, while the other shows the condition of the muddy road later in the 1920s (Figure 8.12).

South of the entrance into Elkhorn Ranch, the highway crosses Sage Creek and then the Gallatin River. The bridge over the Gallatin (MM#32.8) was constructed in 1959 in its present location after the river was rerouted (Figure 8.14). The old highway at that location once cut across pasture land to the west, then sharply angled to the east across the river and then angled back to the south again. This is just another example of how the present highway, greatly improved in the 1950s and '60s, often altered the channel alignment of the Gallatin River.

South of this bridge over the Gallatin, in the floodplain of the river across the road from the Tepee Creek pull-in (MM#32), is a large exclosure (Figure 8.16). This exclosure, initially built in 1948, was meant to demonstrate

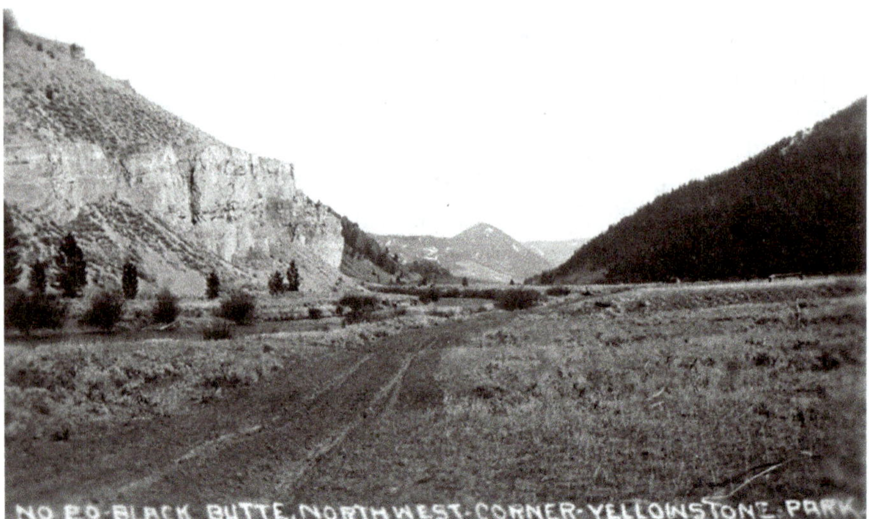

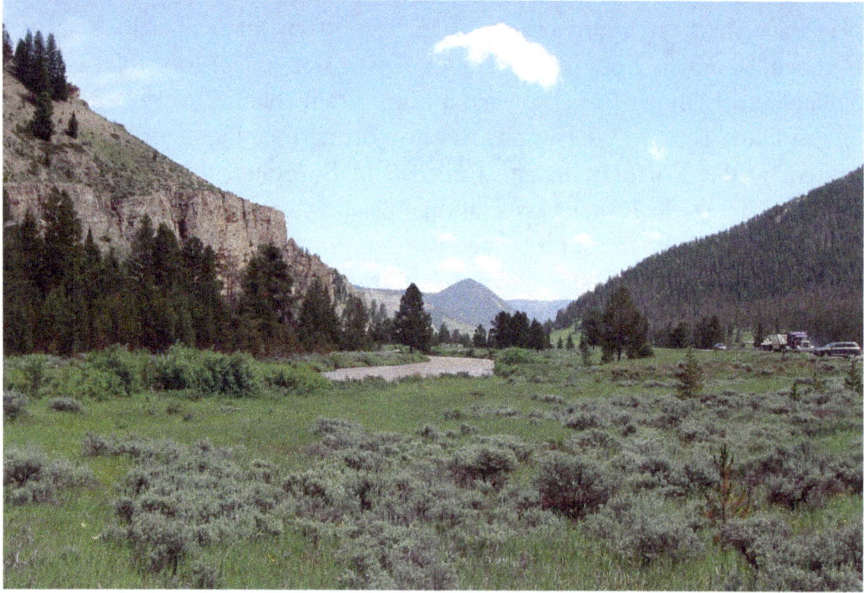

Figure 8.12. Looking south toward Black Butte from the east side of Highway 191 just north of Elkhorn Ranch turnoff (MM#33.1).
Upper photo (1920s): Road conditions seem almost impassable, but by this time the road to West Yellowstone was well traveled. *Gamel family*.
Lower photo (July 2013): Note that there is little or no evidence of the early road, and the new highway passes to the right of the auto seen on right of photo.

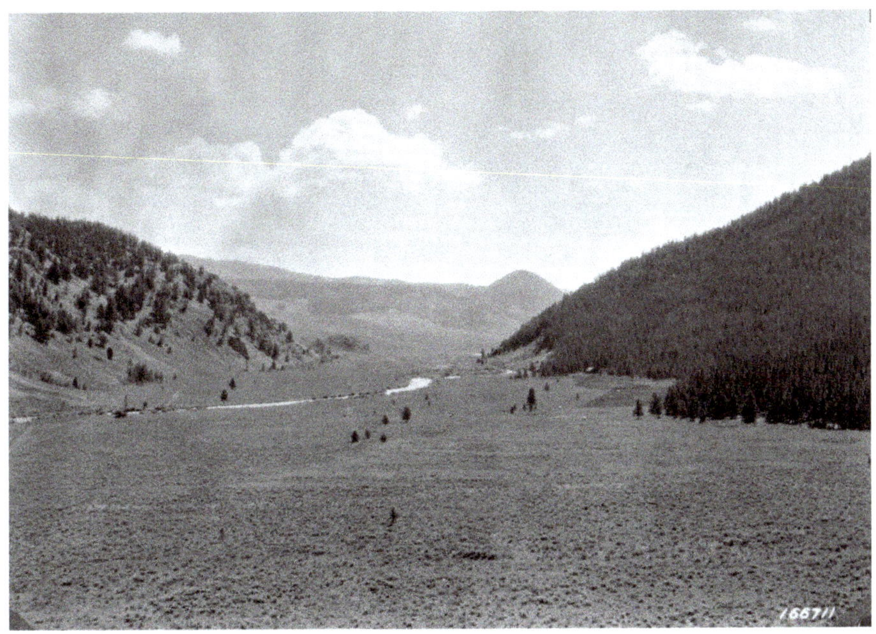

Figure 8.13. View of Black Butte from near Elkhorn Ranch (MM#33.1).
Above photo (circa 1920s): The sagebrush flat in the foreground was part of the "Cow Camp" property purchased by Elkhorn in its early years. The buildings belonging to the original homestead are seen in the distance along the forest edge. The roadway is slightly visible on left of photo. *GHM.*
Below photo (June 2016): Highway 191 cuts through the left side of the valley, and much of the sagebrush has been converted to pasture.

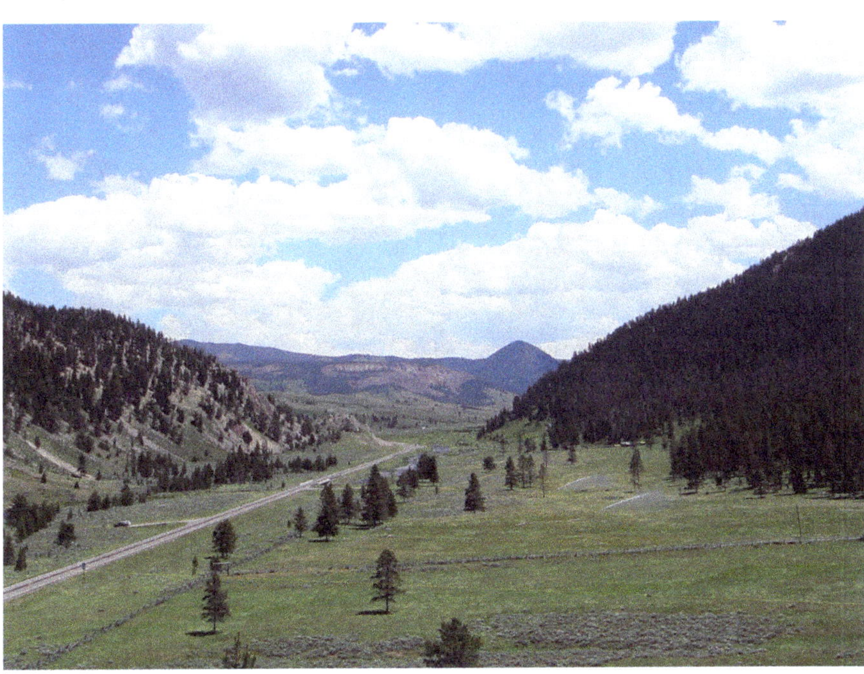

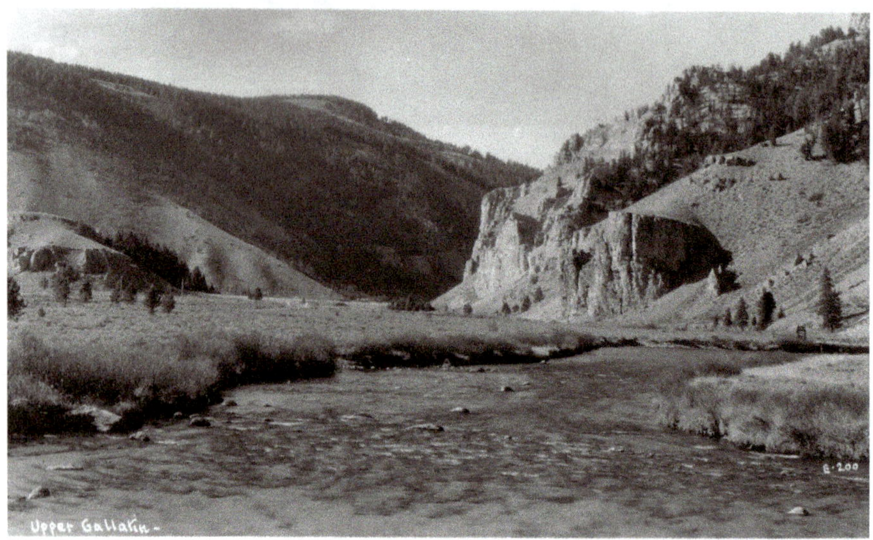

Figure 8.14. View to the north from near the bridge over the Gallatin River (called Tepee Bridge) about a quarter mile south of the Elkhorn Ranch turnoff (MM#32.8).
Above photo (circa 1910–20s): A free-flowing river with no apparent crossing. At this time, the bridge was just upstream (south) of this location, and this photo may have been taken from the bridge. *MOR.*
Below photo (2013): The river channel is dry because the Gallatin River was diverted to allow building of Tepee Bridge in 1959 (bridge on left in photo) with the river crossing at a right angle to the bridge.

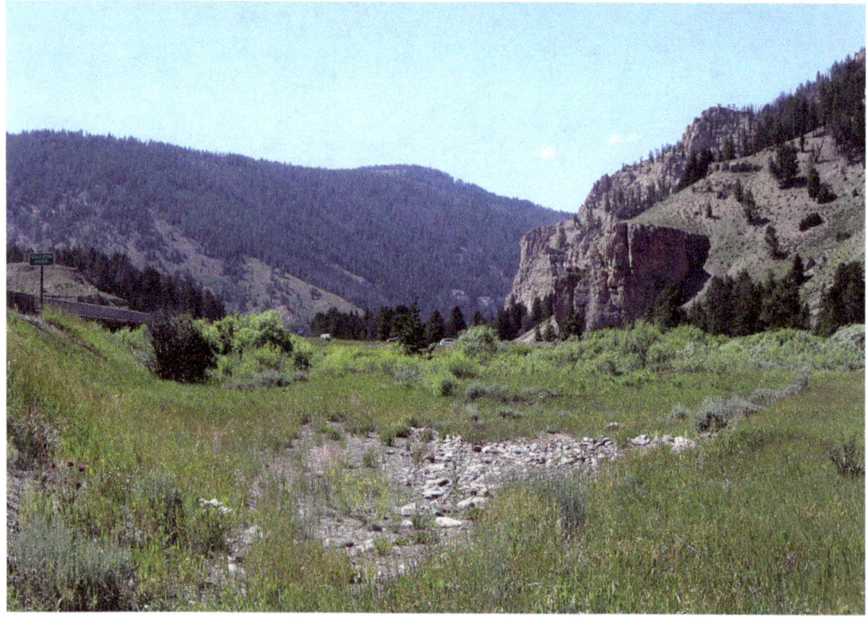

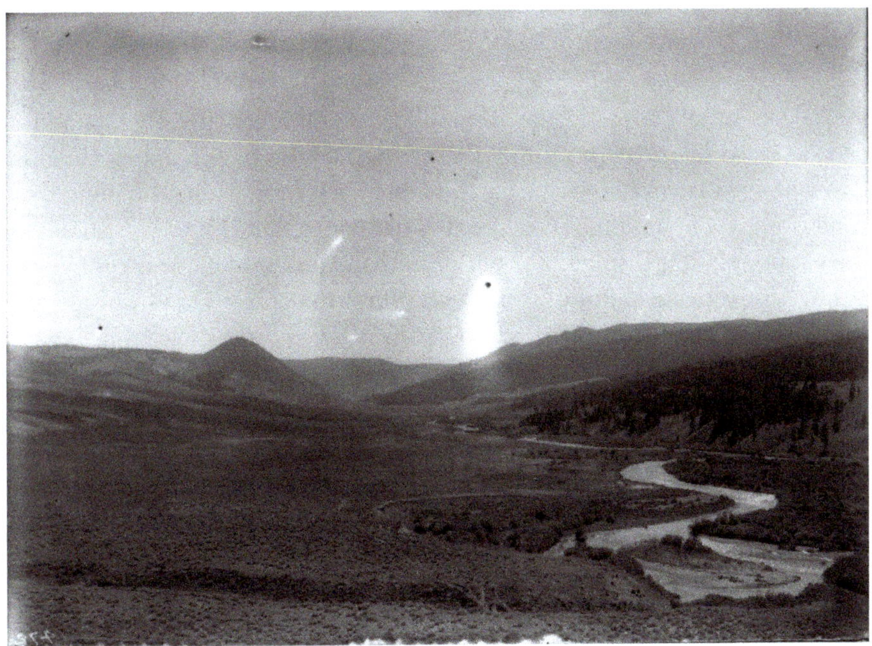

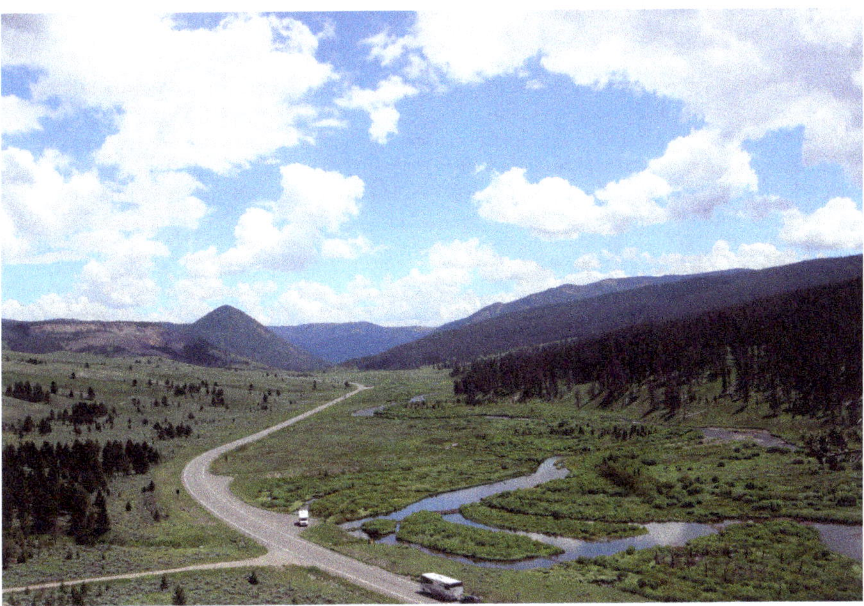

Figure 8.15. Looking south up the Gallatin River Valley toward Black Butte from near Tepee Creek pull-in about one mile north of Yellowstone National Park boundary (MM#32).
Upper photo (circa 1907): Photo shows no distinct road or trail, although the access to the upper Gallatin was often a wagon trail down Tepee Creek from Tom Miner Basin. *MOR*.
Lower photo (August 2013): Highway U.S. 191 cuts across photo headed south into the park. Lodgepole pine has invaded the sagebrush flat and beavers have modified the Gallatin River (in foreground), elevating the water table, which supports a dense willow stand.

the effects of elk browsing on the willow community. It was enlarged a decade or so later. At that time, the elk population in the upper Gallatin River basin was very large. In harsh winters, elk were eating anything they could find—willows, pine trees, et al. That is not the case today (2016), as the elk population is small, a result of climate and predation. It is obvious, if one stops at the pull-off at the exclosure, that the willows outside the exclosure, being lightly browsed and with a high water table from beaver dams, are doing very well, while those inside die back periodically because of competition from high density and no browsing. It is also interesting to note that in 1911, because of low elk numbers and cattle grazing and hunting in the early twentieth century that limited the elk range, the area from the Buffalo Horn/Tepee Creek divide, which is several miles up Tepee Creek south to the park boundary, was closed to grazing and elk hunting with creation of the Gallatin Wildlife Preserve. This area became a Wildlife Closed Area, which then was named a Management Area that was opened in 2010 to limited hunting by lottery.

Figure 8.16. Snowflake Springs exclosure along Gallatin River constructed in 1948 to demonstrate the effects of browsing by the local elk population (2017) (MM#32). The willows now grow all across the floodplain, a consequence of a greatly reduced elk herd in the upper Gallatin and an elevated water table from beaver damming. Willows within the exclosure die back about every ten years from high density and overcompetition for resources, excluding water.

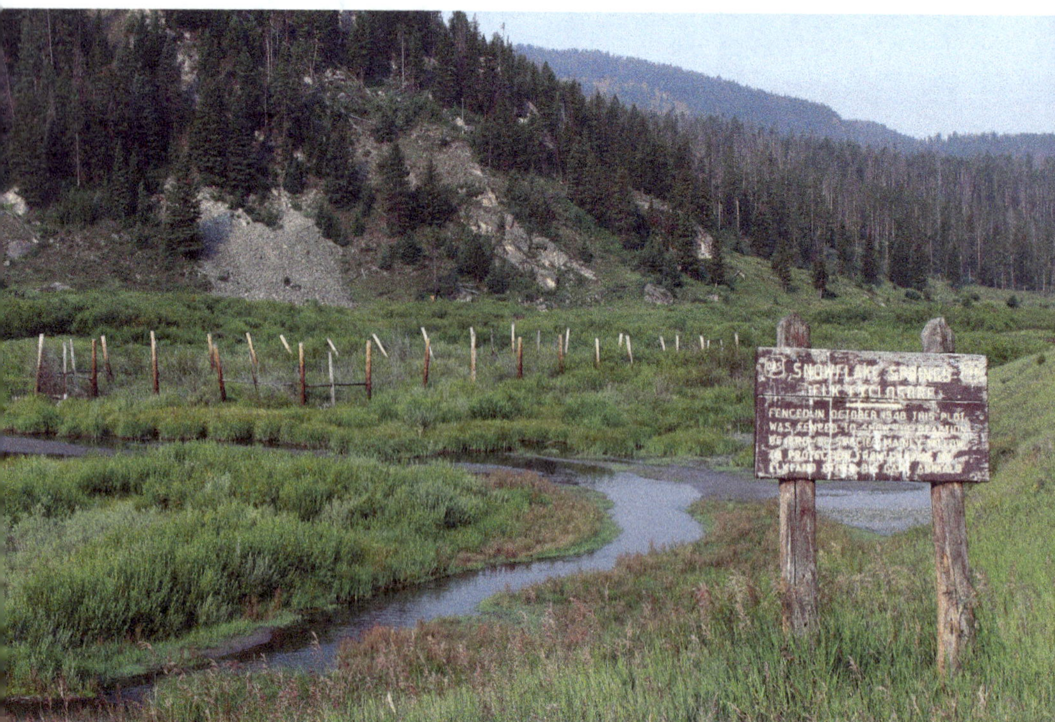

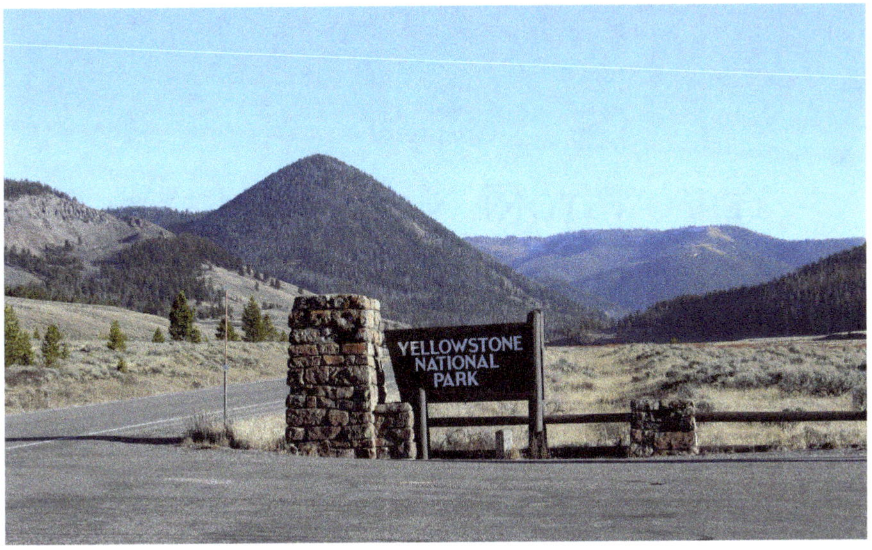

Figure 8.17 (2016). Entrance to Yellowstone National Park along the Gallatin Way (MM#31.2). This entrance location was created when this corner of the park was expanded in 1929. Black Butte is in the background.

The Tepee Creek pull-in (MM#32), across the highway from the exclosure, allows parking for hiking up Tepee Creek Valley. In the early 1900s, before a road reached this location, the Tepee Creek Valley was often the beginning of a trip from the Upper Basin of the Gallatin back to Bozeman. The traveler, often by wagon, went up Tepee Creek over into headwaters of Buffalo Horn Creek and then over the pass into Tom Miner Basin. From there, the trip went up the Yellowstone River Valley over Trail Creek to the west and into Bozeman. This is a reverse trip from that mentioned in Chapter 1 about ways early pioneers accessed the Upper Gallatin.

As mentioned earlier, in 1907, Black Butte was photographed from a vantage point just upslope from the Tepee Creek parking area, showing the condition of the sagebrush-covered rangeland in the foreground (Figure 8.15). Today, much of that sagebrush area is being invaded by lodgepole pine, a process that is happening throughout much of the Greater Yellowstone area. The cause for this invasion may be climatic or reduction in fires. That is uncertain.

A little farther south, the highway enters the northwest corner of Yellowstone National Park (Figure 8.17) (MM# 31.2). This became the northwestern corner of the park in 1929.

Chapter 9

Yellowstone National Park's Northwestern Boundary to Grayling Creek

(MM#31.2 to MM#19.2)

After entering Yellowstone National Park, the Gallatin Way (West Gallatin Highway) continues south toward West Yellowstone (Map 9.1). Until 1929, the northwest corner of Yellowstone National Park was about three miles south of its present location and about a mile north of Specimen Creek (circa MM#28). On March 1, 1929, three days after signing a bill that created Grand Teton National Park, President Hoover signed a bill changing the boundaries of Yellowstone National Park. Along the east side of the park, the boundary changed from a straight north–south line to one that predominantly followed topographic contours. In this northwest corner of the park, the new alignment (see Map 1.3) purposely included an extensive area of a petrified forest representing more than forty different volcanic events from the Absaroka Mountain Range during the Eocene-Oligocene period (50 to 30 million years ago). These volcanic events postdate the Laramide orogeny, the uplifting of the Rocky Mountains (80 to 55 million years ago). Each volcanic event caused mudslides of ash, soil and some lava, which buried forests that were then petrified in place over time. The forests included redwoods, maples, magnolias, oaks, dogwoods and pines, a forest very similar to that in the Southeast United States today except for the presence of redwoods. New forests grew on the new land, some trees being five hundred years old, only to be buried by another volcanic event. These layers were exposed over time as the mountains slowly eroded. This petrified forest in the northwest corner of the park has many more layers than the one on Specimen Ridge near the Lamar River within the heart of

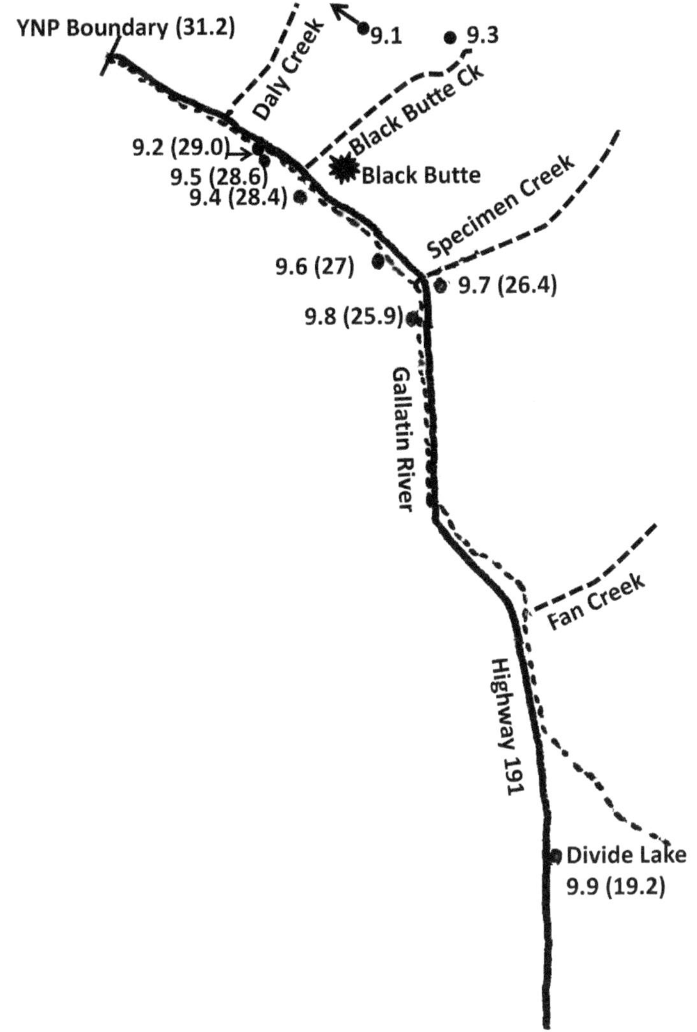

Map 9.1. Yellowstone National Park boundary to Grayling Creek (MM#31.2 to 19.2). Map of photo locations, including those along Highway 191 and the Gallatin River (mile markers in parentheses).

the park. Being available to the public with no constraints on collecting prior to the area becoming park, petrified wood was being gathered and removed for commercial sale.

On the ridge to the east between the head of Daly Creek (MM#30.5) and Tom Miner Basin, there is a very large petrified stump of prehistoric redwood (*Sequoia langsdorfii*), approximately fourteen to sixteen feet (four to five meters)

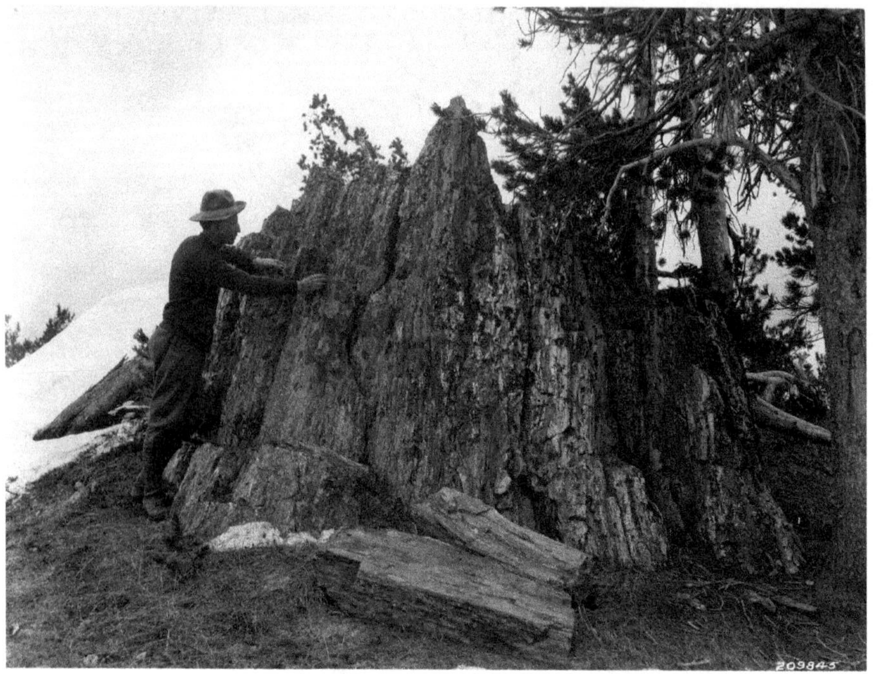

Figure 9.1. Petrified sequoia (fossil redwood) stump (fourteen to sixteen feet in diameter) located on the Daly Creek Sky Rim trail. This may be one of the world's largest petrified stumps, according to Erling Dorf, a paleobotanist who studied fossil forests in Yellowstone National Park.
Left photo (1926): Petrified stump showing petrified logs in front of it, which are missing in the following photo, removed probably before this area was protected by Yellowstone National Park expansion in 1929.
Right photo (2016): The stump looks unchanged except for the missing petrified logs.

in diameter at the base (circa forty-seven feet in circumference) (Figure 9.1). This may be one of the largest petrified stumps in the world, according to Erling Dorf, who visited the location with me in 1964. Dorf was a professor of paleobotany at Princeton University and one of the world's experts on fossil forests. He had extensively studied the fossil forests on Specimen Ridge near the Lamar Valley for many years before his visit to this site.

About a half mile into the park from the northwest entrance there is a pull-off into Daly Creek (MM#30.5). Daly Creek basin is much more open than most forested areas in the region and thus has been a major location for elk in the winter. In the 1950s and '60s, when the Yellowstone National Park northern elk herd, including the Upper Gallatin herd, was considered too large, the number was reduced through eliminating some herds within

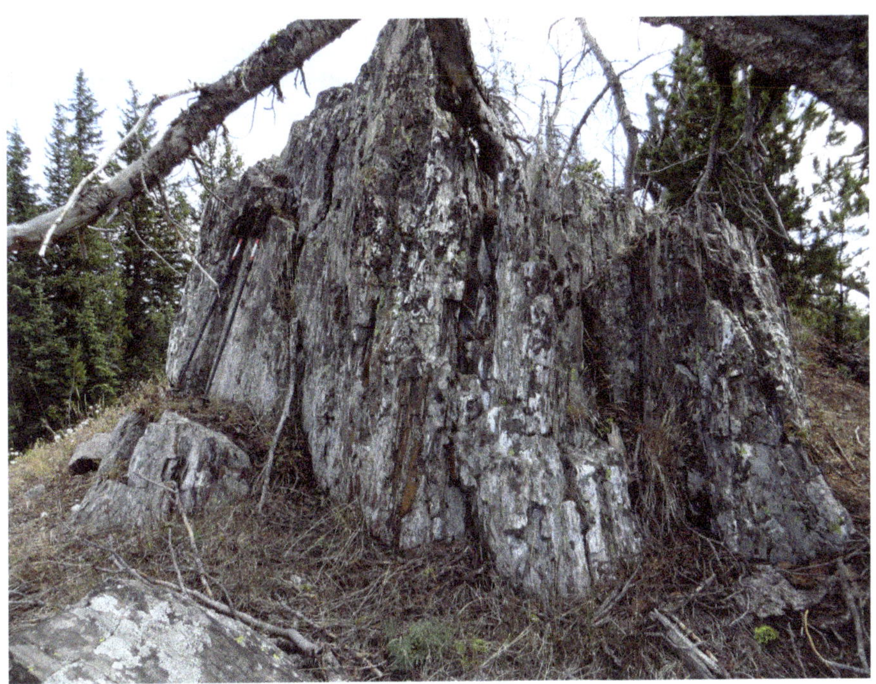

the center of the park through shooting by park rangers and trapping and transplanting elk to other states, for example, Arizona, northern Michigan and even the Appalachians. Trapping and transporting elk were not new to the park at that time. Starting in the early 1900s and continuing well into the 1930s, Yellowstone National Park was a source of elk for zoological parks, as well as reestablishing herds in other locations such as Glacier National Park, Washington and other states. Elk were lured into traps at night with hay or hazed into enclosures during the day. In the early 1960s, Daly Creek was a location of one of the elk traps, a large fenced area like a corral into which the elk were driven, often by aircraft, then put in a shoot, dehorned (if bulls) and loaded onto trucks. There is no longer evidence of the traps in the Daly basin. A hike up Daly Creek can be a very pleasant outing but not on a hot day in summer because it is so open.

Across the Gallatin River from the Daly Creek pull-in is a large open grass-sagebrush-covered area sloping up to the forest and mountains, with Lodgepole Creek flowing through it. Much of this area was homesteaded by E.C. Alderson in 1908. The chimney from Alderson's cabin still stands on the south side of this open area. In the middle of the area where there is a row of trees there once was a sawmill. This forested gully is now referred to as Saw Mill Gulch.

About a mile south from the park entrance, the highway takes a sharp turn to the west around an earthflow that continues to move downhill and cause changes to the roadbed. Just before entering this curve, one can see a location along the river just below the curve where the roadway in 1914 crossed the river. There is still evidence of the abutments built to support a small bridge (Figure 9.2). The old roadway, which originally was located closer to the bench to the east and south of Daly Creek, turned west near the curve "under" what is now elevated highway and crossed the river. The old road is still evident across the river leading away to the southwest from the abutment area. Across the river just south of the curve, there is another earthflow that almost reaches the river. At its base is the remnant of the old county road, most of it having been eroded away by river action or covered by earthflow material.

Black Butte comes up at MM#28.5. Black Butte was a photo point in the past (see the previous chapter for several photos). Black Butte geology is andesite porphyry stock, which was extruded millions of years ago to form the cone-like mountain. Black Butte Creek flows past Black Butte north of the mountain coming from a watershed headed by cliffs with many petrified

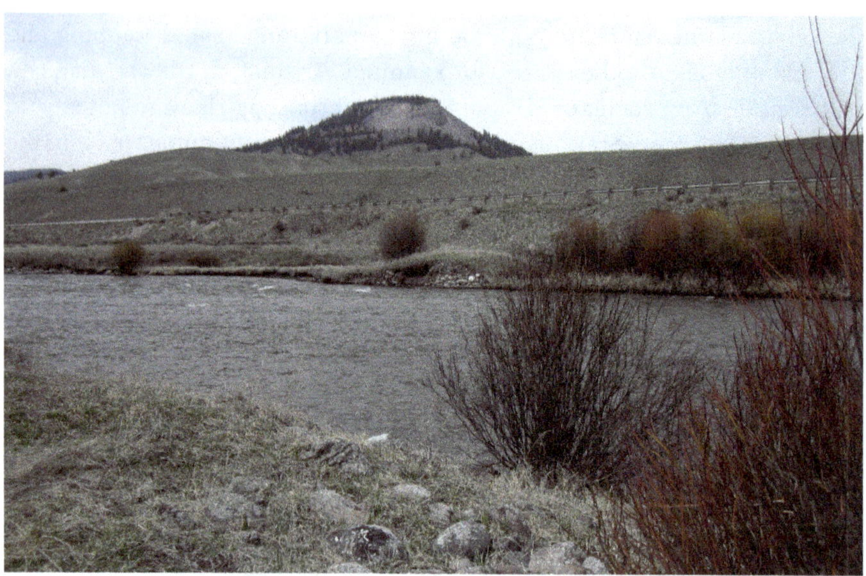

Figure 9.2 (2015). Abutments in foreground and across river for the early county road built in 1911–14 that crossed the Gallatin River (about MM#29) upstream from Daly Creek. This crossing was abandoned in 1918, when the U.S. Forest Service built an improved road along the east side of the river to near Specimen Creek. The present elevated highway with railing is visible above the willows across the river. Crown Butte is in the background.

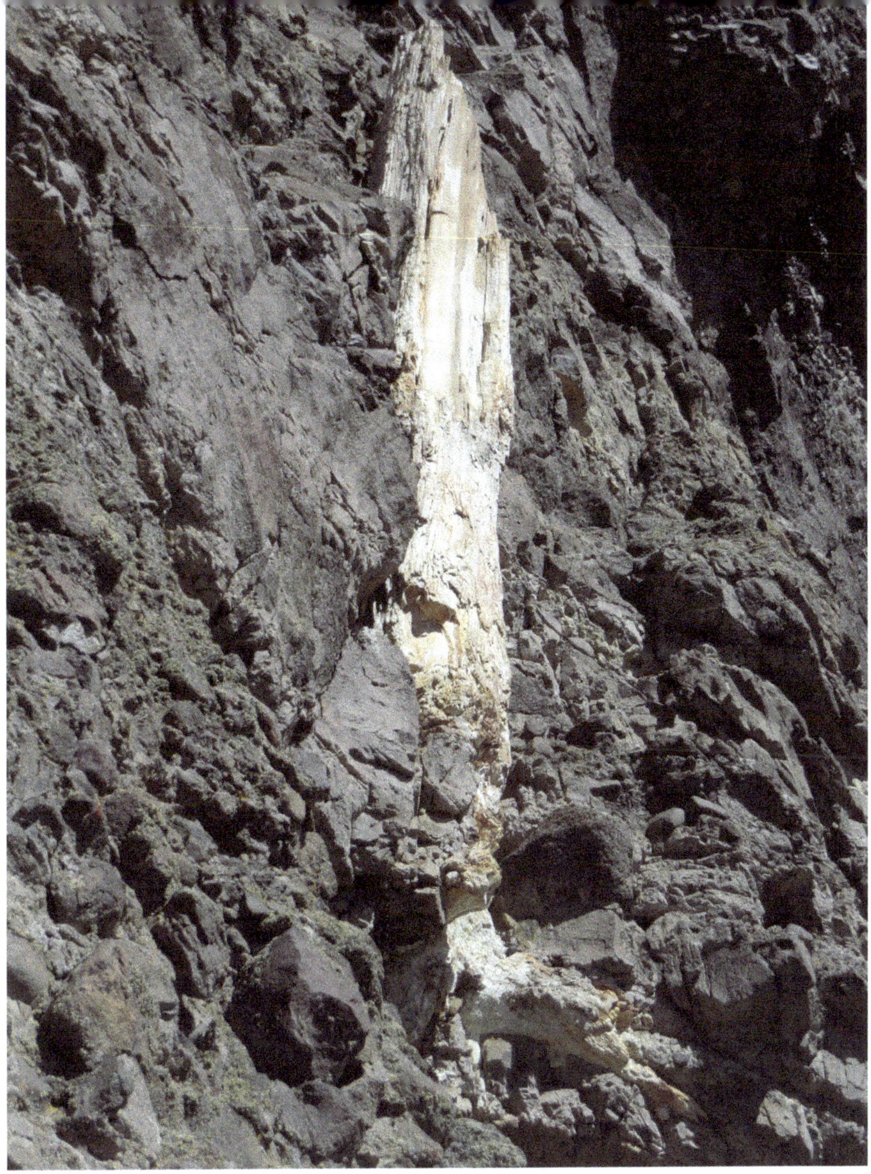

Figure 9.3 (2016). Fossil tree (redwood) in a cliff face of volcanic ash and mud deposit on the side of King Butte at the head of Black Butte Creek in northwestern Yellowstone National Park. The image shows the tree trunk, approximately twenty feet high, and part of the root system, demonstrating that the tree was buried and petrified in place.

tree specimens. If one looks east up the valley, one can see the face of King Butte, which appears to have many horizontal layers. Each of these layers represents a volcanic event. This area and that up Specimen Creek a little farther south may have up to forty-eight layers with petrified trees from different ancient forests. Some layers are thick enough to hold much of a whole petrified tree trunk with roots (Figure 9.3). A pull-off is located across the highway from the Black Butte Trail. The trail follows Black Butte Creek and leads to the cliffs with petrified trees (about two and a half miles). Limited mining occurred in the Black Butte Creek drainage in the early twentieth century. Both hillside mining and hydrologic/sluice mining took place. There is a decaying miner's cabin in a side drainage of Black Butte Creek, and evidence in the cabin (e.g., a Sears Roebuck catalogue from the early 1920s) indicates mining nearly up to the time this area became part of Yellowstone National Park in 1929.

This area along the Gallatin Way was very popular with hunters as Yellowstone National Park, with an apparent abundance of elk, was only a few miles away (Figure 9.4). Although the elk population in this area was declining, hunting continued up until the designation of the area as the Gallatin Wilderness Preserve in 1911, which then excluded all big game hunting. Today, the area near Tepee Creek and west of the river is a Wildlife Management Area with very limited hunting.

Across the valley from Black Butte is Black Butte Ranch. This ranchland once belonged to Nelson Story Jr. of Bozeman, son of Nelson Story, an early pioneer of Bozeman. Nelson Story Jr. acquired several parcels in the

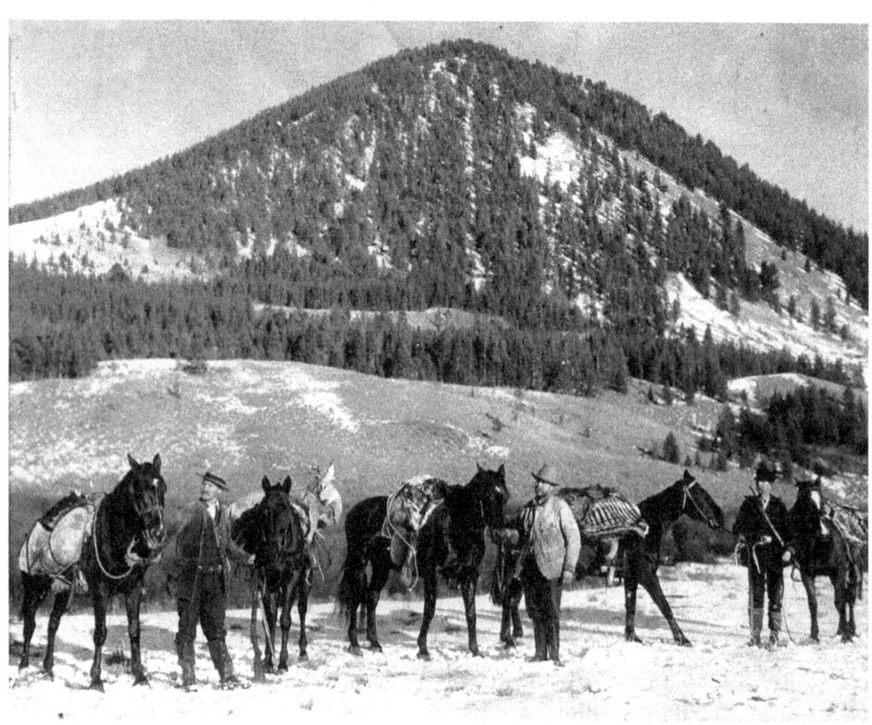

1920s, two of them early homesteads. One homestead belonged to Lester Pierstorff, who homesteaded in 1916, and one belonged to W.C. Alderson, who homesteaded in 1908. Through three land trades with the federal government, Story filled in the holding to the acreage it is today. According to Pierstorff, there once was a two-story house on the property that burned down in 1902. He did not recall who the owner was. The location he describes for the house today has the appearance of a rock footing or foundation. Black Butte Ranch is presently owned by the family of Marc and Doris Patten, my parents, who purchased the land in 1955 from the daughter of Nelson Story Jr. In the early years of Black Butte Ranch, Marc Patten raised quarter horses. The ranch is now a private family ranch owned by the children and families of Marc and Doris.

The use of this land during the early 1900s makes one think about how the Upper Gallatin Canyon might have looked today. In 1914, the early

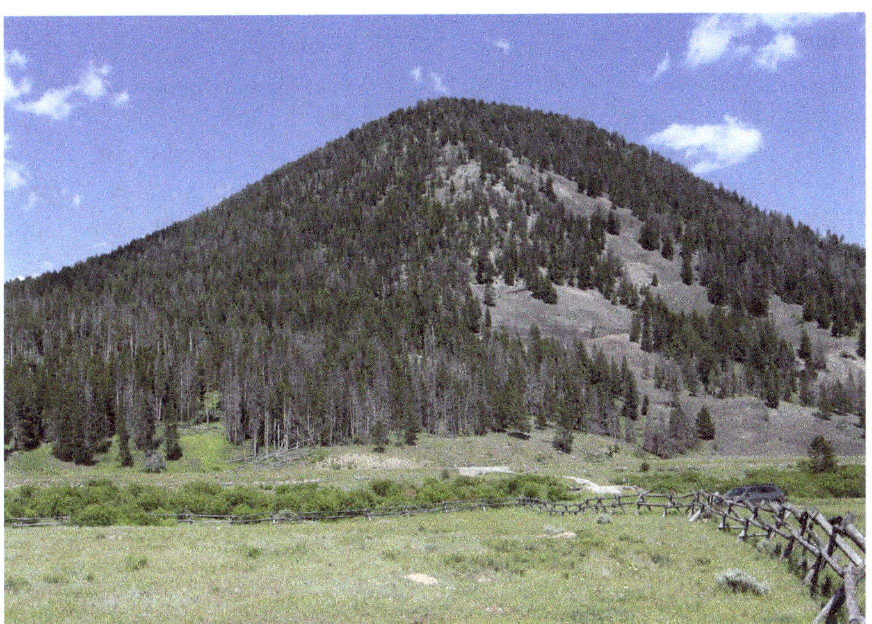

Figure 9.4. Black Butte located in the northwestern corner of Yellowstone National Park (MM#28.4).
Left photo (circa 1910): Hunting party at Black Butte. The person on the left is Albert Schlechten, who photographed many locations in the Gallatin Canyon. Others are Pratt and Schergie. The location is on the bench to the west of the Gallatin River where the county road was located in 1914. The county had acquired a forty-foot right of way in 1911. *GHM.*
Right photo (2015): Black Butte Ranch pastureland with jack fence showing the roadway to the ranch from Highway 191. The forest has expanded on Black Butte, but also much has been killed by mountain pine bark beetle.

county road to the west entrance of Yellowstone National Park (West Yellowstone) passed across the flat terrace to the west of the river above the floodplain across from Black Butte. An improved road was constructed by the U.S. Forest Service in 1918 near its present location on the east side of the river. In the early years of private ownership of these lands, owners would lease land to mining companies that explored for gold along the floodplain of the Gallatin River. There is still evidence of test pits along the floodplain. In 1888, Thomas Michener tried to make a claim on all "unclaimed" properties from West Fork to the park line, which at that time included this area. Although this area didn't prove up, one of the primary purposes for Michener's claims was to stop the Milwaukee Railroad from building a railroad through the Gallatin Canyon to the park. To think, if gold had been discovered, much of the Gallatin River valley from near West Fork to the park boundary might now look like the Alder Gulch floodplain near Virginia City, Montana (Figure 9.5).

Just south of Black Butte Creek, there is a small drainage coming from the east called Wickiup Creek, apparently once called Wigwam Creek and possibly Riley Spring. The name is based on the existence of wickiups (dwellings formed with branches) built by Sheepeater Indians (part of the Bannock Indians) that are still in evidence a short way up the creek. Aubrey Haines, a Yellowstone National Park historian, has argued that the wickiups are likely of Crow or Piegan (Blackfeet) origin. Regardless, these are evidence of the occupation of this area prior to arrival of pioneers, miners and homesteaders.

About where Wickiup Creek crosses under the highway, there was a soldier station built in 1902 to guard this corner of the park against poachers and unpermitted tree cutting. It was also used as a check station after the road was completed, about 1914–15. This check station was eventually manned by soldiers who were stationed at a larger soldier station built in 1910 just south of Specimen Creek (see discussion on this station later). The small check station, according to Lester Pierstorff, who had his homestead on Monument Creek at that time, "was a double log cabin at the Riley Spring on the east side of Specimen Flat three-quarters of a mile north of Specimen Creek." Although the station had a cabin and barn, today there is no evidence of the station, and Riley Spring may be the flow of Wickiup Creek from its valley into the Gallatin River.

On the west side of the river across from Wickiup Creek was another park ranger station (Figure 9.6) built in June 1918 after the 1910 station south of Specimen Creek (see Figure 9.7) burned down in March 1918. Park

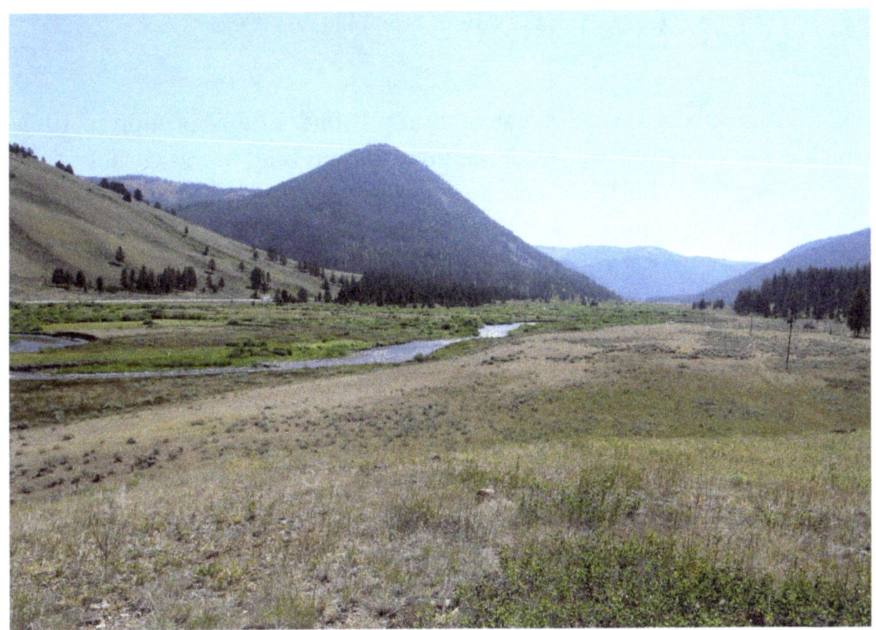

Figure 9.5. Floodplains of two Montana rivers with different historic uses.
Above photo (2016): Gallatin River Valley near Black Butte (MM#28.4) showing a grassy terrace and willow-covered floodplain along the river that are undisturbed by mining. Test pits dug in the terrace in the 1920s showed no evidence of gold, thus no active mining occurred in the floodplain in this area.
Below photo (2016): Alder Gulch tailing piles near Virginia City and Nevada City, Montana. From 1898 through 1922, large floating placer mining dredges chewed up the valley bottom, destroying anything in their path, including several communities, depositing tailings behind them.

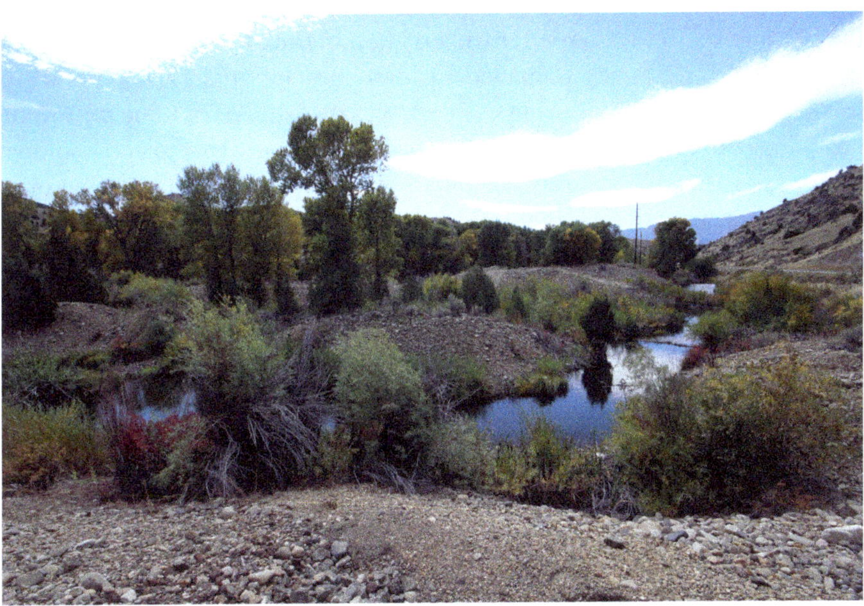

records indicate that a full ranger station was built at this location in 1925, which is incorrect, as there were no more stations built in this corner of the park after 1918. The 1925 record may be a record of an improvement on the 1918 ranger station. The 1918 station, which included a house, barn and corrals, housed a ranger, often with family. Originally, the station was used year-round, but as its condition deteriorated, it was limited to only seasonal summer use, and rangers and their families were offered a house trailer to live in. The rangers who lived here patrolled this corner of the park, which eventually included a large campground at Specimen Creek that was established sometime after the 1929 expansion of the park. The campground was closed and removed in 1968 at the same time the park ranger station and the bridge to the station were razed.

About a half mile farther south is the turn-in for Specimen Creek parking (MM#26.5). Specimen Creek received its name because of the presence of specimens from many petrified trees up the valley, in some places more extensive than on Specimen Ridge in the center of the park. For example, about two miles up Specimen Creek on the slope of a small tributary, many petrified forest layers are evident, with several exposed standing stumps, some very large and some quite tall. The gravels in Specimen Creek usually contain pieces of petrified wood; however, as this is in a national park, none of the petrified wood pieces can be collected or removed from the park.

When considering the history of the Specimen Creek area and the northwest corner of the park, one must remember that in the early days of the park up to 1918, even after the creation of the National Park Service in 1916, the U.S. Army managed Yellowstone National Park. The army was brought in initially during the early years of the park to help prevent poaching, among other problems. To do this, the army placed soldier stations at strategic locations, the northwest corner of the park being one. Prior to construction of the 1918 station used by the park, there were two earlier soldier stations: a small one, mentioned earlier, built in 1902 near Wickiup Creek and used as a check station, and a larger station built in 1910. This latter station, lost to fire in 1918, was on a terrace just southeast across Specimen Creek from the parking area (Figure 9.7). The cause of the fire is unknown but has been blamed on a faulty chimney, disgruntled soldiers or the fact that the army was no longer in charge and the soldiers were being moved with no need for the station, and thus the buildings were burned. As mentioned earlier, in 1918 another station was built, probably by the park, farther north on the west side of the river shortly after the 1910 soldier station burned down. In 1904, during the

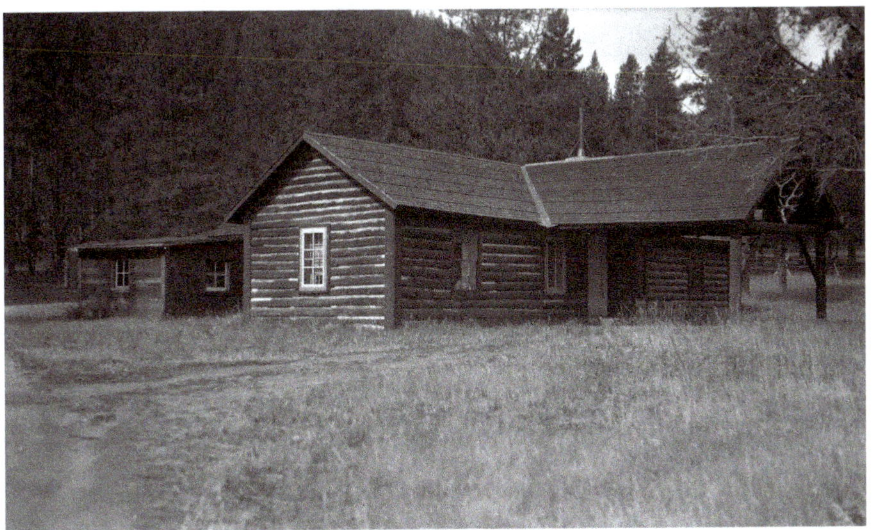

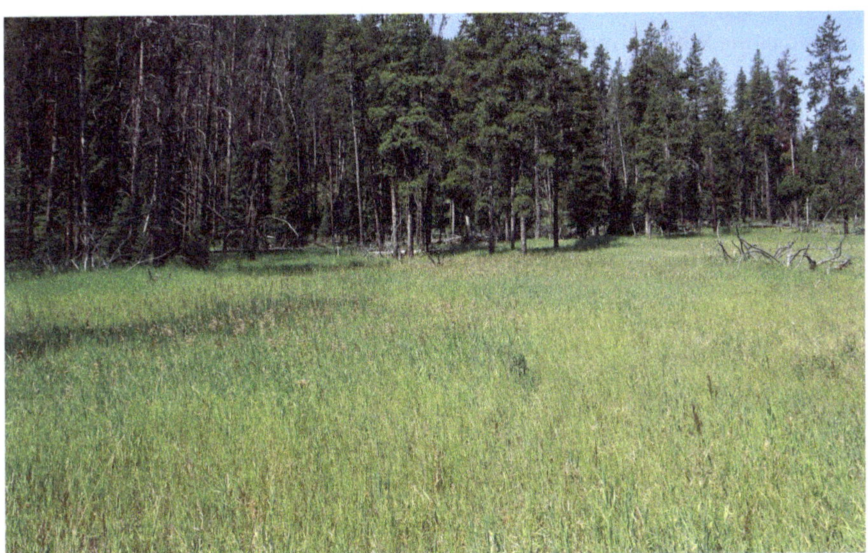

Figure 9.6. Yellowstone National Park Gallatin Station, built in 1918 on the west side of the Gallatin River near the northwestern corner of the park.
Upper photo (circa 1925): The station after only seven years of use. *YNP Photograph Collection, YELL 31670.*
Lower photo (2016): The present condition of the location of the 1918 Gallatin station, with no evidence of the station after it was removed in 1968.

stay of soldiers at the station built in 1902, two soldiers were skiing to the Riverside Station (park headquarters once located on the Madison River, outside the present location of West Yellowstone). On their venture, one was lost in an avalanche a short distance south of Specimen Creek. The creek near where he was lost is now called Snowslide Creek, which flows into the Gallatin River from the west.

One often thinks of this northwest corner of the park and the surrounding national forest as always being relatively pristine except for the presence of the army. However, history tells us differently. In 1863, a group called the Fairweather Party camped at Black Butte Creek. While there, they sank a shaft to bedrock looking for gold. They cut the date on the windlass, which was still there in 1916. Mining up Black Butte Creek was discussed earlier. In the period from 1860 to the 1890s, Kick Rock from Henry's Lake in Idaho built a cabin on Black Butte Creek. No evidence of this cabin exists today.

Up the hill, above the location of the 1918 ranger station on the west side of the river, along the park's north–south boundary, was a fully developed mining camp with cabin, mine adit, water lines from a local spring and other outbuildings. This mine was built and operated by Big Lou Bartholomew (also Lou Bart), a historic character from this region. This mine claim was active well into the 1940s or 1950s. Lou Bart had come to the canyon in 1898, operated a sawmill at Greek Creek and purchased land where Pete

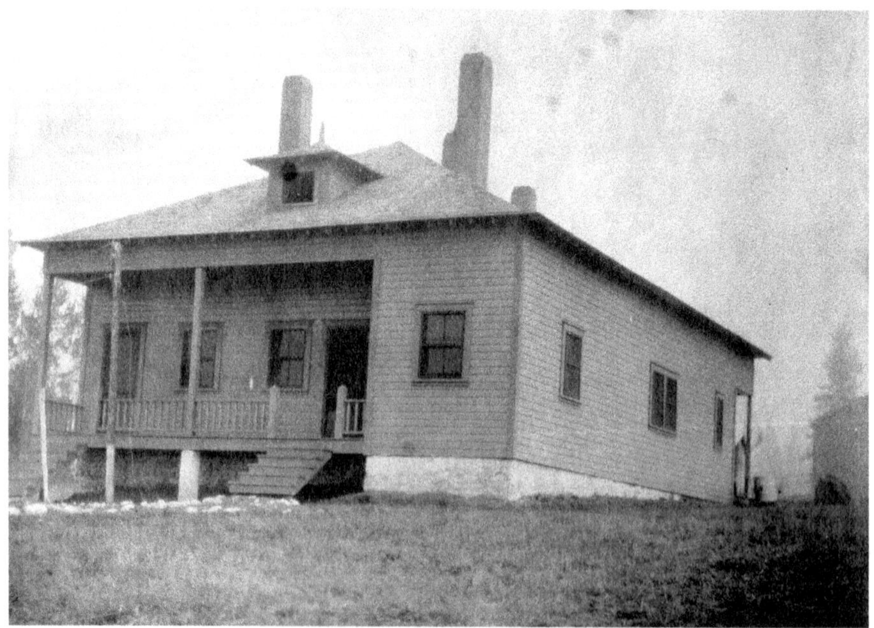

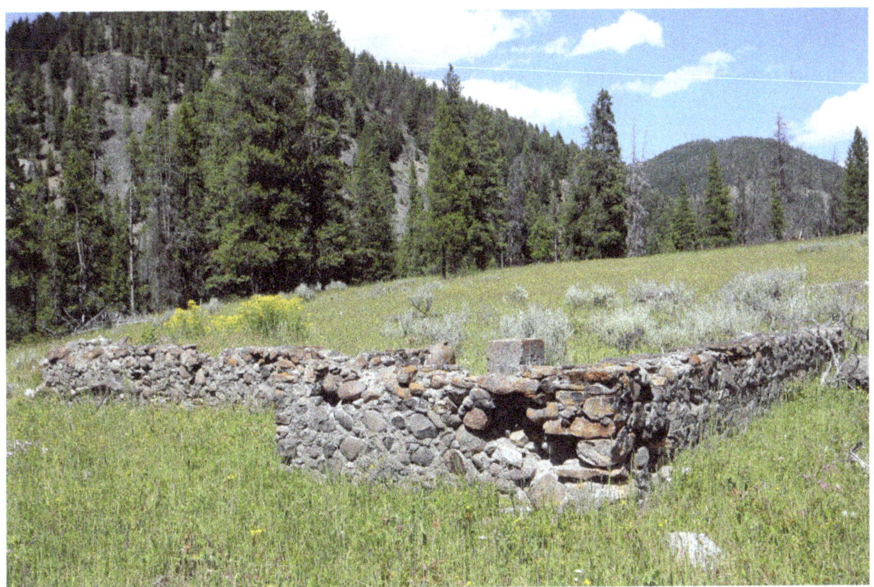

Figure 9.7. Location of the Gallatin Soldier Station in the northwestern corner of Yellowstone National Park (near MM#26.4).
Left photo (circa 1910–18): Soldier station constructed in 1910 and burned down in 1918. In the back right side of picture is the station barn. *YNP Photograph Collection, YELL 203479.*
Right photo (2016): Foundation remains of the building.

Karst eventually settled (see chapter 5). After selling that land, he built two cabins where Rainbow Ranch is now located. When in the upper Gallatin and starting his mining efforts, he decided to attach wings to a bicycle, hoping to fly. He cycled down the roof of a barn and adjacent shed at the Story Ranch (now Black Butte Ranch) and "failed" to fly (surprise). He had announced this effort in Bozeman, and many came out to see the spectacle.

Additional development in that area prior to 1889 include a squatter, possibly a homesteader, who had a claim on the sagebrush flat west across the highway from the Specimen Creek parking. He used this area for a very productive hay field with timothy and clover. When Montana became a state in 1889, this strip of land was ceded to the government, the man was bought out and his buildings were destroyed. It appears that he had diverted some of Specimen Creek for irrigation, as evidence of the irrigation ditch and diversion point take-out is still apparent a short way up Specimen Creek.

Heading south, one crosses Specimen Creek bridge (MM#26.5), built in 1955, replacing an older bridge just upstream built around 1928; the abutments of this bridge are still visible at the river near the parking area.

From there, the road follows a straight southerly route. In the Gallatin Road rebuilding period of the 1950s and '60s, this straight road replaced the old highway that, after crossing Specimen Creek, turned west crossing the Gallatin River and continued down the west side of the valley. Although signs of the bridge over the Gallatin River are not apparent other than slightly raised abutments near the river, one can still see evidence of the bank cuts and roadway along the far side of the valley. Except for highway improvements, much of this area in the park has not changed much since the early part of the twentieth century (Figure 9.8). About three miles south of Specimen Creek at MM#23.6, the new highway crosses to the west side of the Gallatin River on a bridge built in 1955. This was all part of the major roadwork during that period. Here, the road intersects the path of the old road, turning back into the valley from the west. The old roadway is still visible east of the highway from this point south to below the Fan Creek/Fawn Pass parking area (MM#21.9), where its route is across the lower floodplain near Bacon Rind Creek and then to below the parking area. The new road required a new bridge (culvert) for Bacon Rind. The Fan Creek/Fawn Pass parking area built as part of highway improvement allows hikers, horse riders and skiers access to interior areas within this northwest corner of the park.

Along this section of highway, north of the Fan Creek/Fawn Pass parking area, is a turn to the west into a gravel road to Bacon Rind Creek parking (MM#22.7). This road was built into Bacon Rind Creek to service the Bacon Rind Road Camp (mess hall, dorm, bunkhouses and stables), built in 1929–30. The Road Camp was also occasionally used by the CCC after its use for early roadway construction crews and eventually cleaned up by that group. Some of the Road Camp buildings were removed in 1968, at the same time the Gallatin Ranger Station was removed. In 1988, the Bacon Rind dorm (possibly a two-story stable with dorm) was determined not eligible by the Montana Historic Preservation Office and was altered and moved to the west entrance of Yellowstone National Park. I recall seeing the two-story building in the 1950s and '60s and perhaps later, with what appeared to be garage doors (stable doors?). If one hikes up the Bacon Rind trail a short distance from the parking area, one can still find evidence of the "paved" road that served the buildings in that area. Also, there is some evidence of the platforms where bunkhouses and other buildings were located off the paved road.

The highway heading south from the Fan Creek/Fawn Pass parking area is straight until the valley narrows and the forest begins to encroach on

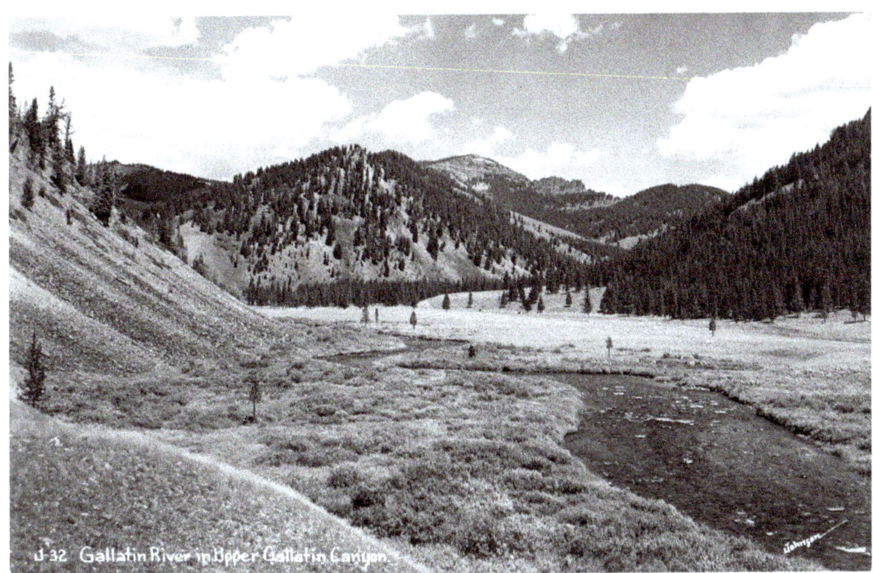

Figure 9.8. Upper Gallatin River Valley looking north toward Specimen Creek valley (across the Gallatin River from MM#25.9).
Above photo (circa 1915–20s): This location is just downstream from where the 1914 road crossed the Gallatin River. One road cut can be seen in the center of the photo near the mouth of Specimen Creek valley (the valley entering from the right center of photo). *GHM.*
Below photo (2016): The new highway constructed in the 1950s and '60s on an elevated roadbed is slightly visible on the other side of the river near the forest (truck is visible on the highway). The river channel has migrated only slightly over one hundred years.

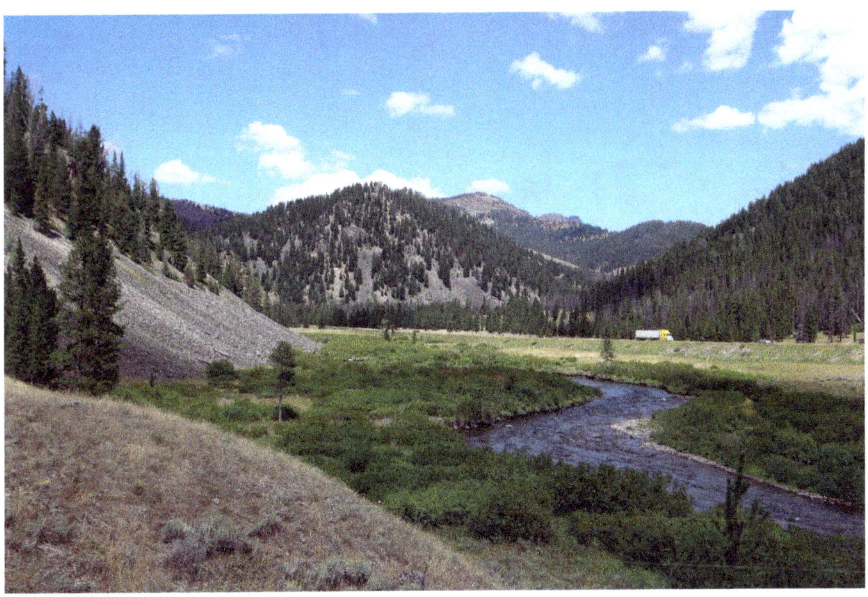

the valley. Some evidence still exists of the old highway route in the open sagebrush areas along the west side of the road. The highway also passes a burned area recovering from the 2003 Rathbone Fire. Extensive numbers of young lodgepole pine are growing up in the understory of this forest. This is a typical recovery process for lodgepole pine forests following fire, as many lodgepole pine trees have serotinous cones (cones that open from heat). This fire moving northeast was stopped at the highway and Bacon Rind Creek valley. The park was determined not to have it extend farther east into the park, where it would burn into areas where there were recent past fires, one in the 1950s or '60s and the big one in 1988. If the fire had jumped Bacon Rind Creek valley to the north, it would have been difficult to stop for many miles, as this forest is dense mature lodgepole pine forest prime for fires.

Along the straightaway heading south from the Fan Creek/Fawn Pass parking area, at MM#20.3 there is a turn-in to the east into a short road leading to a parking area for those heading up the Big Horn Pass trail. This trail goes to the head of the Gallatin River at Gallatin Lake. This trail has a branch that goes to the Fawn Pass Trail and one that heads over Big Horn Pass to Mammoth Hot Springs. This route up the Gallatin and over

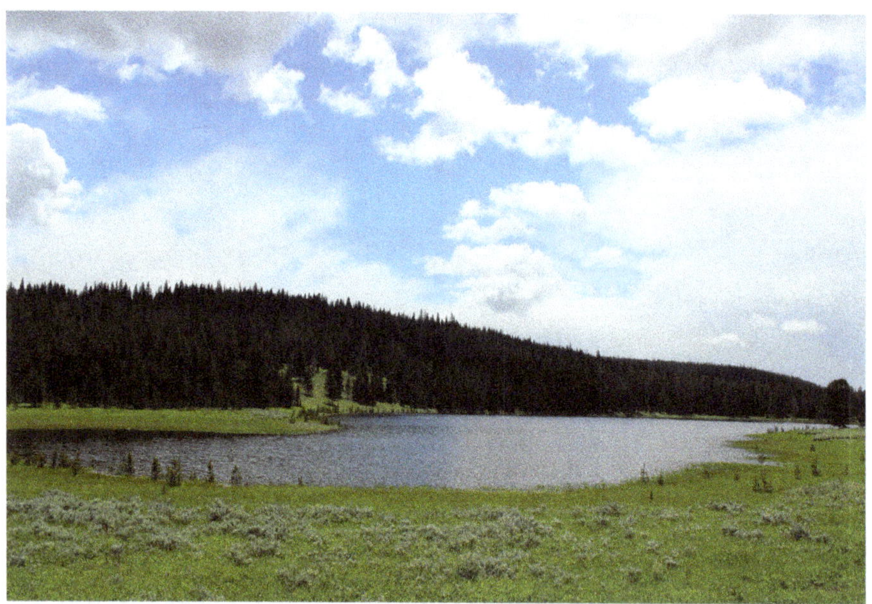

Figure 9.9. Divide Lake (2016) (MM#19.2). Divide Lake falls on the divide between the Gallatin River and Grayling Creek drainages. It is fed primarily by groundwater and is often empty, especially after dry years. Wildlife is often seen around this lake.

Big Horn Pass was proposed in the first half of the twentieth century for a railroad and roadway to the northern part of the park and was a major route used by the Bannock Indians.

Toward the end of this straightaway on Highway 191, and before arriving where the forest narrows, one passes Divide Lake on the east (Figure 9.9) (MM#19.2). The lake is so named because it is on the divide between the Gallatin River and Grayling Creek drainages. This does not look like much of a lake, as it is often empty, with plants growing in the basin. It is a small depression in hummocky glacial drift that lies in front of a glacial moraine. This depression often fills following heavy snowfall years. The lake level is maintained primarily by groundwater; consequently, following several wet years, the lake tends to stay full, or near full, during the summer, whereas following dry years, the lake level drops or the lake eventually dries up. Exceptionally wet springs and early summer rain may also fill the lake. When the lake totally fills, which is uncommon, it drains north into the Gallatin River drainage. On early mornings, one can occasionally see wildlife around this lake, especially when it has water. Leaving Divide Lake heading south, one enters the Grayling Creek drainage.

Chapter 10

Grayling Creek to 287 Junction to West Yellowstone

(MM#19.2 to #0)

The southern section of the Gallatin Way, the road from Divide Lake to West Yellowstone, initially follows Grayling Creek drainage (Map 10.1). This drainage is a relatively narrow canyon, which created some problems for early road builders. The old meandering roadway is still visible in some locations in the forest adjacent to the present highway. Major adjustments made to the highway in the late 1950s and 1960s abandoned the old route and created a relatively straight route along Grayling Creek by cutting into hillsides, straightening out rivers or totally abandoning the old route and creating a substitute route.

About one mile south of Divide Lake, there is a pull-off on the west side of the highway (MM#18.5). This is parking for people who wish to hike (or ski) the hill to the west, which goes to a set of meadows called Sink Creek Meadows. Skiers also use the slopes for telemark skiing. Sink Creek Meadow is so named because the small stream flowing across the meadow flows into a limestone sink, disappearing for several miles and reappearing farther down a small canyon and then crossing meadows in the Gallatin River valley headed toward the Gallatin River.

About a mile farther south (MM#17.5), Grayling Creek emerges from the forest east of the highway, flowing from its headwaters in the park below Mount Holmes (see Map 1.2). From this point until the highway breaks out into the Madison Valley, the river and highway run more or less parallel. Today, there is one exception to their parallel paths. Before the highway was improved in the 1950s and '60s, the highway followed Grayling Creek

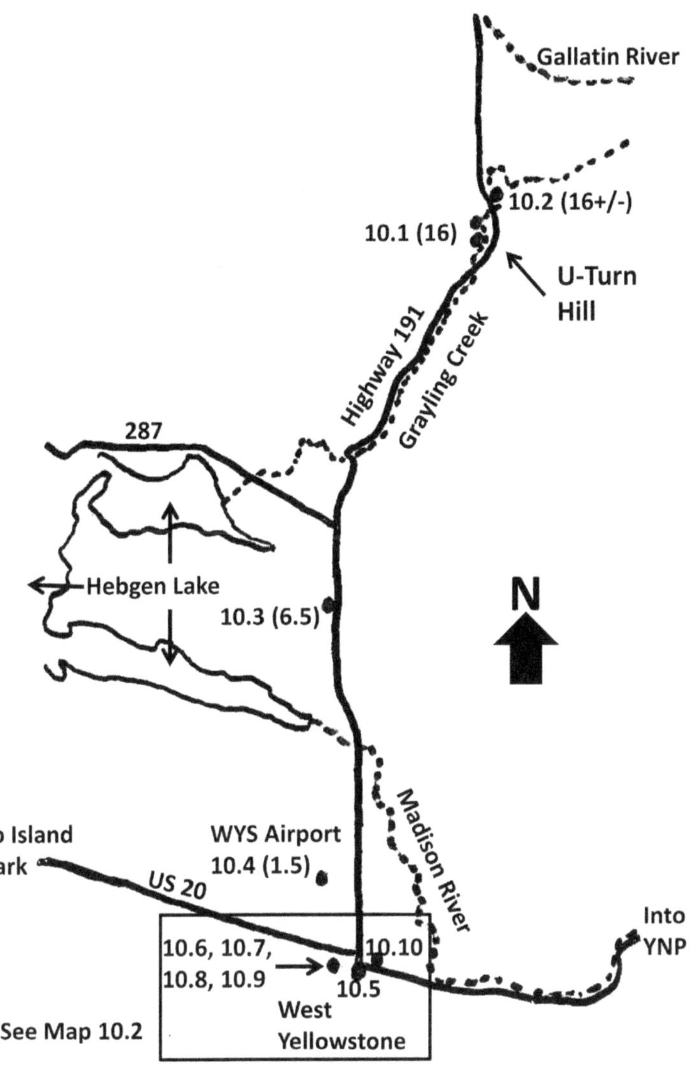

Map 10.1. Grayling Creek to West Yellowstone (MM#19.2 to 0). Map of photo locations including those along Highway 191, the Gallatin River and Grayling Creek and in West Yellowstone (mile markers in parentheses).

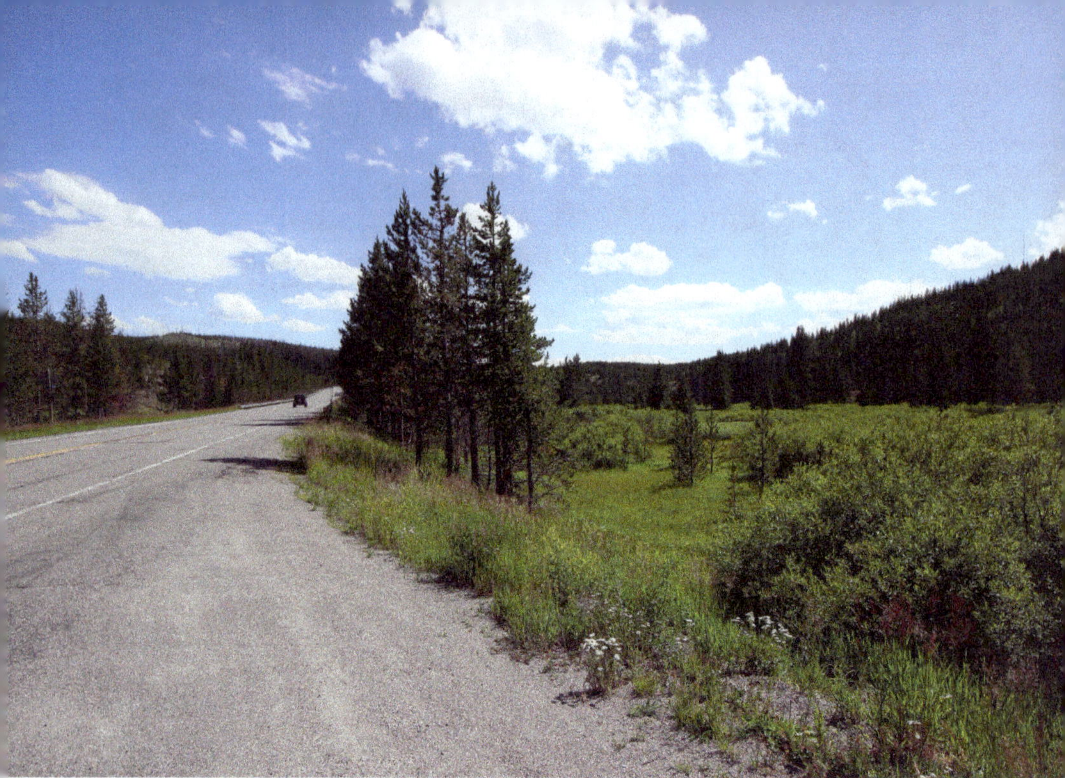

Figure 10.1. U-Turn (Horseshoe Turn) Hill area along Highway 191 (MM#16).
Above photo (2016): Highway 191 heading south over U-Turn Hill. The old highway prior to construction of this hill was through the forested area on the right of photo, some of which is still visible in some places.
Opposite page, upper photo (2015): Highway 191 passing over Horseshoe Turn Hill on the left, with the old highway to the right showing location of the sharp turn crossing a small drainage leading into Grayling Creek. *Photo Image ©2015 Google.*
Opposite page, middle photo (2016): Early roadway, paved in the 1930s, heading north toward the U-Turn (Horseshoe Turn). Note the large rocks on right of roadway to protect cars from plummeting into Grayling Creek Canyon. The roadway was used last in the late 1950s.
Opposite page, lower photo (2016): The U-Turn or Horseshoe Turn on the old highway. This sharp turn was necessary because the roadway followed the contour and went around and over a small drainage that was filled in to develop the roadway. The asphalt is still solid except for invasion of plants in cracks.

above a narrow canyon, west of the present road, where the roadway took a sharp U-turn around a small tributary flowing into Grayling Creek canyon. This U-turn was sharp enough to prevent most big trucks from navigating it. Today, the highway goes over a small hill with a passing lane. The hill to locals is called U-Turn or Horseshoe-Turn Hill, making people wonder how it got that name; now it is obvious, considering what it replaced (Figure 10.1). As one ascends the hill heading south, the old highway is still visible in the forest along the western edge of the valley passing above the canyon. The canyon is being used by the park and U.S. Fish and Wildlife

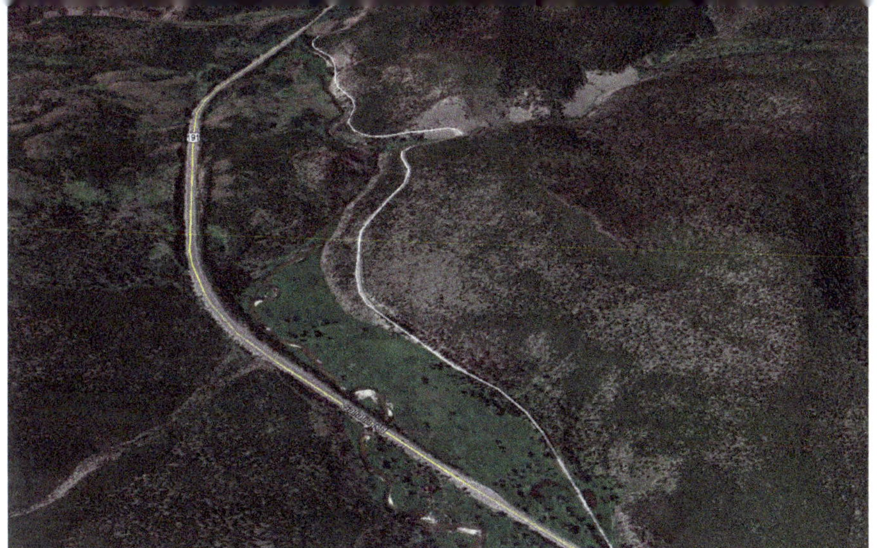

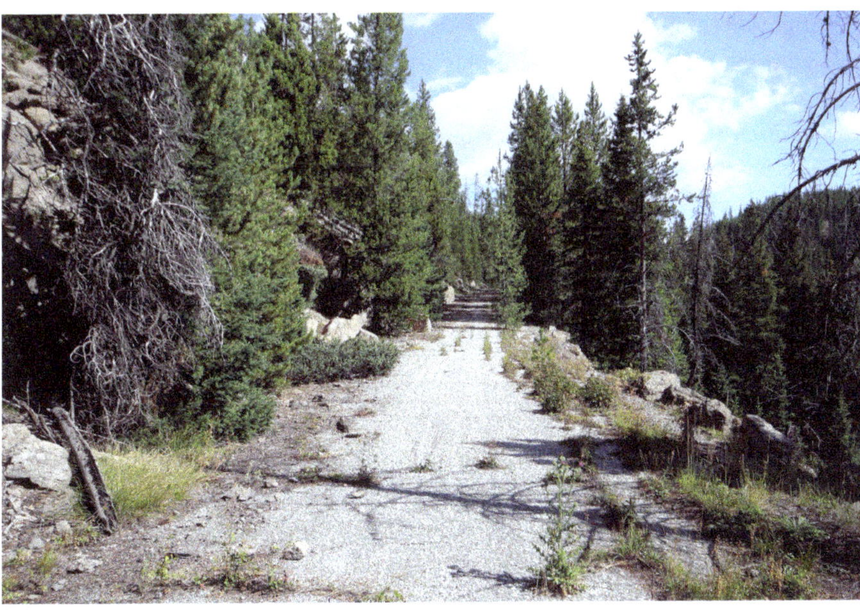

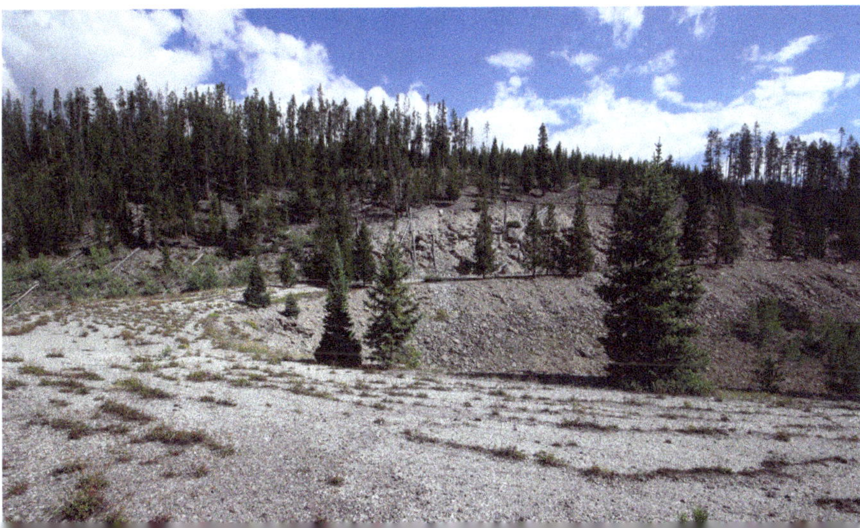

Service (USFWS) for placement of a fish barrier to prevent nonnative fish from moving up Grayling Creek while the park reestablishes native fish in Grayling Creek above the barrier, primarily westslope cutthroat trout and Arctic grayling.

On both sides of this section of Highway 191 and from the old road, one can observe the recovering forest from the 1988 Yellowstone National Park fires (Figure 10.2). This area was burned by the North Fork fire, the portion of the larger 1988 fire that burned much of western Yellowstone National Park, reaching as far east as Tower Junction. This fire started outside the park in Idaho along the western boundary of the park. That fire was man-caused, but by the time it moved into the park, weather conditions in 1988 were so conducive to fire expansion—that is, high temperatures and winds—that it was impossible to extinguish the fire. Ironically, the day before the North Fork fire was started, July 22, Yellowstone National Park determined it had to begin to try to suppress any new fire within the park, but the North Fork fire had started outside the park. The North Fork fire stopped moving northwesterly (three miles an hour due to strong winds) on September 11, 1988, when rain and snow began to fall. That was the end of the 1988 fires. If one can imagine, the willow stand along the highway to the west just before ascending U-Turn Hill was completely burned to the ground because the fire was so hot (Figure 10.2). This was considered a wetland area with plenty of moisture and resistant to burning. As one might note, the willow stand is completely recovered, whereas the forest still shows young lodgepole pine growing up among burned trees—a natural recovery process for these forests.

Along this stretch of the highway, Grayling Creek flows first on the east side of the highway and then flows through a culvert near where the first photo in Figure 10.1 was taken to the west side of the valley. On the south side of U-Turn Hill, Grayling Creek returns to the east side of the highway. At MM#10.9, the highway leaves Yellowstone National Park. Shortly after this, the highway crosses a newly constructed bridge over Grayling Creek (MM#9.7), which replaced one just downstream; the location of the old bridge is apparent. The old bridge was on a very sharp, dangerous curve, most dangerous in winter. From the bridge, the highway rises out of Grayling Creek drainage and breaks out into the Madison-Hebgen Lake valley with broad vistas toward Lion Head Peak in the Targhee Range to the southwest and into the park to the east. At the top of the rise just as the viewshed expands, there is a small cemetery to the east, Fir Ridge Cemetery (MM#9.3). This cemetery has been used as

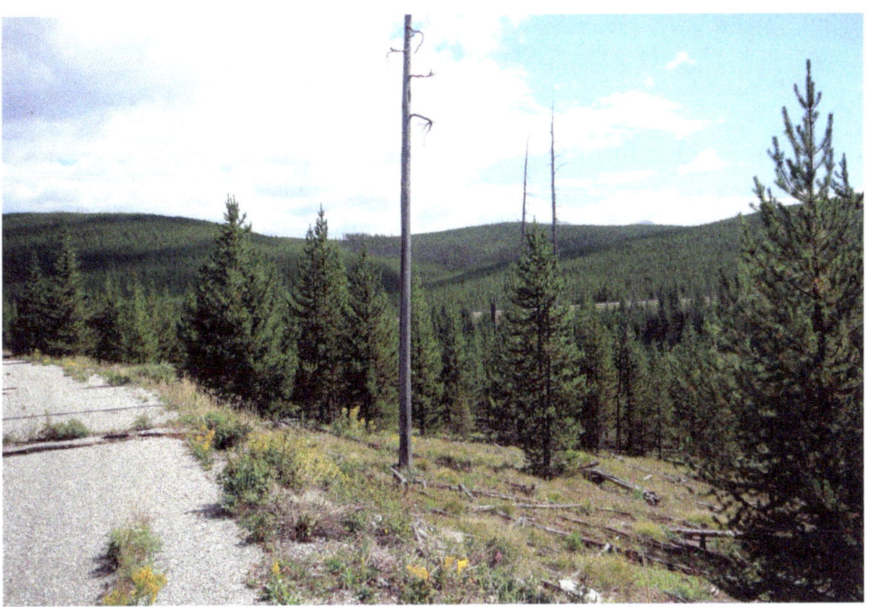

Figure 10.2. Forest and willow recovery evidence from the 1988 Yellowstone National Park fire along Highway 191 from MM#17.5 to MM#15.
Above photo (2016): View from old highway (see Figure 10.1) west of Highway 191 looking at the north end of today's U-Turn (Horseshoe Turn) Hill (gray line in photo). Forest recovery is evident in the distant hills, where unburned lodgepole pine forest is taller than recovering pines. Burned trees from the 1988 fire are evident in the photo where the living trees are mostly recovery trees following the fire.
Below photo (2016): View west from pull-off on the north end of Horseshoe Turn Hill showing tall unburned trees in distance with pine regrowth around them. A dense stand of willow grows in foreground. This area was burned to the ground by the 1988 fire.

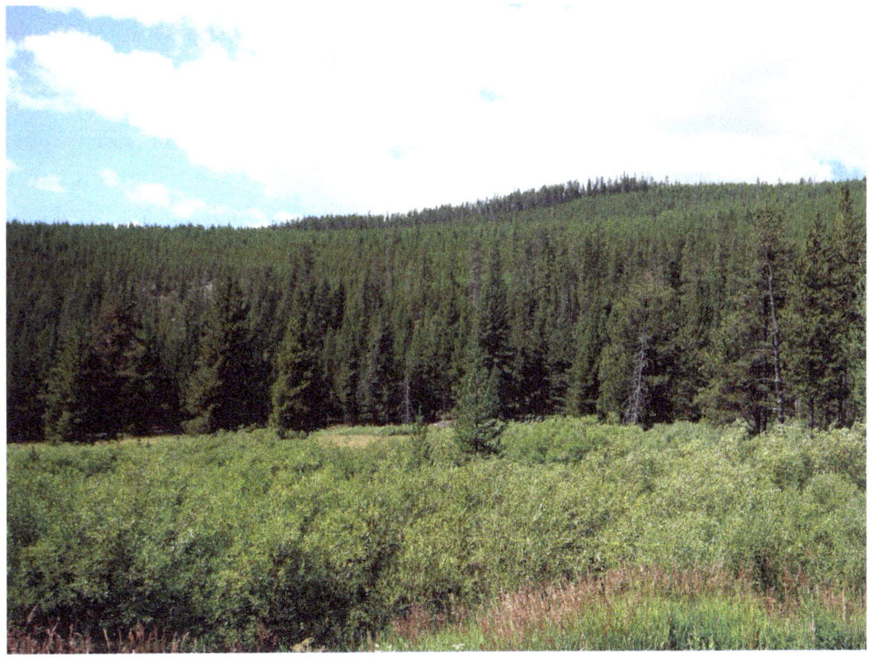

the burial location for many local people over many decades. It is also a parking area for hiking to Gneiss Creek in the park.

Dropping into the Madison River basin, there are new developments to the west, an example of the expansion of habitation in this area. Starting at the point of entering the basin, one should look out for bison that occasionally use the roadway for migrating out of the park. This is true for the whole highway stretch from here to West Yellowstone and is most common in seasons other than summer, when the bison move back into the park where forage has improved.

U.S. Highway 191 junctions with U.S. Highway 287 (MM#8.3) at the bottom of the hill. Highway 287 heads west toward Ennis, Montana, and the Madison River Valley, a broad valley with many ranches. Along Highway 287, the road passes evidence of the 1959 Hebgen Lake earthquake, eventually arriving at the USFS Earthquake Lake Visitor Center before leaving the Madison River canyon. The earthquake at 11:37 p.m. on August 17, 1959, had a magnitude of 7.3 to 7.5 on the Richter scale. It resulted in formation of the Hebgen Lake fault scarp, about a nine- to ten-foot (circa three-meter) displacement, running parallel to and north of the highway, with another fault scarp near Red Canyon, a nineteen-foot (circa six-meter) displacement. These displacements caused major damage to the roadway. The quake also caused a resistant rock holding part of the south canyon wall just near the western end of the canyon to break off. The material behind and above the broken rock flowed into the valley and up the other side with hurricane force, burying a campground and plugging the canyon forming Earthquake Lake (Quake Lake). Including those lost in the campground, twenty-eight individuals were lost due to the earthquake, a small number considering its magnitude. The earthquake also caused displacement in the Madison River Valley where Hebgen Lake is located. The northern side of the lake dropped several feet, while the southern side was elevated. The lake went into an oscillating seiche, a wave that moves back and forth across the lake surface, that damaged houses and facilities along the side of the lake and topped Hebgen Dam, built in 1914, causing little damage to the dam. The rush of water down the canyon and the wind that accompanied the slide, along with the earthquake's shifting of the land, caused more damage and some deaths. The water rapidly moving down the canyon plus continued releases from the dam formed a lake behind the earth flow, soon to be called Earthquake Lake (or Quake Lake), which blocked Highway 287. As the water rose behind this natural dam, there was concern that this dam might fail, which would cause a flood down the valley and inundate Ennis. Consequently, a sluiceway was cut through the quake dam to lower Quake Lake. The once flooded trees on the edge of the lake, now dead, are evidence of the original height of the lake. A side note: my wife and I were camped that night in the Hilgard Mountains just north of the slide area. We fortunately camped in an elevated location near Crag Lake, as massive amounts of rocks poured off the mountains into a valley adjacent to that area, burying everything in their path. All night long, after the initial shock, aftershocks could be heard and felt about every fifteen minutes. Lying on the ground, we would first hear a roar, followed by the ground shaking. Initially, we thought the rockslides might have caused the shaking, but we soon realized we were in the middle of a major earthquake.

Back at the junction of U.S. Highways 191 and 287, going south U.S. 191 heads onto a flat landscape covered by dense lodgepole pine forests. Areas of this forest have been clear-cut over the years. The first road through this area was just a narrow cut through the forest, but with highway improvement, the roadway and shoulders were widened, and now the route is a wide swath through the forest (Figure 10.3). At MM#3.6, the highway drops into the Madison River floodplain, crossing the river over a bridge initially built in 1911–13 and replaced in 1968. The Madison River in this area is often used for swimming or floating, as the water is warmer than most mountain rivers because the river is fed by the Gibbon and Firehole Rivers in the park, both rivers being warmed by inflows from adjacent hot springs, especially the Firehole. The river is outside Yellowstone where it goes under the highway, and thus, people can float this reach with tubes, kayaks, canoes or other boats.

South of the bridge over the Madison River, there are several side roads leading to resorts and one into the Baker's Hole Campground. This campground abuts the Madison River. Years when the grizzly bears were common in the area, the campground was limited to hard vehicles and campers—no tents. Also, in the early and mid-twentieth century, the town of West Yellowstone had its dump not far from Baker's Hole Campground. This dump was a major attraction for locals and tourists, as it attracted local black and grizzly bears. In the evening, one could park, with headlights shining into the dump, a large excavated hole, and watch the bears (mostly grizzlies) rummage through the trash. In the late 1960s to 1970, the dumps in Yellowstone as well as West Yellowstone were closed because food availability at the dumps tended to cause grizzlies to become habitualized to human food, often with dire consequences. This ended one of the attractions the park depended on in its early years. To entertain

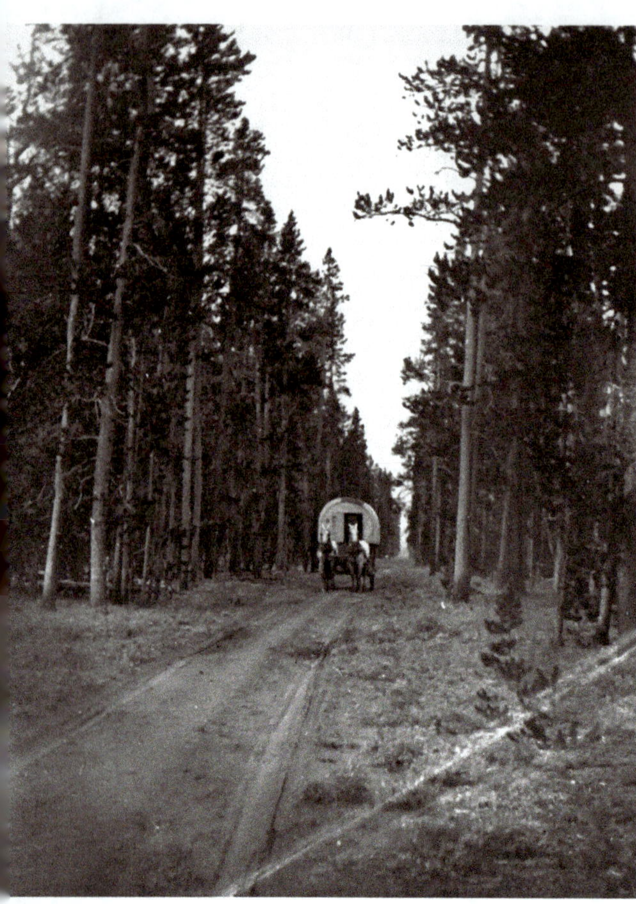

Figure 10.3. Road into West Yellowstone (lower photo MM#6.0).
Left photo (circa 1910–14): Roadway cuts through dense lodgepole pine forest. *YHC.*
Below photo (2016): Roadway is greatly widened, allowing a broad shoulder.

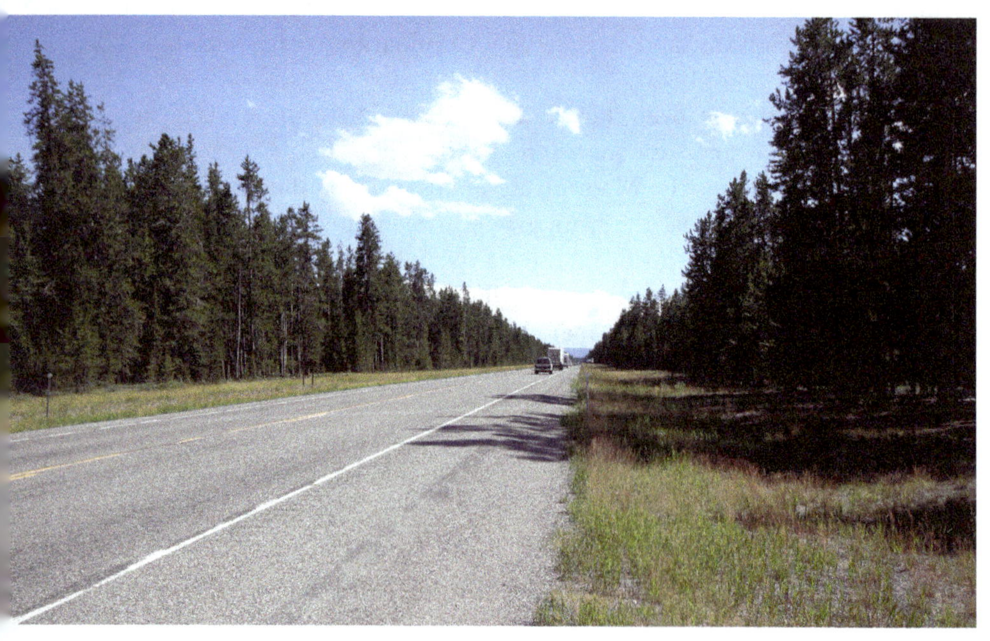

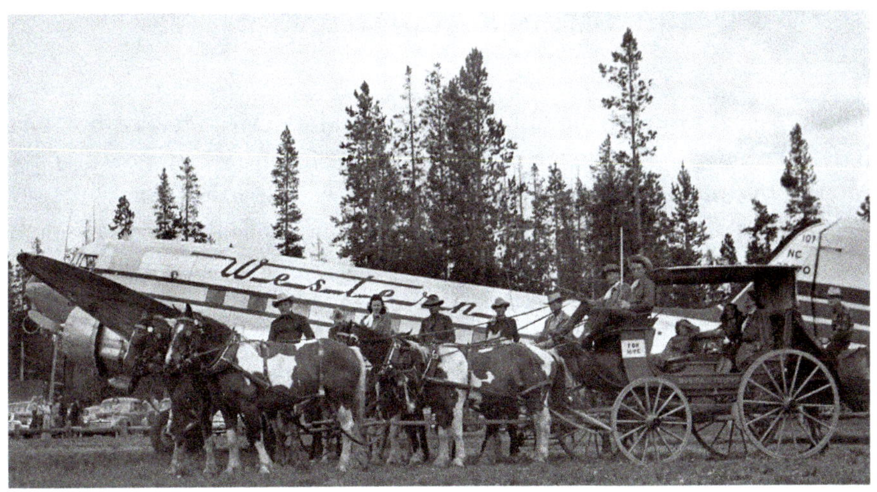

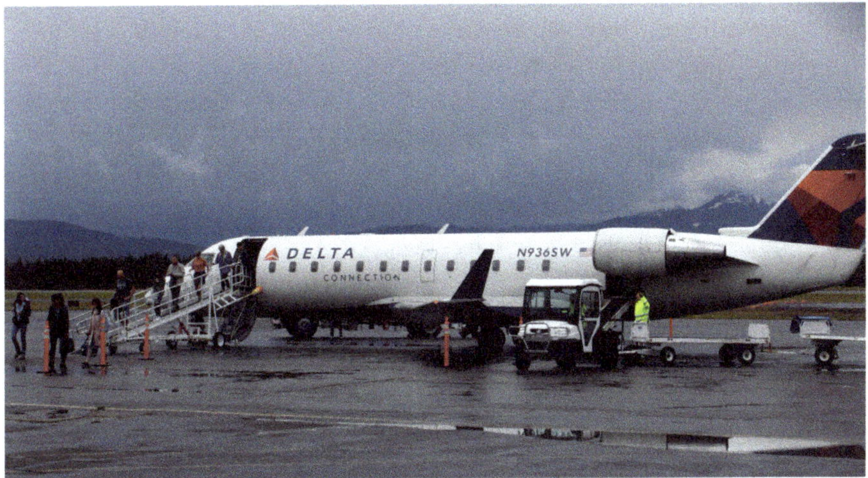

Figure 10.4. Airports at West Yellowstone, Montana.
Upper photo (circa 1940s): A Western Airlines DC-3 at old airport. *YHC.*
Lower photo (2017): Commercial jet airliners now serve the new airport. Delta's CRJ 200 unloads passengers in stormy weather.

visitors, the park set up "picnic" tables for bears (mostly black bears) and spread garbage on the tables. Spectator stands were erected for viewing the bears forage. Even feeding bears along the roads in the park was not discouraged. Eventually, all these practices were forbidden, and the bears moved into the backcountry for natural forage. This didn't keep some of the bears from continuing to visit campgrounds where odors from human cooking and food waft through the air.

About two miles south of Baker's Hole Campground is the West Yellowstone Airport. This airport opened in June 1965 with one runway.

This replaced a smaller airstrip on the west side of West Yellowstone that had two runways. The old airstrip, officially opened in 1935, is now used for snowmobile races, summer expositions, rallies, etc. At its inauguration, only one landing strip was ready for use. The final landing field was five hundred feet wide by five thousand feet long in the shape of a block letter V. The airport included a Scenic Airways private hangar, a gasoline pump and an airplane repair shop. Scenic Airways provided air tours and charter services over the park. National Parks Airways provided the regular scheduled air and mail service until 1937, when it was purchased by Western Air Express. Western Air Express was renamed Western Airlines in the spring of 1941 (Figure 10.4, previous page). Shortly after that, service to West Yellowstone was classified as nonessential due to the war effort. Western Airlines resumed air service in 1946. However, the trees at the end of the runway grew to be dangerously tall, and for safety reasons, Western ceased service in the fall of 1947. Air services to West Yellowstone would not resume until 1965 with the completion of the second (and current) airport.

West Yellowstone, with its new airport, has been served over the years by several airlines. There was a time when one could fly into West Yellowstone in the summer from Salt Lake City (Western Airlines, which merged with Delta and then added Aspen Airway) and Denver via Casper, Wyoming

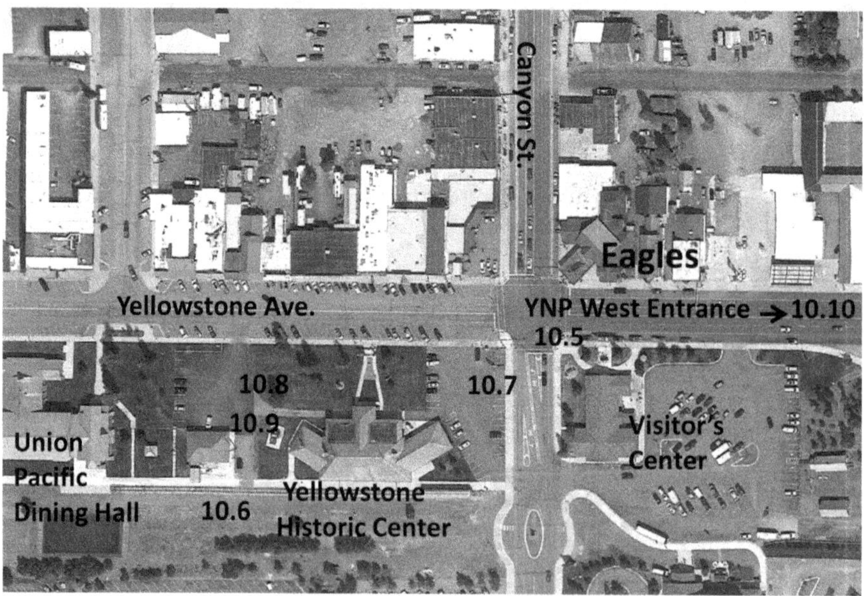

Map 10.2. Downtown West Yellowstone with photo locations. *Map Image ©2016 Google.*

(Frontier Airlines). Today (2017), only Delta Air Lines/Skywest serves West Yellowstone from Salt Lake City, and only in the summer. The airport is also home to the U.S. Forest Service Interagency Fire Center, a location that houses smoke jumpers and other forest firefighting equipment.

From the airport road intersection, it is less than two miles into the town of West Yellowstone, a town that is very much a tourist center serving the west gate of Yellowstone National Park (Map 10.2). In the early years, there were no paved roads, and during heavy snows in winter, it was difficult to get into or out of town. The town had many bars, some dance halls and a few shops, Eagles being one of the early shops if not the first one. In 1908, on a plot of forestland near the new train station at the west entrance to Yellowstone National Park, Sam Eagle and his business partner Alex Stuart built a general store that would later become known as Eagle's Store or just Eagles (Figure 10.5).

The town was very much an old western town, which enchanted the tourists of the day, and yet it had Union Pacific Railroad train service from Idaho, which began in 1908 and ended in 1960 (Figure 10.6). In the summer, the train brought tourists to the town who would be met at the Union Pacific Depot (now the Yellowstone Historic Center) and transported into the park. Horse-drawn carriages were used (Figures 10.7 and 10.8) until vehicles were allowed in the park starting in 1915 (Figure 10.9). The Union Pacific also had a dining hall for the tourists; the building is now used for large meetings. Today, the town is bustling with tourists, summer and winter. Motels and hotels of all sizes abound, and there is an Imax Theatre and the Grizzly and Wolf Discovery Center. The animals housed here can no longer be let back into the wild for many reasons; they are recovered "orphans," not "well behaved" or have had bad encounters with humans in the past. To learn more about the history of this area, one should visit the Yellowstone Historic Center in the old train depot, which has a museum and is open in summer.

From West Yellowstone, one can return to Bozeman via U.S. 191 and "rediscover" all the interesting attributes of the Gallatin Way; head into Yellowstone National Park through the west gate (Figure 10.10); or head west to Idaho on U.S. 20, passing through Island Park and locations south.

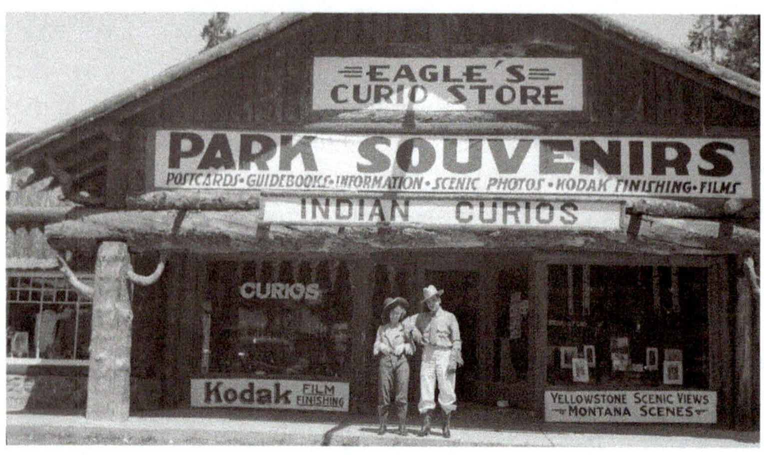

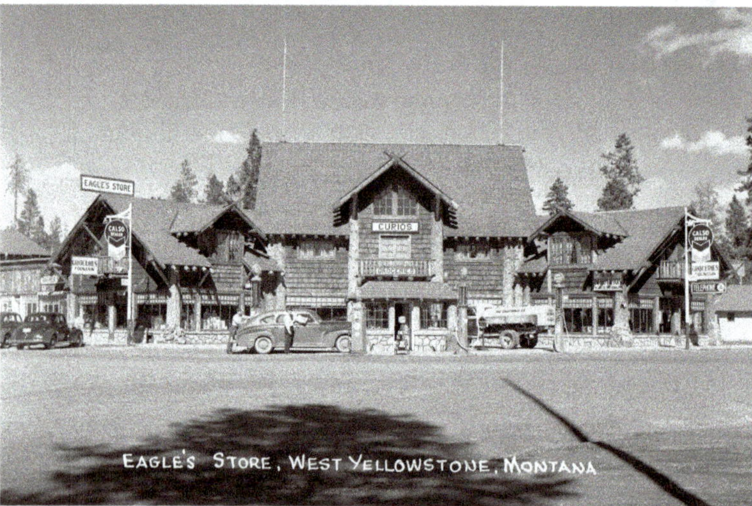

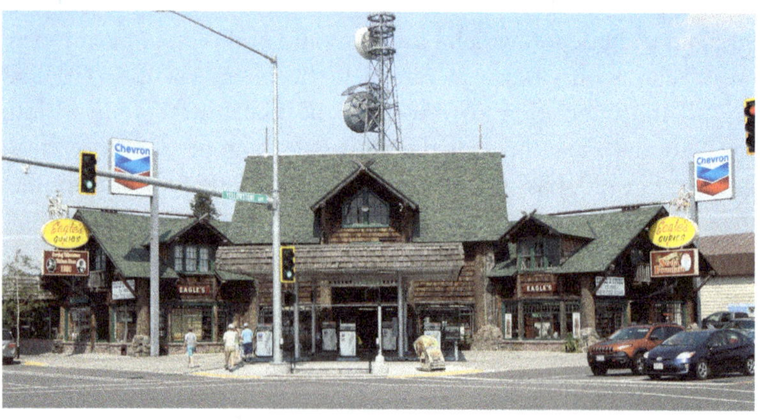

Figure 10.5. Eagles Store in West Yellowstone, Montana. *Upper photo* (early 1900s): This may be the original Eagles Store, which was built in 1908, enlarged in 1913 and then razed in 1927 to build the present store, which was completed in 1930 and designed by Bozeman architect Fred F. Willson. *MOR.* *Middle photo* (August 1939): Eagles Store after the business was open for over thirty years. This store was built in 1930. *MOR.* *Lower photo* (August 2016): Eagles Store in the modern era, showing little change over seventy-seven years except for modern structures such as the microwave/cellphone tower and stoplights.

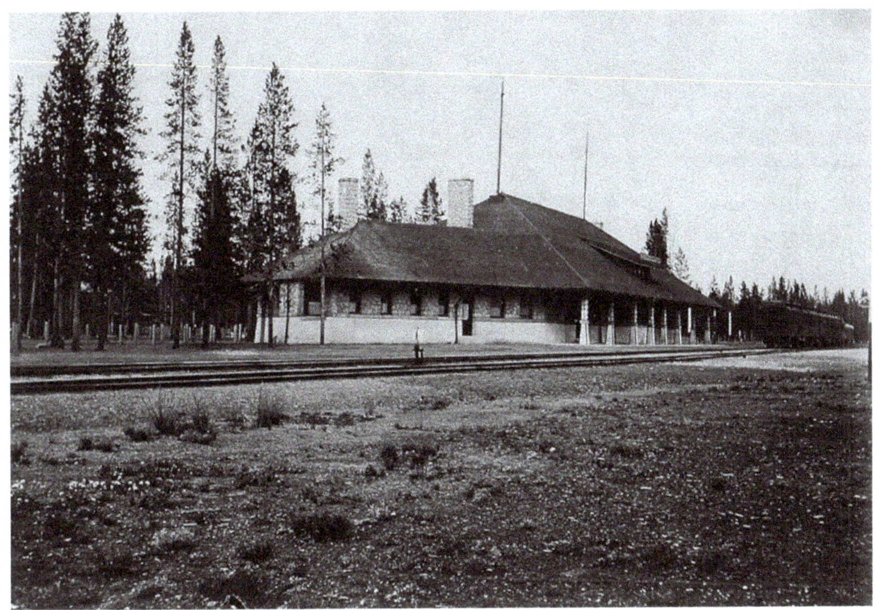

Figure 10.6. Tracks on south side of Union Pacific Train depot building, West Yellowstone, Montana. The train from Monida, Idaho, served the west entrance to Yellowstone National Park from 1908 to 1962.
Above photo (circa 1910–20): Train parked near the south side of depot soon after the depot was constructed. *YHC.*
Below photo (2016): Remaining remnant of a single train track with a representative passenger car on the south side of depot, which now houses the Yellowstone Historic Center.

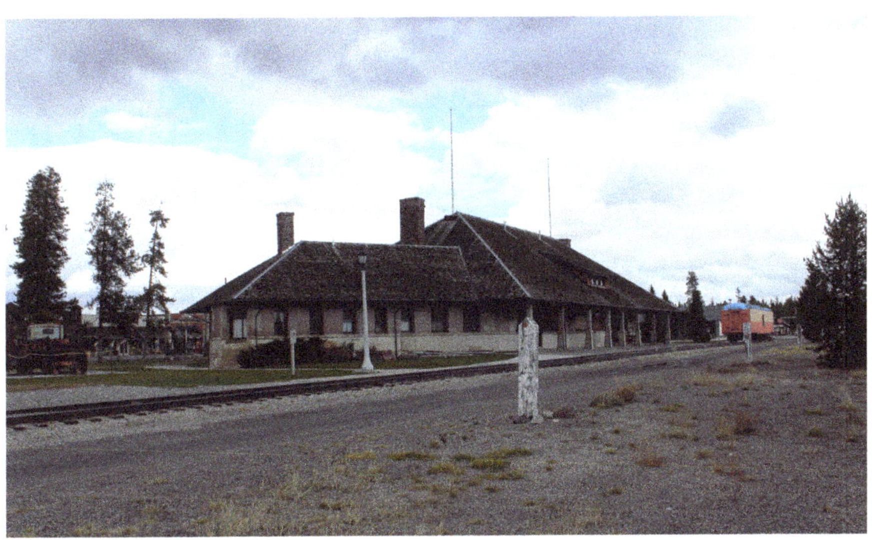

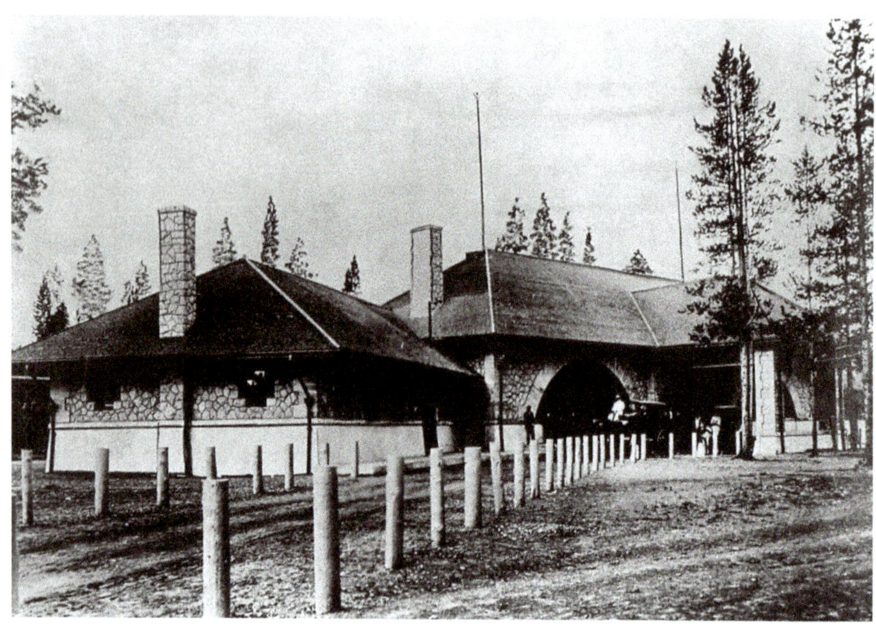

Figure 10.7. Union Pacific train depot building at West Yellowstone; east end. *Above photo* (circa 1910): Depot in its early days, when horse-drawn carriages picked up passengers for their trip through the west entrance into Yellowstone National Park. *YHC.* *Below photo* (2017): Depot building now houses the Yellowstone Historic Center; showing historic yellow touring bus.

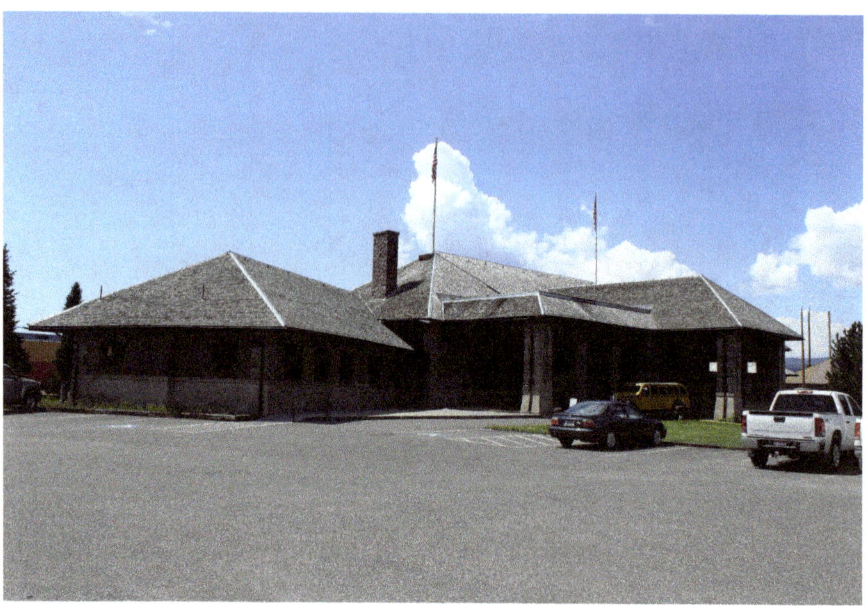

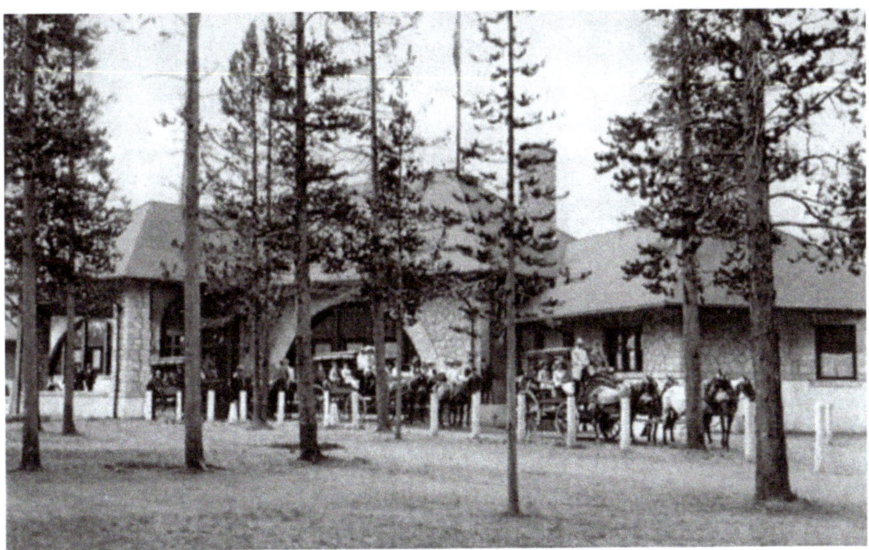

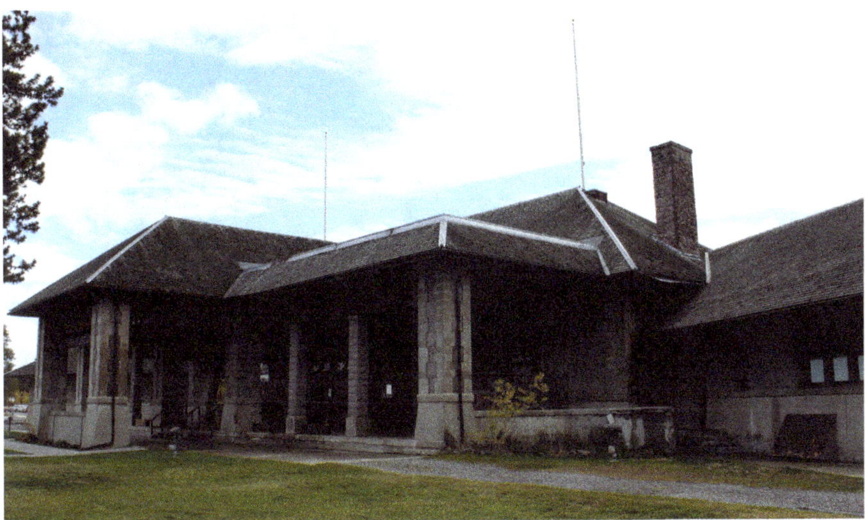

Figure 10.8. West Yellowstone Railroad Depot west end and entrance.
Upper photo (circa 1910): Passengers being picked up at depot by horse-drawn carriages for beginning of a trip into Yellowstone National Park through the west entrance. Horses were used as the park did not allow autos within the park until 1915. *YHC.*
Lower photo (2016): The depot now houses the Yellowstone Historic Center and has no roadway leaving the west side of the building.

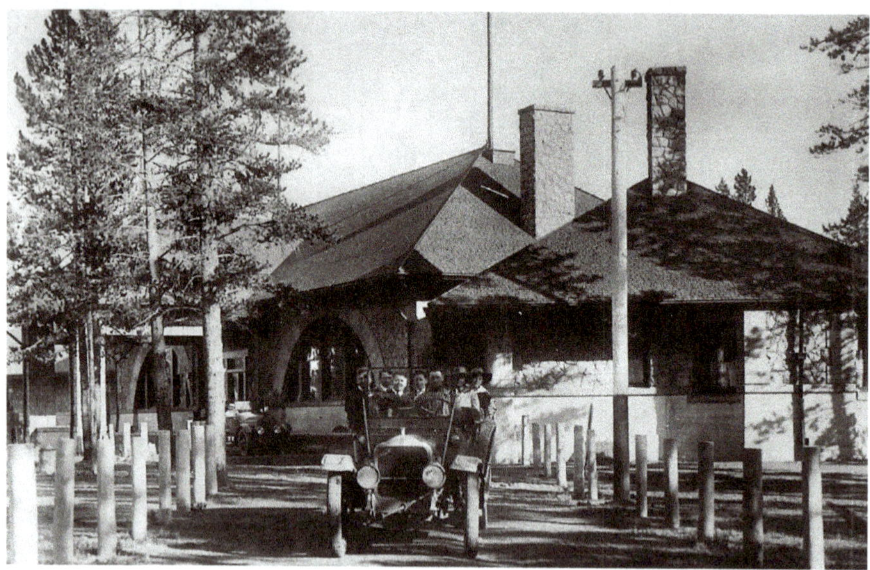

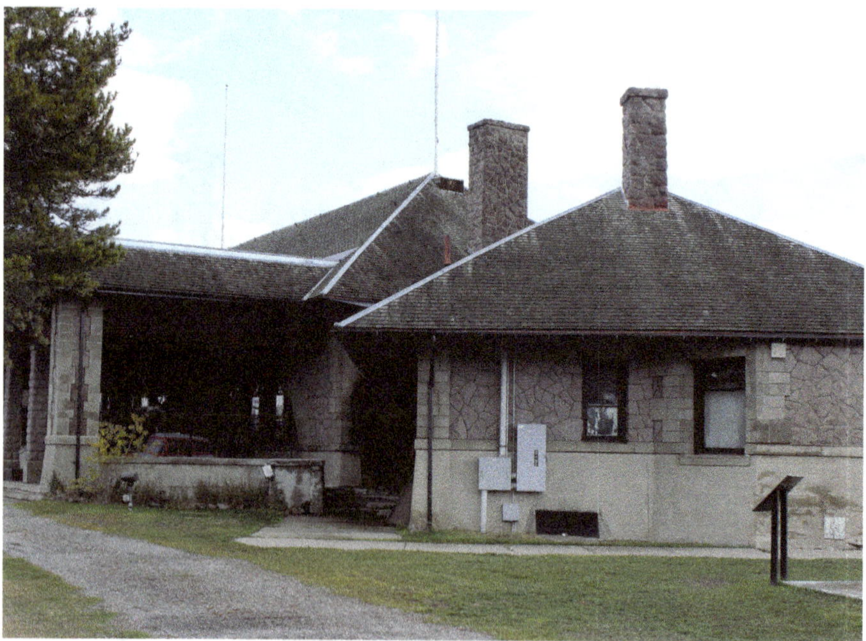

Figure 10.9. West Yellowstone Railroad Depot west end and entrance.
Upper photo (circa 1920s): Passengers being picked up in a "bus" for trip into the park. Vehicles were allowed in the park starting in 1915. *YHC.*
Lower photo (2016): West side of the depot with a walkway closed to traffic.

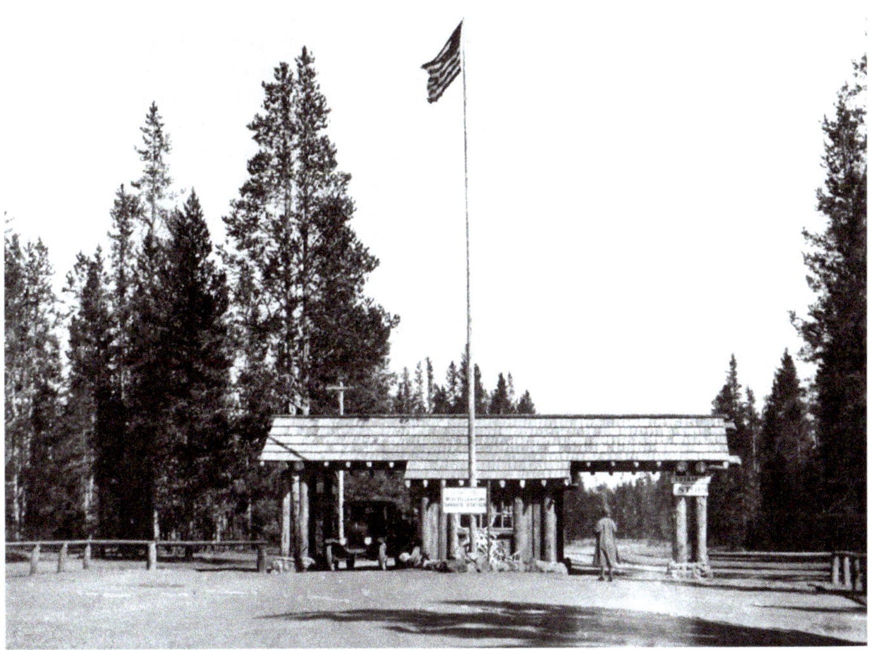

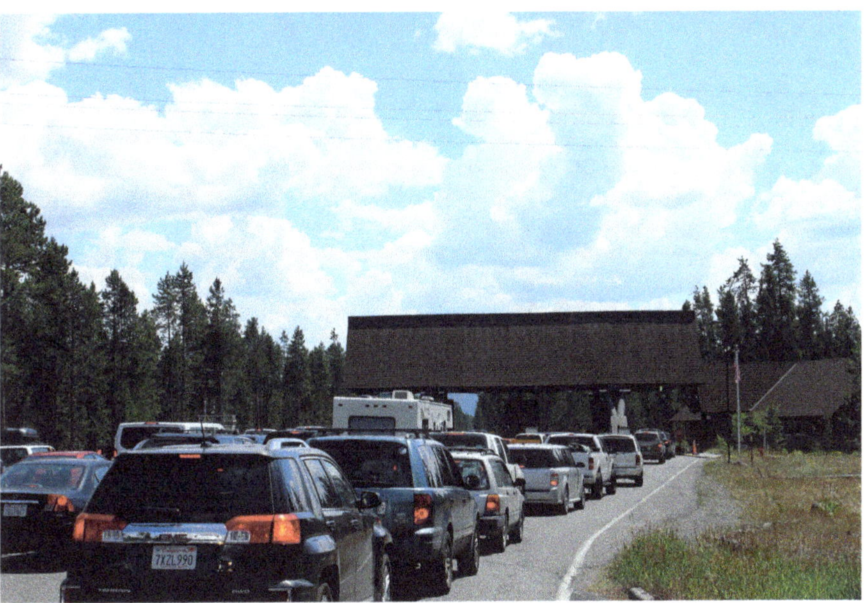

Figure 10.10. West entrance gate to Yellowstone National Park.
Upper photo (circa 1915–20): West entrance when there was limited traffic. Note there is an entrance and exit booth. In 1924, a combined check station and ranger station was built at the west entrance. *YH*C.
Lower photo (2017): Entrance with upgraded booths, three for entering and a non-booth road for exiting. The backup of vehicles is common in the summer when all entry booths have long lines.

Appendix A

Geographic Location of Repeat Photo Points

Most photo points are the same for historic and recent photos. Unknown locations are so indicated.

Figure #	Latitude (N)	Longitude (W)	Elevation (ft.)	
1.1	Unknown			
1.2	Unknown			
1.3	Unknown			
1.4	45°09'34.67"	111°14'55.50"	6297	
1.5	Unknown			
2.1	45°31'31.95"	111°14'57.18"	5200	
2.2	45°30'65.2"	111°16'13.17"	5247	
2.3	45°35'36.27"	111°11'53.71"	4951	
2.4	45°28'44.05"	111°16'12.91"	5258	
2.5	45°28'24.31"	111°16'11.66"	5284	
2.6	45°27'32.53"	111°14'53.85"	5320	
2.7	45°27'30.03"	111°14'49.43"	5309	
2.8	45°27'31.67"	111°14'31.36"	5280	

Figure #	Latitude (N)	Longitude (W)	Elevation (ft.)	
2.9	45°27'29.76"	111°14'48.25"	5313	
2.10	45°26'16.66"	111°14'01.06"	5417	
2.11	45°26'21.22"	111°13'56.83"	5386	
3.1	45°26'00.97"	111°13'58.88"	5400	
3.2	45°25'45.92"	111°14'02.04"	5493	
3.3	45°24'56.81"	111°13'56.81"	5426	
3.4	45°24'54.40"	111°13'53.75"	5491	
3.5	45°24'54.40"	111°13'53.75"	5491	
3.6	45°24'27.60"	111°13'33.21"	5525	
3.7	45°24'34.33"	111°13'34.65"	5534	
3.8	45°24'26.05"	111°12'27.10"	5526	
3.9	45°24'26.22"	111°13'16.81"	5553	
4.1	45°24'19.89"	111°13'13.13"	5532	
4.2	45°23'39.22"	111°12'21.56"	5599	
4.3	45°23'06.16"	111°11'35.14"	5723	
4.4	45°23'10.06"	111°11'37.46"	5690	
4.5	45°23'25.89"	111°12'02.43"	5603	
4.6	45°22'51.71"	111°11'02.28"	5658	
4.7	45°22'42.01"	111°10'24.73"	5671	
4.8	45°22'15.11"	111°10'28.41"	5722	
5.1	45°21'06.27"	111°10'19.49"	5734	
5.2	45°20'49.51"	111°10'21.61"	5888	
5.3	45°20'49.32"	111°10'23.41"	5754	
5.4	45°20'48.66"	111°10'24.16"	5737	
5.5	45°20'40.80"	111°10'26.02"	5739	
5.6	45°20'32.85"	111°10'11.39"	5919	

Figure #	Latitude (N)	Longitude (W)	Elevation (ft.)	
5.7	Unknown			
5.8	45°17’53.59”	111°12’14.50”	5886	
6.1	45°16’01.01”	111°15’14.54”	6129	
6.2	45°15’56.22”	111°15’14.68”	5996	
6.3	45°16’22.30”	111°17’31.23”	6259	
6.4	45°15’50.07”	111°15’19.75”	6010	
6.5	45°15’48.17”	111°15’13.40”	6001	
6.6	45°14’42.32”	111°5’04.83”	6055	
6.7	45°13’36.38”	111°14’43.63”	6108	Historic School
6.7	45°13’44.57”	111°15’02.15”	6110	New School
6.8	45°12’43.56”	111°14’51.72”	6162	
7.1	45°11’51.19”	111°14’13.22”	6181	
7.2	45°11’38.35”	111°14’15.13”	6212	
7.3	45°11’40.89”	111°14’13.96”	6205	
7.4	45°10’32.96”	111°14’36.23”	6279	
7.5	45°08’22.08”	111°14’12.12”	6366	
7.6	45°08’13.73”	111°14’10.33”	6372	
7.7	45°06’58.05”	111°13’31.86”	6454	
7.8	45°06’46.00”	111°13’45.37”	6537	
8.1	45°06’05.26”	111°13’09.28”	6504	
8.2	45°06’06.02”	111°13’06.56”	6486	
8.3	45°06’06.18”	111°13’07.85”	6485	
8.4	45°05’00.69”	111°12’32.02”	6562	
8.5	45°04’13.73”	111°18’38.76”	7020	
8.6	Unknown			

Figure #	Latitude (N)	Longitude (W)	Elevation (ft.)	
8.7	45°06'24.14"	111°13'19.80"	6466	
8.8	45°04'50.91"	111°22'25.52"	7020	
8.9	45°03'57.69"	111°17'30.73"	6941	
8.10	45°04'10.76"	111° 11'27.88"	6615	
8.11	45° 04'01.02"	111°11'26.21"	6734	
8.12	45°04'07.38"	111°11'27.88"	6618	
8.13	45°04'01.02"	111°11'26.21"	6734	
8.14	45°03'54.45"	111°10'54.42"	6637	
8.15	45°03'47.15"	111°10'11.35"	6798	
8.16	45°03'43.20"	111°10'13.40"	6667	
8.17	45°03'15.26"	111°09'20.35"	6697	
9.1	45°05'42.50"	111°04'54.02"	9532	
9.2	45°03'42.32"	111°07'55.69"	8367	
9.3	45°01'45.89"	111°04'48.53"	8577	
9.4	45°02'19.64"	111°07'31.51"	6811	
9.5	45°02'18.72"	111°07'33.25"	6836	
9.5	45°19'11.06"	112°02'18.97"	5309	
9.6	45°01'07.40"	111°05'42.46"	6871	
9.7	45°00'41.18"	111°04'42.58"	6864	
9.8	45°00'10.87"	111°05'42.46"	6975	
9.9	44°54'51.96"	111°03'10.51"	7259	
10.1	44°51'55.44"	111°03'13.26"	7072	
10.2	44°52'25.50"	111°02'44.16"	7053	
10.3	44°45'56.90"	111°06'48.94"	6587	
10.4	44°41'11.10"	111°06'54.48"	6646	
10.5	44°39'31.18"	111°05'58.02"	6679	

Figure #	**Latitude (N)**	**Longitude (W)**	**Elevation (ft.)**	
10.6	44°39'28.82"	111°06'05.33"	6680	
10.7	44°39'30.47"	111°05'59.49"	6680	
10.8	44°39'30.27"	111°06'03.85"	6682	
10.9	44°39'30.20"	111°06'04.42"	6681	
10.10	44°39'25.32"	111°05'28.10"	6686	

Appendix B

Mile Markers of Gallatin Road (West Yellowstone to Canyon Entrance)

0.0	West Yellowstone
1.6	West Yellowstone Airport
2.7	Baker Creek Campground
3.6	Madison River Bridge
4.2	West Yellowstone dump
8.3	Junction with Highway 287 (also Duck Creek)
9.3	Fir Cemetery (trail to Gneiss Creek)
10.9	YNP Boundary sign
16	Top of Horseshoe Turn (U-Turn) Hill
18.5	Telemark Meadow parking pull-off
19.2	Divide Lake
20.3	Big Horn/Upper Gallatin parking access road
21.9	Fawn Pass parking area.
22.7	Bacon Rind Creek road
23.6	Bridge over Gallatin River north of Bacon Rind
26.5	Specimen Creek parking
27	Wickiup Creek
28.4	Black Butte
28.5	Black Butte Creek
30.5	Daly Creek
31.2	YNP northwest boundary

32	Tepee Creek
32.1	Snowflake Springs exclosure
32.8	Tepee Creek Bridge
33.1	Elkhorn Ranch (33133 Gallatin Road)
33.7	Taylor Fork Road
34	Taylor Fork
34.1	Covered Wagon Ranch (34035 Gallatin Road)
34.6	Pulpit Rock
36	320 Ranch (205 Buffalo Horn Creek Road)
37.1	Cinnamon Lodge (37090 Gallatin Road)
38.8	Palisades
41	Buck Creek
41.5	Red Cliff Campground
41.7	Cliff north of campground turnoff
42.9	Halfway Point/Corral and Rainbow Ranch (42950 Gallatin Road)
43.1	Halfway Point curve north of Rainbow Ranch
44.3	Buck Creek Ridge Road
45.1	River House (45130 Gallatin Road)
45.3+/-	Ophir School
46.6	Buck's T-4
47.9	Lone Mountain Trail (Big Sky turn-in)
49.8	Jack Smith Bridge
51.5	Green (High's/Markley) Bridge
53.2	Portal Creek Road
53.9	Durnam Bridge (to Durnam Meadow)
55.3	Karst
55.8	Moose Creek Bridge
56.2	Moose Creek Flat Campground
57.3	Swan Creek Bridge (campground turnoff)
58.2	Greek Creek Campground
59+/-	Sagebrush Point
59.6	Kitchen Rock
60	Rocky Hillside
61	Cascade Creek cabins overlook
61.1	Curve into thirty-five-mile-per-hour bridge from south
61.3	Thirty-five-mile-per-hour bridge
62.3	House Rock
63.7	South end of Beckman Flats

64	Beckman Flats (center at Montana Whitewater 63960 Gallatin Road)
65.2	Squaw Creek Road (Storm Castle Road)
65.9	The Inn (originally Castle Rock Inn) (65840 Gallatin Road)
66.9	Rockhaven (66850 Gallatin Road)
67.1	Milwaukee Railroad Arch location
68.2	Spanish Creek
69	Spanish Creek Road
70.3	Harringer Bridge at canyon entrance
70.3	Entrance to canyon

References

Bozeman Daily Chronicle. Articles on Pete Karst and dude ranching.

Burlingame, M.G. "A Brief Chronological Sketch of the Gallatin Canyon." *Bozeman Daily Chronicle*, February 15, 16, 17, 1970.

Cooper, Walter. Memories of what seems to be his daughter (filed as author unknown in Dr. McGill Collection, MSU). Date unknown.

Cronin, Janet, and Dorothy Vick. *Montana's Gallatin Canyon: A Gem in the Treasure State*. Missoula: Montana Press Publishing Co., 1992.

Culpin, Mary Shivers. "History of Construction of Road System in Yellowstone National Park 1872–1966." National Park Service. *Historic Resource Study*, vol. 1, 1994.

Forest History Society. Third Episode, Gallatin National Forest. 1940s. *Memoirs of a U.S. Forest Service Employee in the Gallatin District: dates 1915–1919. (date unknown)*. Recollections of Clyde P. Fickes on his experiences with the U.S. Forest Service in Montana 1915 to the 1920s, including the West Gallatin River drainage. Photos by Smith Riley.

Hayden, F.V. *Sixth Annual Report of the USGS of the Territories Embracing Portions of Montana, Wyoming, Idaho and Utah Being a Report of the Progress of the Expeditions of the Year 1872. United States Geologist. Conducted Under the Authority of the Secretary of the Interior*. Washington, D.C.: Government Printing Office, 1873.

Malone, Michael P. "The Gallatin Canyon…and the Tides of History." *Montana: The Magazine of Western History* 23, no. 3 (Summer 1973): 2–17.

McGill, Dr. Caroline. Memoirs. Museum of the Rockies Archives.

Miller, Grace Nutting. Transcript of taped memories over several sittings, 1979. Content: memories of family, friends and starting the Elkhorn Ranch.

Montana Cowboy Hall of Fame. "Introducing 2012 Montana Cowboy Hall of Fame Inductee…Peter F. Karst." montanacowboyfame.org/uploads/3/5/1/5/35150022/peter_f._karst_.pdf.

Montana State University Library. Photographs and text from an 1899 expedition to Yellowstone National Park by a group of twelve Harvard students. One of the travelers' great-granddaughter Lisa Rickenbaugh donated an album of expedition photos to MSU's library.

Pierstorff, Lester. Transcript of an interview in 1939 by Vic Benson, founder of Covered Wagon Ranch. Content: memories of Pierstorff's experiences and knowledge of the canyon and its people back to 1888.

Scott, Kim Allen. "Blood Money: The Montana Bankers Association and the Bozeman Bank Robbery of 1932." Pioneer Museum, Bozeman, MT, #7063 (August 2013).

Shea, Paul. Images of America: *West Yellowstone*. Charleston, SC: Arcadia Publishing, 2009.

Smith, Phyllis. *The Flying D Ranch Lands of Montana: A History*. Bozeman, MT: Gallatin County Historical Society and Pioneer Museum, 2001.

Strickler, Jeff, and Anne Marie Mistretta. Images of America: *Big Sky*. Charleston, SC: Arcadia Publishing, 2012.

West Yellowstone Historic Center. "West Yellowstone: A Town at the End of the Line."

Wylie, W.W. *History of Yellowstone Park and the Wylie Way Camping Company*. N.p., 1926.

About the Author

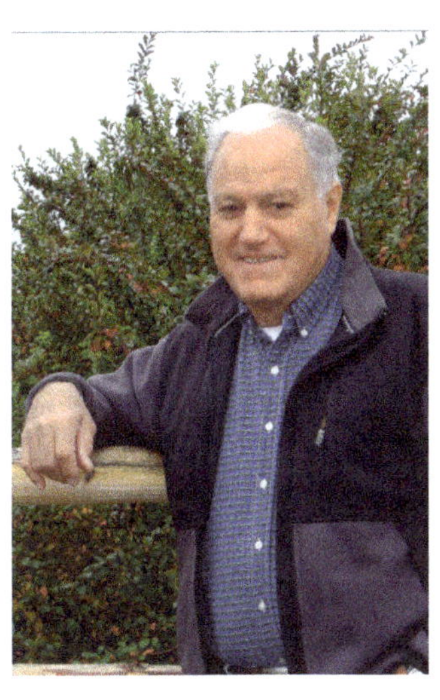

Born in Michigan, Duncan Patten spent many summers in the West with his family. The Gallatin Canyon was a favorite destination until his parents moved permanently to the Gallatin. Patten did all his graduate work in the upper canyon area and has continued research in the area ever since. Dr. Patten is a hydroecologist and private consultant in riparian, wetland and watershed ecology. He is emeritus professor in the College of Life Sciences at Arizona State University. He was a research professor with the Department of Land Resources and Environmental Sciences at Montana State University in Bozeman from 1997 to 2014 and director of the Montana University System Water Center. At Arizona State University, he was a faculty member from 1965 to 1995 and director of the Center for Environmental Studies. Dr. Patten holds a PhD from Duke University, MS from University of Massachusetts–Amherst and AB from Amherst College. His research interests include arid and mountain ecosystems, especially the understanding of ecological processes of watersheds, and riparian, wetland and riverine ecosystems. Dr. Patten was president of the Society of Wetland Scientists and business manager of the

Ecological Society of America. He is a Fellow of the American Association for the Advancement of Science, the Ecological Society of America and the Arizona/Nevada Academy of Sciences. He has served on the National Research Council Board on Environmental Studies and Toxicology; and Commission on Geoscience, Environment and Resources; as well as twelve NRC committees. He also served on the U.S. Environmental Protection Agency's National Science Advisory Board. Patten now resides in Bozeman, Montana, with his wife of sixty years, only one hour from his family's ranch on the upper Gallatin River bordering northwest Yellowstone National Park.

www.ingramcontent.com/pod-product-compliance
Lightning Source LLC
LaVergne TN
LVHW010933100826
845153LV00001B/17

9781540233561